RECORD ALL MONSTERS!

The Book of the Essays from the Podcast

By Robert L. Kelly

Dedicated to, in no particular order for the most part:

Derek M. Koch

Emma Fox Wilson

Fr. Bob Wild

Hollywood Video

Haruo Nakajima

Hasting's Books and Music

The Highwaymen, but mostly Johnny Cash & Waylon Jennings

Masaru Sato

Bill Corbet, Kevin Murphy, & Michael J. Nelson

Joel Hodgson, Trace Beaulieu, & Frank Conniff

Leonard Maltin & Roger Ebert

The Coen Brothers & The Shaw Brothers

Noriaki Yuasa

Shinichi Sekizawa

Tomiyuki Tanaka, Ishiro Honda, & Akira Ifukube

Marion C. Cooper & Willis O'Brien

And especially
Eiji Tsuburaya, Marcel Delgado,
My wife, and my mom (wooooo!)

With Special Thanks to:

Derek M. Koch

Emma Fox Wilson

Quenton Dougherty & Parker Verret

Anri Hata, Frank Jones, & Kento Hata-Jones

John LeMay

Ryan Lengyel

Travis Alexander, Michael C. Hamilton, Nathan Marchand, & Everyone at Kaiju Ramen

Stephen White

Jon Margheim & Austin Ford

Kaiju Hime

Brian Livingston

Ray Hanly

Nathanael Ross Smith & Molly Hardwick Smith

Dr. Bill Tsutsui

Dr. Emily Zarka

Aubrey & Amberly

The Doctors Bagnulo & their Wonderful Daughters

And Richard Kelly

With Acknowledgments to:

Ryan Lengyel

John LeMay

The Classic Horror Film Message Boards

Ed Godziszewski

Steve Ryfle

Stuart Galbraith IV

August Ragone

Dr. Bill Tsutsui

Dr. Emily Zarka

Bob Eggleton

Matt Frank

PART I: THE EPISODES 13

   Chapter 1: King Kong 15
      A Quick Look at The Lost World (1925): 18
   Chapter 2: The Beast from 20,000 Fathoms 20
   Chapter 3: Godzilla vs Godzilla, King of the Monsters 23
      A Quick Look at Luigi Cozzi's Godzilla 26
   Chapter 4: Godzilla Raids Again 27
   Chapter 5: Rodan 30
      A Quick Look at Half-Human 32
   Chapter 6: The Giant Claw 35
   Chapter 7: Varan the Unbelievable 38
   Chapter 8: The Giant Behemoth 41
      A Quick Look at DINOSAURUS! 43
   Chapter 9: Konga 45
   Chapter 10: Reptilicus 47
   Chapter 11: Gorgo 49
      A Quick Look at The Colossus of New York 52
   Chapter 12: Mothra 54
   Chapter 13: King Kong vs Godzilla 57
   Chapter 14: Mothra vs Godzilla 60
   Chapter 15: Ghidorah the Three-Headed Monster 64
   Chapter 16: Frankenstein Conquers the World 67
   Chapter 17: Gamera 69
   Chapter 18: Invasion of Astro-Monster 72
   Chapter 19: The Magic Serpent 75
      A Quick Look at the Daimajin Trilogy 77
   Chapter 20: Gamera vs Barugon 80
   Chapter 21: War of the Gargantuas 83
   Chapter 22: Ebirah, Horror of the Deep 87
   Chapter 23: Gamera vs Gyaos 89
   Chapter 24: The X From Outer Space 92
   Chapter 25: Gappa, the Triphibian Monster 94
      A Quick Look at The King Kong Show 96
   Chapter 26: King Kong Escapes 98
   Chapter 27: Yongary, Monster from the Deep 101
      A Quick Look at Three Kaiju Films from Outside Japan 103
   Chapter 28: Son of Godzilla 106
   Chapter 29: Gamera vs Viras 109
   Chapter 30: Destroy All Monsters 111
   Chapter 31: Gamera vs Guiron 114
   Chapter 32: The Mighty Gorga 115
      A Quick Look at The Valley of Gwangi 117

Chapter 33: Godzilla's Revenge (All Monsters Attack)..119
Chapter 34: Gamera vs Jiger..130
Chapter 35: Space Amoeba..132
Chapter 36: Voyage into Space...134
Chapter 37: Gamera vs Zigra..136
Chapter 38: Godzilla vs Hedorah..138
Chapter 39: Godzilla vs Gigan...141
Chapter 40: Godzilla vs Megalon..143
Chapter 41: Godzilla vs Mechagodzilla..146
Chapter 42: Terror of Mechagodzilla..153

PART II: THE RECORD ALL MONSTERS GAME SHOW QUESTIONS AND ANSWERS..... 157

APING THE APES: Game for King Kong..159
FAMOUS RAY'S ORIGINAL QUOTES: Game for The Beast from 20,000 Fathoms..... 160
THE GEOGRAPHY THAT I STANDS TO YOU SUPERIOR: Game for Godzilla vs Godzilla, King of the Monsters... 161
WHAT'S IN A NAME: ANGUIRUS EDITION: Game from Godzilla Raids Again........... 162
TYRANNOSAURUS-SEX: Game for Rodan... 163
EL SANTO CONTRA EL CACA DEL TORO: Game for The Giant Claw....................... 164
VARAN THE UNAVAILABLE: Game for Varan the Unbelievable................................ 165
WHAT'S IN A NAME: DINOSAUR EDITION: Game for The Giant Behemoth............... 166
BATMAN OR NOT, MAN?: Game for Konga... 167
YOU CAN'T DO THAT IN A MONSTER MOVIE: Game for Reptilicus......................... 168
FATHER OF THE BRIDE OF FRANKENSTEIN: Game for Gorgo................................. 169
FAIRY TALE OR FAKE-Y TALE: Game for Mothra... 170
KING KONG VS GODZILLA: Game for King Kong vs Godzilla................................... 171
WHAT'S IN A NAME: CELEBRITY EDITION: Game for Mothra vs Godzilla................ 172
WHEN WORLDS COLLIDE: Game for Ghidorah the Three-Headed Monster............... 173
FRANKENSTEIN OR FRAUDENSTEIN: Game for Frankenstein Conquers the World 174
YOU KNOW, FOR KIDS!: Game for Gamera..175
WHAT'S IN A NAME: ALIEN EDITION: Game for Invasion of Astro-Monster............... 176
ANIMANIA!: Game for The Magic Serpent..177
BACK IN THE HABIT, CRUISE CONTROL, ELECTRIC BOOGALOO: THE GAME: THE SEQUEL: Game for Gamera vs Barugon...178
O! BROTHER, WHERE ART THOU?: Game for War of the Gargantuas..................... 179
CHANGING OF THE GUARDIANS OF THE GALAXY: Game for Ebirah, Horror of the Deep...180
MONSTER BLOOD: Game for Gamera vs Gyaos..181
X MARKS THE SPOT: Game for The X from Outer Space.......................................182
REMAKE OR RE-FAKE: Game for Gappa the Triphibian Monster............................183
DR. WHO?: Game for King Kong Escapes... 184
WHAT'S IN A NAME: INTERNATIONAL TITLE EDITION: Game for Yongary, Monster from the Deep... 185
SON OF GODS: Game for Son of Godzilla...186
FORMULA FRENZY: Game for Gamera vs Viras..187

DESTROY ALL BAND NAMES: Game for Destroy All Monsters 188
  WHAT'S IN A NAME: GAMERA MONSTER EDITION: Game for Gamera vs Guiron ... 189
  MIGHTY MIX UP: Game for The Mighty Gorga 190
  WE HATES IT!... OR DO WE?: Game for Godzilla's Revenge 191
  WHAT'S IN A NAME: SURGERY EDITION: Game for Gamera vs Jiger 192
  YOG OR NOG?: Game for Space Amoeba 193
  GAME SHOW: MOVIE: THE SERIES: THE GAME: Game for Voyage into Space 194
  SHARK JUMPING: Game for Gamera vs Zigra 196
  NEW HOTNESS OR OLD AND BUSTED: Game for Godzilla vs Hedorah 198
  TUMMY TROUBLE: Game for Godzilla vs Gigan 200
  CALLOUSED THUMBS UP OR DOWN?: Game for Godzilla vs Megalon 202
  WHAT'S IN A NAME- ROBOT EDITION: Game for Godzilla vs Mechagodzilla 203
  MY CANADIAN-ROBOT GIRLFRIEND GOES TO A DIFFERENT SCHOOL: Game for Terror of Mechagodzilla 204
PART III: SUNDRY THINGS 207
  SPECIAL EDITION GAME SHOW FOR 1ST MONSTER KID RADIO APPEARANCE .209
  WRITTEN ESSAYS FOR PODCASTERS ASSEMBLE 210
    PODCASTERS ASSEMBLE SEASON 4 EPISODE 1: KING KONG (1933) 211
    PODCASTERS ASSEMBLE SEASON 4 EPISODE 2: GODZILLA (1954) 213
    PODCASTERS ASSEMBLE SEASON 4 EPISODE 3: GODZILLA (1998) 213
    PODCASTERS ASSEMBLE SEASON 4 EPISODE 4: KING KONG (2005) 216
    PODCASTERS ASSEMBLE SEASON 4 EPISODE 5: GODZILLA (2014) 218
    PODCASTERS ASSEMBLE SEASON 4 EPISODE 6: KONG: SKULL ISLAND 219
    PODCASTERS ASSEMBLE SEASON 4 EPISODE 7: GODZILLA: KING OF THE MONSTERS (2019) 220
    PODCASTERS ASSEMBLE SEASON 4 EPISODE 8: KING KONG VS GODZILLA (1962) 221
    PODCASTERS ASSEMBLE SEASON 4 EPISODE 10: BEST AND WORST OF GODZILLA AND KONG 223
  Godzilla vs The World: The "Villains" of Destroy All Monsters 225
Selected Bibliography 229

PART I: THE EPISODES

Chapter 1: *King Kong*

"Listen - I'm going out and make the greatest picture in the world. Something that nobody's ever seen or heard of. They'll have to think up a lot of new adjectives when I come back." - Carl Denham, *King Kong*, 1933

Those words from Carl Denham feel almost prophetic nine decades later, as *King Kong* is an unqualified classic, and broadly considered one of the greatest films of all time. Even if you haven't seen it, (which, if that's the case, you should stop reading, remedy that, and then rejoin us) you probably know the story: A giant gorilla is brought from his island home where he fought dinosaurs and was worshiped as a god to New York, escapes his captors and is shot dead in the streets because he fell in love with a woman.

King Kong can be looked at in a number of ways, and has been read as everything from a tragic fairy tale to a political commentary, and you can find brilliant people saying brilliant things about it almost anywhere you look. The angle I want to look at *Kong* from, however, is as the first born of a new breed of movie: The Giant Monster Movie.

Some people point to Harry O. Hoyt's adaptation of Sir Arthur Conan Doyle's novel *The Lost World* as the beginning of the genre, but there's a key difference, one that makes *Kong* stand out. While *The Lost World* is a fantasy, the animals depicted in it are based on the then current understanding of very real animals, the dinosaurs. The titular monster of *King Kong* is a 20 foot tall gorilla, as Denham said, "something that nobody's ever seen or heard of!". So, despite the similar starting point of a Lost Prehistoric World being equally fantastic in each film, the difference between the two is what is *unknown*. We knew about dinosaurs, but before 1933 nobody knew what King Kong was. And now, you'd be hard pressed to find someone who didn't.

Kong is the father of all who came after, and you could draw a direct line from him to pretty much any giant monster you've ever seen on screen, like a bad parody of biblical genealogy: "King Kong beget the Rhedosaurus, and the Rhedosaurus beget Godzilla, and Godzilla beget Gamera, Yongary, and Guilala…" and so on and so forth.

Of course, all of these monsters were made by people, and that same, unbroken line of succession can be found in the real world of special effects artists making these movies. In the case of Willis O'Brien, his heir would be at the helm of the next step in the evolution of the Giant Monster Movie.

I want to say a few words about Willis O'Brien here, since he's such a hugely influential figure who is going to be stepping out of the narrative for the time being. He made his first stop-motion film in 1915 at the age of 29, a six minute short called *The Dinosaur and the Missing Link,* a light farce where a dinosaur kills an ape man and a caveman child takes credit for the deed, winning acclaim from his elders and a kiss from a cave girl. This short caught the attention of Thomas Edison, who commissioned a series of prehistoric shorts in the same vein as *The Dinosaur and the Missing Link*, which led to O'Brien's work on 1918's *The Ghost of Slumber Mountain. Slumber Mountain* was not a happy production for O'Brien, or "Obie" as his friends called him. The film's producer, Herbert M. Dawley, cut it down to just shy of 12 minutes from Obie's 45 minute version, and then claimed credit for the stop-motion effects[1]. 2 more films were made from the discarded footage, a sequel, *Along the Moonbeam Trail* in 1920, and a documentary, *Evolution* in 1923. O'Brien received little credit or financial compensation for any of these projects.

At last, and unusually, O'Bi caught a lucky break. The ill-fated productions with Dawley caught the attention of director and screenwriter Harry O. Hoyt, who hired him for the visual effects on *The Lost World.* The film was a hit, and included 11 stop-motion animated dinosaurs, designed after the paleo-art of Charles R. Knight. After the success of *The Lost World,* Hoyt and Obie started on another dinosaur epic: CREATION.

It's September in 1931, a new executive at RKO, the company producing *Creation*, has been brought on board to cut upcoming features from the studio's slate. In a shed on the corner of the RKO's studio lot is an ongoing production that has hemorrhaged one hundred thousand dollars over the past few years, Hoyt and Obi's *Creation*.

When the new executive, a man named Merian C. Cooper was hired, he accepted the job on one condition, that he could make a movie he'd dreamed of, one in which a "giant terror gorilla" fought a Komodo dragon. Now, as Cooper watched the effects footage that had cost a hundred thousand dollars from O'Brien's creation, he had two realizations: 1. *Creation* had taken up half of a prestige picture's budget to create a few minutes of dinosaur footage, and 2. This Willis O'Brien guy just might have what it takes to bring his "Giant Terror Gorilla" movie to life. So, in December of 1931, RKO Pictures shut down Harry O. Hoyt and Willis O'Brien's *Creation,* And greenlit Marien C. Cooper, Ernest B. Schoedsack, and Willis O'Brien's KING KONG.

That's where we'll leave Willis O'Brien for now, don't move the level gauges, we need to see where we left him when we come back. That's a stop motion animation joke. There's one more behind the scenes story I want to tell, or, rather, illuminate, and I need to give a little bit of background information on myself before I do. My last name may be Kelly, but I am Hispanic, primarily of Mexican descent. So imagine my delight when I came across this anecdote while watching the seven part making of documentary on my King Kong Blu-Ray:

---

[1] In the time since the original version of this essay was released as a podcast, friend of the show Ryan Lengyl has pointed out that the Dawly v O'Brien situation is much more nuanced than this.

"The Kong puppets, and as well as a lot of the miniature trees and all that stuff, and the dinosaurs were made by this guy named Marcel Delgado"

"Marcel Delgado was a kid studying at the Art Center, I believe, and Willis O'Brien found him- he met Marcel in a grocery store, and- and just happened to see some of his work. And, uh, Delgado was very reluctant to come and work for Willis O'Brien because he didn't think the work would be steady. He offered him work on *The Lost World* a number of times, and Marcel went, 'Ah, you know, I don't want to work on a lot of movies, I got a good job in a grocery store.'"

"And O'Brien had to tempt him with, uh, with, you know, a $75 a week offer to come and sculpt for him, you know. And even at that, Delgado didn't want to do it until he saw the workshop. He walked in and said, 'Here it is, it's all yours. Do what you will'"[2]

Marcel Delgado at home with one of the Kong armatures in the late 1960s/early 1970s

And then this a few moments later:

"The matte paintings in *King Kong* were crafted by a team of skilled artists that included Byran Crabb, Henri Hilink, and a man who would continue to work alongside O'Brien for the next twenty years."

"Mario Larinnga was a very good artist in the art department there at RKO when O'Brien started to work on *Creation*, and he sort of discovered his talents and moved him on to his crew."[3]

Both men would work with Obie during the rest of their careers, over 20 years in both cases. This may not mean a lot to some people, but to me, it means a lot. Here, at the birth of my favorite movie genre, are men who contributed to bringing it to life, who look like me, with whom I share heritage. Mexicans were there at the very beginning, and we're here now. 2013's *Pacific Rim,* was directed by Guillermo del Toro, another Mexican. He won the

---

[2] *RKO Production 601: The Making of 'Kong, the Eighth Wonder of the World.'* Directed by Dan Brockett, 2005.
[3] *RKO Production 601: The Making of 'Kong, the Eighth Wonder of the World.'*

Academy Awards for Best Director and Best Picture at the 90th Oscars for his romantic monster movie, *The Shape of Water*.

A lot has happened with *King Kong* since 1933, a sequel from the same year, *Son of Kong*, that's, uh, not as good. Two remakes, which we will hopefully cover in due time, and a recent reboot that's supposed to crossover with the new Godzilla franchise in 2021. On top of all that, there are countless rip-offs, cash ins, pop culture references, a Rankin-Bass cartoon series, toys, model kits, and other things I can't think of off the top of my head, and can't be bothered to look up.

This is where it all started, so this is where we're starting too.

A Quick Look at *The Lost World* (1925):

From time to time, there will be films, tv shows, or other media that I don't feel merit a full episode of the show, but do deserve a brief analysis or review due to their impact on Giant Monster Movies. Today's film, Harry O. Hoyt and Willis O'Brien's *The Lost World,* is one such movie.

Released in 1925, *The Lost World* laid a lot of the groundwork for what would come in the genre. We have the scientist nobody believes, the journalist and his buddy, the woman who proves useful as early iterations of the stock players of Kaiju movies on an expedition that would inspire the makers of *King Kong, Mothra, and Gorgo* to bring monsters or their friends to a major city in which they may wreak havoc.

The similarities were known as *Kong* began production and Serge Bromberg of Lobster Films

A scene from The Lost World *(1925)*

theorizes, in the essay accompanying their 2017 Blu-Ray, that there were wide reaching ramifications born from that knowledge. In 1929, *The Lost World*'s producers at First National Pictures agreed to remove it from circulation and destroy all existing prints and negatives. The only surviving components of the film were shortened, five reel versions owned by Kodak to sell for home projection[4]. This is the version of the film that most people living today have seen. In the early 90s, several different, nearly complete versions were

---

[4] Bromberg, Serge. *The Lost World: Secrets of the Restoration*. Flicker Alley, 2017, pg 5

recovered from George Eastman's collection and The National Film Archive of the Czech Republic[5], and this is the reason the full, 10 reel version of the film is available to be viewed today.

The reason I didn't include this movie as a full episode on the podcast is because its stated goal is to present realistic dinosaurs to the public as they might have been, even taking their designs from the paleoart of Charles R. Knight, which had been and still is featured in museums as prestigious as the Smithsonian Institute. This makes it rather different from a monster movie, even if the bones look quite similar. Think about it like a dimetrodon, the mammal-like reptile often confused with dinosaurs. It isn't one, but without it there to catch the eye of many a three year-old in a baggie of plastic dinos, that interest might not have flourished.

And of course, this source material had its own source material, in the novel of the same name by Sir Arthur Conan Doyle, probably most famous for being the creator of Sherlock Holmes. There's a well known story that he took a reel of Willis O'Brien's effects footage to be exhibited without explanation to the Society of American Magicians. The New York Times declared the next day on their front page, that if these were fake animals, as they were, "They were masterpieces."

And so is this film. It's captivating and fast paced, and the dinosaurs look great. While we recognise them as monstrous mis-imaginings of animals today, at the time, this was as real as it could get.

---

[5] *Secrets of the Restoration*, pg 12

Chapter 2: *The Beast from 20,000 Fathoms*

George Ritchie: [referring to the A-bomb test] You know every time one of those things goes off, I feel as if I was helping to write the first chapter of a new Genesis.
Professor Tom Nesbitt: Let's hope we don't find ourselves writing the last chapter of the old one.

Well, it's not the first chapter, but, like Buzz Aldrin said, "second comes right after first!"[6]. In the intervening 20 years between *King Kong* and this film there was a little something called World War II, which ended abruptly when America decided to stop boxing with gloves and begin boxing with a gun in both hands. That opponent, Japan, would see the event in a very different light for obvious reasons, but in America we decided that disproportionate force wasn't the only thing atomic energy was good for. More on that later.

Elsewhere, two 13 year old boys named Ray, one in California, one in Arizona, saw *King Kong*. That's gonna be a recurring theme throughout our history of Giant Monster Movies. Anyway, these Rays both had their lives changed forever, and they decided to work in movies. The Californian Ray, Ray Harryhausen, wanted to pursue a career creating the kind of magic and monsters he'd just born witness to, while the Arizonan Ray, Ray Bradbury, wanted to write fantastic stories like *Kong*. It wasn't long after the Bradbury's moved to Los Angeles that the two Rays met and formed a line of friendship that would last the rest of their lives. That's a math joke.

Ray Harryhausen with the armature of the title character in Mighty Joe Young

At one point, a friend arranged for Harryhausen to meet Willis O'Brien, who advised him to take some sculpting and anatomy classes to really excel at his craft. Not long after, he got a job animating George Pal's Puppetoons, which were animated with a series of differently posed figures, as opposed to traditional stop motion's use of one poseable figure. Meanwhile, he and Bradbury joined Forrest Ackerman's Science Fiction League[7]. Then that pesky World War II we were talking about earlier cropped up. Bradbury didn't serve due to

---

[6] *The Simpsons*, Season Five, Episode 15 "Deep Space Homer"
[7] Eller, Jonathan R., 'L.A. High and the Science Fiction League', *Becoming Ray Bradbury* (Champaign, IL, 2011; online edn, Illinois Scholarship Online, 20 Apr. 2017), https://doi.org/10.5406/illinois/9780252036293.003.0003, accessed 1 Sept. 2023.

poor eyesight[8], but Harryhausen served under Frank Capra in the US Army's Special Service division, where he would save the extra rolls of 16mm film that were left over. Once the war ended, Harryhausen used the salvaged film to produce his famous fairy tale shorts[9].

1947 was a big year for both men. Bradbury had his first collection of short fiction, *Dark Carnival* published[10], and Harryhausen served as assistant director of visual effects to Willis O'Brien on the wonderful gorilla movie, *Mighty Joe Young.* They were well on their way to becoming two of the most Famous Rays in all of history.

In 1951, Harryhausen was working on his first film as head special effects technician, *Monster from Beneath the Sea.* Now, I've heard this story told a couple of different ways, but in each version, Harryhausen convinces the producers of the film that Bradbury would be a good script consultant.

When Bradbury reads the script, he recognizes elements of his short story, *The Beast from 20,000 Fathoms.* He brings it up to the producers on the way out, and, the next day, receives a telegram with an offer to buy the story's motion picture rights. They changed the name of the movie to match the story and, voila! *The Beast from 20,000 Fathoms*[11]. His name was used in the film's advertising, and he was given an onscreen writing credit. "Suggested by the *Saturday Evening Post Story* by Ray Bradbury".

The rhedosaurus rampages through New York City

According to his introduction for the 1981 book, *They Came from Outer Space: 12 Classic Science Fiction Tales That Became Major Motion Pictures,* Bradbury was not too happy with *The Beast* as an adaptation of his story, or a film in general, but loved his friend's work on bringing the dinosaur, called the Rhedosaurus, which was made up for the film, to life[12]. As much as I respect him as a writer, I have to disagree with Bradbury here. I think that *Beast*

---

[8] *A Week to Remember: Ray Bradbury*.
https://www.lapl.org/collections-resources/blogs/lapl/week-remember-ray-bradbury. Accessed 1 Sept. 2023.
[9] "Ray Harryhausen Timeline." *Timetoast Timelines*, 29 June 1920,
https://www.timetoast.com/timelines/ray-harryhausen-408d72dc-bd1b-475a-9dfb-6b75f617b1fc.
[10] *A Week to Remember: Ray Bradbury*.
https://www.lapl.org/collections-resources/blogs/lapl/week-remember-ray-bradbury. Accessed 1 Sept. 2023.
[11] The Rhedosaurus and the Rollercoaster: The Making of "Beast." Directed by Ray Harryhausen, 2003.
[12] Wynorski, Jim, editor. *They Came from Outer Space: 12 Classic Science Fiction Tales That Became Major Motion Pictures*. Doubleday, 1980.

From 20,000 Fathoms is a lot of fun, and important as well, as the first *atomic* dinosaur movie.

Lee Van Cleef as the military sniper who kills the rhedosaurus

And that's the word I want to come back to: Atomic. The attitudes toward atomic energy in this film are incredibly different from what you might be used to. It's extremely casually referenced as the force that unleashes, but doesn't create, the film's monster. As a matter of fact, an atomic weapon saves the day! A radioactive isotope is loaded into a bullet, effectively a miniature atom bomb, and fired by a sniper into an open wound in the monster's neck. The sniper, by the way, was an early role for Lee Van Cleef of spaghetti western fame.

The monster's demise is tragic, like the demise of all Giant Movie Monsters is, but this isn't the last time we see the Rhedosaurus on screen. True, there were no *Beast From 20,000 Fathoms* sequels or spinoffs, but he does make an appearance on the losing end of a battle with a T-Rex in 1977's *Planet of the Dinosaurs*, a dumb but fun survival flick that has some fairly well realized stop motion dinosaurs.

And of course, just like *Beast* is the Son of *King Kong,* the Rhedosaurus has his own children, and we'll be talking about the biggest and arguably most famous one in our next chapter, but hopefully from an angle you might not have given too much thought.

Chapter 3: *Godzilla* vs *Godzilla, King of the Monsters*

What can I say that hasn't been said about 1954's *Godzilla?* Or even its now much maligned 1956 US import version, *Godzilla, King of the Monsters*? Given the amount of ink spilled over the original's importance as a film and an allegory, I kind of feel like talking about this movie at all is almost a waste of my time and yours. I doubt I will say anything you haven't heard before, but given the fact that my goal with the podcast this book is based on is to talk about the history of Giant Monster Movies, how can I ignore the movie that inarguably changed literally everything about the genre? The film that introduced Godzilla, my favorite monster ever, to the world, and whose many sequels would come to dominate the landscape of this particular genre all the way to the present day, almost 70 years later?

Well, I'm going to talk about it anyway. And I'm going to urge you to stay and to listen, or, as it may be, keep reading, because I'm going to try to say something here that is nuanced and difficult to explain. Something related to my central belief that Giant Monster Movies should be fun. 1954's *Godzilla* is a masterpiece of atmospheric filmmaking and deserves all of its accolades. 1956's *Godzilla, King of the Monsters*, though now derided as an abysmal edit of a glorious masterwork, was and is a GOOD and NECESSARY film, and the one I watch more often of the two. Please, hold your tomatoes until the end, it's very hard to read what I'm writing with all the pulp in my eyes.

The world's first look at Godzilla

Let's start by looking at the market for foreign films and Japanese films in particular in the 1950s. Most of this information I'll be sharing comes from David Kalat's excellent commentaries on the Criterion Collection's 2011 Blu-Ray, which included both versions of the film. In 1952, Akira Kurasawa's iconic film *Rashomon* was released in the US. It was the highest grossing Japanese film in the States at the time. It's total US gross? Two hundred thousand dollars. That's just shy of two million dollars in today's money. It won the Academy Award for Best Foreign Language Film, for cryin' out loud![13] That's a miserably small amount of money for a film of that prestige. For context, let's look at the winner from the 2020 Oscars, Bong-Joon Ho's *Parasite,* which pulled in 53 million at the box office. Or, just for fun, five and a half million in 1952 money.[14]

---

[13] Kalat, David, "Commentary", *Godzilla, Spine #594, The Criterion Collection,* Disc 2, Directed by Ishiro Honda (Japan, Toho Studios, 1954, 1956, 2011) Blu-ray
[14] Inflation figures researched through https://www.bls.gov/data/inflation_calculator.htm

I know we mostly think of foreign films being subtitled as a recent and respectful innovation in presenting them, but this was the norm in the late forties and early fifties. Not out of respect for the original work or its artistic merit, but because it was cheap. Dubbing a film could increase the cost for the distributor up to ten times as much. You only dubbed a movie you *really* thought was something special. Joseph E. Levine felt that way about films in general, and wanted to make foreign films accessible to general audiences. He'd had hits with Roberto Rossellini's *Open City* and *Paisan,* and Vittorio De Sica's *Bicycle Thieves,* and when he saw Ishiro Honda's *Godzilla,* he thought he could make another hit out of it[15]. But the story was very uniquely Japanese, and the film's attitudes toward the h-bomb and radioactive fall-out, both intellectual and literal, were extremely different from what they were stateside. Just take a look at the last chapter's movie, *The Beast from 20,000 Fathoms*, for an illustration of that.

It's a great disservice, actually, to only call it Ishiro Honda's *Godzilla*. The film is a testament to the collaborative nature of filmmaking. Ishiro Honda certainly left his stamp on the film as director, bringing his experience as a documentarian and prisoner of war, but producer Tomoyuki Tanaka, who had the initial idea for the film, Akira Ifukube who composed the score and created the monster's iconic roar, Eiji Tsuburaya, who created the special effects that brought Godzilla to life, and Haruo Nakajimi, the man in the Godzilla suit, all left indelible marks on the film, and by extension, the franchise, and by FURTHER extension, the genre. There are better sources on them than this book, and we'll have a lot of time to talk about their roles throughout it. In my opinion, they're the most important players in the whole story, and Tsuburaya in particular holds a special place in my heart. But to try to do justice to their hard work and genius in this short space is even more foolish than trying to impart the importance of *Godzilla* at this late date in an early episode of a brand new podcast.

Raymond Burr as newsman Steve Martin in the 1956 US localization of Godzilla

Levine knew that, given the cultural differences between Japan and the US, he would need more than a dub job to make the film accessible. This was a film from a nation we'd been at war with just 9 years ago, after all. Enter Terry O. Morse, an editor and director with a background in cheapie noirs who'd worked as a film doctor before. The casting of Raymond Burr, whose career up to this point consisted mostly of playing heavies and minor villains in gangster and crime pictures, as our American hero was another on the surface strange decision that seems to me to be a minor stroke of genius, or at least, one of terrific luck.

As David Kalat once again points out, instead of the 1954 version's straightforward storytelling, Morse and Levine borrow a flashback structure in the style of film noir to let us

---

[15] Kalat, "Commentary", *Godzilla*

know the height of the stakes from the very beginning[16]. I'm not clear on whose idea it was to recut the film in the way they did, but I feel like all signs point to Morse. Our hero is buried in rubble when we arrive, and he tells us how he got there. The heart of both versions of the movie is Godzilla's second attack on Tokyo. Though, the initial attack on the city includes an undeniably *Kong* inspired and undeniably excellent train sequence. The second attack is an unrelenting 13 minute release of all of the previous tension and dread that had been building up to this point. In terms of innovations in the genre, the alleged point of this alleged "podcast", I guess the biggie here is Godzilla's atomic breath weapon. Nothing like it had ever been seen in the genre before, and the same goes for *Godzilla* itself.

The level of effort and thought Morse put into importing *Godzilla* is remarkable. And that's really how I believe we need to look at this version of it: as a labor of love. The final product was overall very respectful to the tone, story, and spirit of the original, and it was WILDLY successful as the first Japanese film in the US to be a bona fide hit at the box office, earning two million dollars, only the fourth foreign film in American history to pass the million dollar mark. That's almost nineteen million in today's money. Look, I know box office success is not any real indication of a film's quality, after all, the last *Transformers* movie made six hundred and five million dollars, but grant me a further indulgence in the following barely coherent rant:

Godzilla is a brilliant movie, but I've hopefully proven that the market for foreign films in the US was absolutely abysmal under normal circumstances, and simply subtitling it and releasing it to the American public would have consigned it to playing arthouses for wealthy snobs who would have snubbed it for the crime of being about a giant monster instead of some dude slowly killing himself with cigarettes and ennui. Without *Godzilla, King of the Monsters,* my favorite monster might not have reached such a wide audience as soon as it did. It was a NECESSARY decision.

Times have changed, and *Godzilla* has been given its due, but so often at the expense of its American version. But here's the thing, *you don't have to denigrate one to admire the other.* Many critics accuse this edit of robbing the film of its power and transforming it into a standard Giant Monster Movie[17], but the charge holds no water, like a rusty colander. The fact of the matter is that there was barely such a thing as a Giant Monster Movie at the time. I like *Godzilla,* and I like *Godzilla, King of the Monsters.* To do so is no great paradox. Thematic darkness doesn't equal quality, and the kaiju community's attempts to be taken seriously have resulted in us shooting ourselves in the foot, robbing us of our right to enjoy the sweet but empty calories that make up the bulk of the genre, which is a fruit in this sudden and mixed metaphor, so that we can impress our dietician friends by eating the bitter but nutritious rind.

One final point on the US version's merit: in 1957, Terry O. Morse's *Godzilla, King of the Monsters* was released to a warm reception in Japan, with the English dialogue subtitled in

---

[16] Kalat, "Commentary", *Godzilla*
[17] As much as I love *Dark Corners Reviews* on YouTube, series host and writer is way out of line in describing it as "the horribly recut *Godzilla King of Monsters*" in their retrospective on the 1954 film, which i still recommend: Godzilla 1954 Retrospective // DC Classics. www.youtube.com, https://www.youtube.com/watch?v=YOm1hMfNPG4&list=PL1DHoBtqR2tPtFvT1ge6PIPsHJNvLOG52&index=28. Accessed 24 Aug. 2023.

Japanese, and it was this version that took the world by storm in the late 1950s. *Godzilla* is indisputably the better film and everyone knows that now, but it was the US version that truly made Godzilla the *King of the Monsters*.

A Quick Look at Luigi Cozzi's *Godzilla*

Luigi Cozzi had seen *Godzilla, King of the Monsters* as a child when it was released in Italy as *Godzilla il Re dei Mostri* in July of 1957, and it stuck with him. Twenty years later, after directing a few episodes for Italian genre film titan Dario Argento's TV Show, *Door into Darkness*, as well as a few giallo films of his own, Cozzi had been showing classic sci-fi movies at his own theater in a kind of festival series, and he decided he would like to show the original 1954 Japanese version of *Godzilla*. So, he approached Toho's distribution office in Rome, who he had worked with on getting his most recent film, *Take All of Me*, released in Japan, where it had been a respectable hit.

Due to the international distribution deal Toho had worked out back in the 50s, only Terry Morse's American edit was available to Cozzi. He wasn't thrilled, but he'd work with what he had. His Italian distributor wasn't thrilled either, but not for the same reason; *Godzilla, King of the Monsters* was in black and white, and that may have flown back in the fifties, but this was the late seventies, man! Don't nobody wanna see no black and white movie! So they gave him three weeks to colorize the film. Three weeks is not enough time to do anything well, especially not colorize a movie frame by frame, as the best version of the process is done, but he didn't want to merely tint the movie either, so a bizarre middle ground was reached: The film was tinted in different areas for each scene. So, the night sky might be tinted purple, and the fiery foreground of burning buildings surrounding Godzilla would be red or orange.

Other changes were made too, additional shots of real plane crashes and evacuations were added in to supplement the model-based effects footage, and a truly 1970's Italian style opening sequence was added, with lively electronic music playing over actual footage of the aftermath of the Hiroshima bombing, including the bodies of people killed in the blast. Depending on who you ask, it was either a modest hit or a modest flop. Toho approved all of his cuts, but on condition that ownership of the film and all of its components lapsed to them after seven years.

Cozzi's filmography looks pretty familiar to fans of cheap sci-fi and fantasy films of the late 70s and early 80s: the *Star Wars* knock-off *Starcrash*, the *Alien* knock-off *Contamination*, and two live action Hercules movies starring Lou Ferrigno. This sticks out like a sore, tie-dyed thumb, and if you really want to appreciate the care Joseph Levine and company took in importing Godzilla for western audiences, that's the only reason I'd recommend checking out Cozzi's version, except as a historical oddity. But I will give him his due. This is a labor of love gone wrong, but a labor of love nonetheless, one that briefly brought Godzilla back to the big screen during his 9 year hiatus, and for that, at least, we should be a little grateful.

Chapter 4: *Godzilla Raids Again*

In November of 1954, *Godzilla* presented a thoughtful and complex meditation on Japan's experience of being on the receiving end of the atom bomb. An allegory in which the representation of that oppression is a victim of it as well. In May of 1955, *Godzilla Raids Again* presented two monsters fighting among historical landmarks.

In a lot of ways, *Godzilla Raids Again* is a kind of insignificant movie. Its storyline is derivative of the previous movie, and it takes itself just as seriously. Which is unfortunate, because it's not as good, and doesn't do its job quite as well. What it *does* do well is also its major innovation in the history of the genre: making giant monsters fight each other.

Godzilla and Anguirus duke it out on the docks of Osaka

In the very few movies of this kind up to now, the focus had been on single monsters rampaging in a city. *King Kong* had included a few famous skirmishes between Kong and other Skull Island residents, notably the t-rex fight, but the centerpiece of the film really had been his destructive dawdle through New York City. Likewise, the Rhedosaurus in *Beast from 20,000 Fathoms* had no contact with any monstrous animals. The closest thing we get to another creature is the big fake sauropod skeleton in the background of a few scenes. *Godzilla* had innovated in part by increasing the level of destruction in the rampage to match that of the atomic bomb. Kong and the Rhedo had done comparatively little damage.

Aside from this admittedly major story innovation, *Godzilla Raids Again* bears all of the hallmarks of a cheap quickie sequel. Ishiro Honda isn't directing, replaced by the workman Motoyoshi Oda. The only returning actor is Takashi Shimura in a cameo as his character from the previous film, Dr. Yamane.

Well, that isn't quite accurate. Two more actors returned, Haruo Nakajima and Katsumi Tezuka, who had taken turns in the Godzilla suit in the first movie. Both had been working as stuntmen and extras for Toho for some time, Nakajima since the late forties and Tezuka, who was 43 by the time this film had come out, since the early thirties. According to various sources, but primarily according to Nakajima himself, he took the lead in developing how Godzilla moved after studying the movements of bears and elephants at the zoo[18].

---

[18] Galbraith, Stuart. *Monsters Are Attacking Tokyo! The Incredible World of Japanese Fantasy Films.* 1st ed, Feral House, 1998. Pg 69

Apparently special effects director Eiji Tsuburaya liked his portrayal, because he had the younger man continue as Godzilla, while assigning Tezuka to the part of Godzilla's first ever opponent, Anguirus.

Anguirus is one of my favorite monsters in the annals of Giant Monster Movie-dom. He has a great roar, made from distorting the sound of a saxophone. Anguirus is also a wonderfully designed monster. Based on the dinosaur family of ankylosaurs, he has a spiky outer armor, usually referred to as his carapace, that his creators originally intended to fly open like beetle's wings, but after it was decided that they looked bad flopping around during the fight scenes, they were fastened down and together[19]. You can still see them separate a few times during the main battle in Osaka about halfway through the film.

If you're somewhat familiar with this genre but haven't seen this film, you may be surprised that the fight between Godzilla and Anguirus comes at the halfway point instead of the climax. The fight acts like Godzilla's second attack in the first movie. You may also be surprised that Godzilla flat out kills Anguirus, biting down on his neck until blood flows, then lighting him on fire with his atomic breath when the body falls into the water. The finale comes when our heroes move to another part of the country, rather than helping to rebuild Osaka after Godzilla's fight with Anguirus. They work spotting schools of fish for a cannery, and one of them spots Godzilla "walking" along an ice shelf.[20]

Godzilla isn't killed, there's no oxygen destroyer or magic bullet here. Instead, he's buried under mountains of ice, loosened by a daring bombing raid inspired by one of our main character's accidental deaths,

Warner Bros.' poster for the US version, retitled Gigantis the Fire Monster

crashing his plane above Godzilla's head. It has none of the impact of Dr. Serizawa's sacrifice in the previous film.

While writing this, I keep noticing the phrase, "the previous film". It's kind of sad that this movie (which isn't awful, it's perfectly fine) is so overshadowed by the previous film. *Godzilla* was one of the most powerful genre movies made up to that point, with its thinly veiled

---

[19] *Godzilla 1954-1999 Super Complete Works*. Shogakukan. 1 January 2000. pp. 80, 130. ISBN 978-4091014702.
[20] I used quotation marks here because this effect was achieved by way of a wind up toy that wasn't working, so it's just standing there. It's great and I love it.

atomic allegory, and one of the most thrilling too, thanks to its startling and brilliant scenes of, as the US trailer put it, "dynamic violence".

Apparently, when American producer Paul Schreibman decided to import the movie in 1959, he was also worried about the shadow of "the previous film". He wanted people to think they were getting a brand new monster, so he retitled it *Gigantis the Fire Monster*, swapped Godzilla and Anguirus' roars, and made a whole bunch of other baffling choices[21]. Initially he and his fellow producers received permission from Toho to film new special effects sequences with the original suits for a version that would have done away with all of the human storyline called *The Volcano Monsters,* where Godzilla and Anguirus would have stood in for a plain old t-rex and ankylosaurus[22], which I can pronounce however I want because Latin is a dead language[23].

Since this film made money in Japan, but not as much as Toho had hoped it would, it was decided that they should try to make movies about other Giant Monsters. So we'll leave Godzilla here, buried in ice for the next seven years/9 chapters. While this movie kind of crawled along, Toho's next one would really soar.

---

[21] Ragone, August. *Eiji Tsuburaya: Master of Monsters: Defending the Earth with Ultraman, Godzilla, and Friends in the Golden Age of Japanese Science Fiction Film*. Pgs. 46-47 Chronicle Books, 2007.
[22] Ragone, *Master of Monsters*, pgs. 46-47
[23] https://www.babbel.com/en/magazine/fact-vs-fiction-is-latin-a-dead-language

Chapter 5: *Rodan*

Godzilla had been a huge hit for Toho studios in 1954. Its sequel, *Godzilla Raids Again*, had also been a hit the next year, but not as successful as the previous film. So, presumably the thinking was "Monsters are in, but maybe we need this Ishiro Honda guy specifically directing these movies", because they brought him back for *Rodan* in 1956, and didn't let another director take a shot at it for ten years.

I know it has seemed that I was centering the American side of things over the past few chapters dealing with Japanese Monster Movies, but we had very little time to talk about Joseph E. Levine, and we're going to get to talk about Ishiro Honda, Tomoyuki Tanaka, Akira Ifukube, and Eiji Tsuburaya over a much longer period. I want to handle their stories properly and respectfully, so I didn't feel right trying to cram all of that into 3 pages while also covering the story of how Godzilla reached America. So here we are now, talking about one of the Four Fathers of Godzilla, Ishiro Honda.

I wanna give a little bit of background on Ishiro Honda as a person before we look at him as a filmmaker. He probably would have liked that the very first thing that comes to my mind when I hear his name is the word "pacifist". Well, the first word after "Godzilla", which he might have been less happy about. He was the son of the son of a Bhuddist monk, the family sold vegetables from the temple to get by. His oldest brother, Takamoto, became a military doctor and sent newspapers and boy's adventure magazines from the cities, instilling a love of science in young Ishiro[24]. Both of these influences can be seen in his work as a director and a writer.

Ishiro Honda in 1968

Honda's temperament on set was serene, patient, and flexible, making the best of what was available. He went to film school in 1931, which led to his being hired by Photographic Chemical Laboratories, later Toho Studios, serving as assistant director for the first time in 1934[25]. He was drafted into the Imperial Japanese Army that fall. Two years later, a failed coup by Honda's commanding officer and others resulted in his unit being sent to Manchukuo, a puppet state of the Japanese Empire in China at the time, on a wild goose chase after a Chinese resistance leader[26]. The remainder of his 18 month enlistment would be spread out over the following years, next being recalled in 1939[27]. During WWII, Honda

---

[24] Ryfle, Steve, and Ed Godziszewski. *Ishiro Honda: A Life in Film, from Godzilla to Kurosawa.* Wesleyan University Press, 2017. Pg 5
[25] *A Life in Film,* pg 19
[26] *A Life in Film,* pg 16
[27] *A Life in Film,* pg 26

remained in China, fighting the resistance there, and managing what were called Comfort Stations.[28] [29]

Honda was lucky in the war. His deployment in 1944 was bound toward the Philippines, but his unit missed the boat, and they were sent to China, where the fighting was less intense. On his last deployment, a shell landed near him, but didn't go off. He kept it on his desk for the rest of his life. He was taken prisoner, but according to the book *Ishiro Honda: A Life in Film from Godzilla to Kurosawa*, he only ever said of that time that he was treated well by his Chinese captors[30]. When Japan surrendered, he remained behind for seven months, overseeing the return of power to Chinese officials. He was well liked by the locals, who invited him to stay when his service ended. He gave it some thought, but decided to return home to Japan, hoping his wife and children survived the war, and that Toho was still in business and had a job for him. As a parting gift, some of the villagers presented him with rubbings of proverbs from area temples. One read: *Read good books, say kind words, do good deeds, be a good person.* He would often write these for himself on the backs of his scripts.[31]

He returned to his wife and family, and there was a job for him at Toho. In 1949, he served as chief assistant director to Akira Kurosawa on his film *Stray Dog*[32]. The same year, he directed his first film, a documentary called *Ise-Shima* commissioned by that prefecture's officials to boost tourism. He directed several more documentaries, including *Story of a Co-op,* which he also wrote[33]. In 1951, he directed his first feature film, *The Blue Pearl,* which was about pearl divers and featured extensive underwater photography, a first in Japanese Film. He directed 2 films in 1952, and two more in 1953, including *Eagle of the Pacific*, where he would work with Special Effects director Eiji Tsuburaya for the first time[34]. And that's where we'll leave him for now, on the very brink of *Godzilla*, and we'll return to what makes *Rodan* work so well. Part of which is Ishiro Honda.

In a lot of ways, *Rodan* is not very similar to *Godzilla* or *Godzilla Raids Again*. Whereas all three begin with accidents, disappearances, or deaths, the two earlier Giant Monster Movies from Japan brought out their monsters relatively quickly. Godzilla shows up about 20 minutes into his debut feature, and almost immediately in the sequel. We don't see the titular monster of *Rodan* until it's more than halfway over, almost forty minutes in. Before that, it's a murder mystery in a mining town with some giant, atomic bugs called "meganulon". The slow build really pays off when we see Rodan for the first time in a flashback, hatching from his egg.

Once the ball gets rolling, what we see is some of the best monster action the genre has to offer up to this point. We wind up getting TWO Rodans attacking the city of Fukuoka before

---

[28] *A Life in Film*, pg 27-29
[29] I was hesitant to discuss this when the initial podcast version of this chapter was released, as I felt I was not equipped to talk about this. In that episode I recommended an article by "Fae" at "Something Ghoulish". That "Fae" was Fae Basir, and that "Something Ghoulish", is now PHASR, and the article can be found by going to https://phasrmedia.com/reconciling-ishiro-hondas-past-in-the-present/
[30] *A Life in Film*, pg 31
[31] *A Life in Film*, pg 32-33
[32] *A Life in Film*, pg 48-49
[33] *A Life in Film*, pg 46-47
[34] *A Life in Film*, pg 72-75

returning to their volcano lair above the mining town where it all began. The Japanese Self Defense Force (the JSDF from here on out, forever and anon) fire at the volcano, hoping to bury the monsters and trigger an eruption. One Rodan is able to escape, but the other is caught in the smoke and collapses into the molten lava. The other cannot bear to leave its mate behind, and plunges down to join them. They both burn to death.

Oh, man. One of the major through lines in Giant Monster Movies up to *Rodan* is that the monster cannot get a happy ending. Kong was gunned down by airplanes (or was it beauty killed the beast?). The Rhedosaurus had a radioactive bullet put in its chest. Godzilla was revealed to be as much a victim as anyone else before the oxygen destroyer reduced it to bone dust, and the second Godzilla was buried in ice after a fight for its life. They're all tragic figures. The last of their kind. But then here comes Rodan. Or, rather, here come the Rodans, two monsters with just each other, the tragedy doubled with their loss. Instead of facing the world alone, they stay with their doomed love. A gothic romance with Giant Monsters.

Rodan meets resistance as he attacks Fukuoka

In 1957, the King Brothers brought *Rodan* to the States and had a good run with it[35], giving it an extensive TV ad campaign[36]. This was their first foray into the world of Giant Monster Movies, but it wouldn't be the last. Just introducing some key players who will be important a little later on.

A Quick Look at *Half-Human*

From time to time, there will be films that are influential to the time we occupy in this history of Giant Monster Movies, but for one reason or another, don't quite qualify for a full episode. There are several reasons *Jû Jin Yuki Otoko*, AKA *Half Human: A Story of the Abominable Snowman*
Falls under this category, and once I'm through explaining what this film is, I'm sure you'll see what I mean.

Like I said in our episode discussing *Godzilla Raids Again,* Ishiro Honda was otherwise occupied and unable to direct that film. It is widely believed that he was busy developing

---

[35] Staff (May 30, 1958). "Toho's Science-Fiction Team Completes Another Thriller; Tint Entitled 'The H-Man'". Far East Film News. Tokyo, Japan: Rengo Film News Co., Ltd.: 15. OCLC 6166385.
[36] Staff (April 4, 1958). "Rodan". Far East Film News. Tokyo, Japan: Rengo Film News Co., Ltd.: 4. OCLC 6166385

32

Project S, which stood for "Snowman", which had begun production around the same time as 1954's *Godzilla*. *Half Human*, as I'll be referring to it now, was written by Takeo Murata, who had worked on the screenplays for both *Godzilla* and *Godzilla Raids Again*, with science fiction writer Shigeru Kayama, who had also been on the writing team of the first Godzilla film. In addition to that, he had penned several stories about the cryptid Orang Pendek, a three foot tall ape man from the jungles of Sumatra.

A scene from the climax of Half Human

Two of these stories, according John Lemay's *Big Book of Japanese Monster Movies: The Lost Films*, were "Revenge of the Orang Pendek", and, "Fate of the Orang Pendek", served as the basis for the screenplay, in which an expedition in the Japanese Alps searching for the Abominable Snowman goes wronger and wronger. I know that's not a word, but that's what happens. The expedition is buried in an avalanche, and when one of the explorer's sister comes along with her boyfriend to look for them, a group of carnies and rural mountain people give them more trouble than they were expecting.

This movie had obsessed me for almost seven years at the time of this writing, so forgive me if this quick look isn't quite as quick as most others. I first heard about this movie in the summer of 2014, as I was doing my own bigfoot research, traveling down from Ontario and through New Jersey, back home to Texas and then up to Illinois. None of these places are known for bigfoot sightings, but that's not why I was traveling; my travels were incidental to the entirely academic research I was doing for a short story I wrote that hasn't been published. In my research, I encountered Will Laughlin's review of the original Japanese version of this film on his website, braineater.com. That in turn led me to the review of the film's Americanized release by Lyz Kingsley on the website andyoucallyourselfascientist.com.

I have always had a love for movies that present something forbidden, dangerous, or perverse, more out of curiosity than an actual interest in what was being depicted. Why do I bring this up with Half Human? Toho has self imposed a ban on this movie, due to its insensitive portrayal of the Burakumin peoples, a cultural minority within Japanese society made up of people who worked near and around death, such as undertakers, executioners, meat cutters, and slaughterhouse workers, who were placed at the bottom of the social system in Edo period Japan. And while official discrimination against the Burakumin ended with the Meiji Restoration in 1871, the societal effects of their longstanding status as outsiders reach all the way to the present. All you have to do in order to see that illustrated is watch their scenes in this film, portrayed as inbred mountain hicks with very visible physical

Half Human's American theatrical release poster

deformities. The ban on the film, or fuin, meaning seal in Japanese, dates back to the late 80s, when it was being considered for a home-video release. Outside of a few repertory screenings, such as an Ishiro Honda film festival in 1997, the film is still officially unavailable worldwide.

Sometime in the 90s, a timecode-stamped version of the film was leaked online, and if you know where to look, can be easily found. Now that I have tracked down the film, both versions, it doesn't quite live up to my expectations. Between a very simple story without much nuance, too much hiking, and the much more problematic than expected portrayal of the Burakumin, even the Japanese version suffers. But with Ishiro Honda at the helm, it feels like more of a sequel to *Godzilla* than *Godzilla Raids Again* does. Of special note is the abominable snowman himself, portrayed in a great suit that features an expressive face-mask designed by Ohashi Fuminori and performed by him under the name Sanshiro Sagara. Would that Toho's version of King Kong looked this good in 7 years.

And finally, the less said about the American version the better. It is as bad as you've heard, if you've heard of it at all. Seek this one out if you're curious, but only the genuine article, and be aware of its many problems. No amount of John Carridine is worth that mess.

Chapter 6: *The Giant Claw*

When I began outlining this series, I knew I wanted to talk about *The Giant Claw*. I wanted to talk about how producer Sam Katzman had worked for poverty row studio Monogram in the 1940s and had learned how to cut corners like a pro there[37]. I wanted to talk about how in 1955, Sam Katzman and fellow producer Charles Schneer hired Ray Harryhausen to create a giant octopus for their movie *It Came from Beneath the Sea*, but paid him so little that he could only give the thing six legs[38]. I wanted to talk about how when Katzman wanted to make his giant bird-monster movie, partially inspired by the success of *Rodan* the previous year, he decided Harryhausen would be too expensive, and hired a visual effects team in Mexico City to bring the creature to life[39]. I wanted to talk about leading actor Jeff Morrow's humiliating experience watching the movie for the first time, hoping nobody recognized him after they started laughing at the ridiculous beast the characters on screen kept reacting to with sheer terror, sliding lower into his seat as the film played on[40]. I wanted to talk about how Katzman's corner cutting (say that five times fast) resulted in a perfectly serviceable b-monster movie being assigned a place on the cinematic scrapheap of history.

Columbia Pictures wisely elected to leave the monster's face off of the poster

And then I watched the movie again.

First of all, the above stories are so well known that to do more than lightly touch on them would be boring for longtime cult movie geeks, and for people who might be hearing them for the first time, they're more or less true! And fun! Second of all, not only are those stories incredibly well known by now, but so is The Giant Claw itself. I mean the monster. Everyone's seen it in youtube videos of the worst movie monsters even if they haven't seen the movie itself. But what I began thinking about while I watched it, with this show's lens as a history of Giant Monster Movies and their development as a genre, was how much bad science is in it. About 40 minutes into the movie, a boxy looking man with pointy ears and

---

[37] "Sam Katzman: He Makes The Serials." Sunday Herald, 20 Sept. 1953. Trove, http://nla.gov.au/nla.news-article18511872.
[38] Dalton, Tony. *Ray Harryhausen: An Animated Life*. London: Aurum, 2003, p. 73.
[39] Smith, Richard Harland. "Articles: 'The Giant Claw'." Turner Classic Movies. Retrieved: April 8, 2015.
[40] Smith, "Articles: The Giant Claw"

the world's tiniest mustache explains that THE MONSTER BIRD IS FROM OUTER SPACE. AND HAS AN INVISIBLE ANTIMATTER SHIELD THAT MAKES IT IMPERVIOUS TO ALL WEAPONS AND KEEPS IT FROM SHOWING UP ON RADAR. AND THAT IT SOMEHOW OPENS THE SHIELD TO ATTACK. Also, in the same scene, you can see someone behind the camera's shadow on Jeff Morrow's chest. They're scratching the back of their head.

Look, it's easy (and fun!) to sit on our couches and laugh at the obvious puppet who looks like somebody plucked Big Bird's older brother. It's easy to make fun of the movie's bad, bad, bad science. I'm no science guy, but even I could tell it doesn't make any sense. It's also easy for some of you to make fun of the inconsistencies in the types of aircraft used in each scene. I'm also not an airplane guy, so they all look the same to me and this part passes muster. There are only four kinds of airplanes. Little shooty ones, little shooty ones shaped like triangles instead of airplanes, big ones that too many people get shoved into so they can travel, and old time-y, shoot down King Kong and Snoopy ones. Sometimes, these ones have propellers. If you'd like to correct me, send you airplane related enquiries to recordallmonsterspod@gmail.com and I promise not to ignore them. Make sure to put the word "airplane" in the subject so I know not to ignore it.

But enough about my willful airplane ignorance. I'm trying to say that it's easy for us to make fun of bad effects and bad science in a pretty bad movie, but the fact is we're still talking about *The Giant Claw* over sixty years later, so it must have done something right, even if everything we see on screen is wrong. Our two leads, the aforementioned Jeff Morrow and the lovely Mara Corday[41], have great chemistry together, and have a great scene of some rapid-fire flirting that would be at home in a romantic comedy from the previous decade. It's a shame that the same scene starts with him kissing her without her consent, which I'm sure most modern audiences will find off putting. I know I did.

The real reason I wanted to include *The Giant Claw* in my history of Giant Monster Movies is precisely because it is so bad in those areas I've already mentioned. That's what has kept it around for so long. The chemistry between our leads is surprisingly good, but it's not what people remember. People remember that goofy buzzard's head swinging down

The Giant Claw, in all her dopey glory

towards the camera in the same footage being repeated over and over, and they remember that the only thing people can compare a large object to in the entire world is a battleship for some reason. This is a movie where suspension of disbelief is pretty much impossible, because everything has been played too straight while being too ridiculous in practice. It illustrates the importance of the special effects teams working closely with the A-unit to make a movie successful on its own terms, something *the Giant Claw* certainly is not.

---

[41] I think she's very pretty and she makes me blush.

But it is successful, just not on its own terms. It's a little bit like Rocky Balboa at the end of his first movie, winning or losing doesn't matter, what matters is that he did it. Being a good movie doesn't matter for *The Giant Claw*, that fact that we have it to watch and enjoy and poke gentle, loving fun at is enough to justify it. *The Giant Claw* may not be an A-list monster or even a B-list monster, but it has its fans, and I count myself among them. It's too much fun to be mad at for stinking, and I really had a good time. So here, on the bathroom wall that is the book of essays from my podcast, I'll leave a little graffiti as my final word in this chapter: for a good time, watch *The Giant Claw.*

Chapter 7: *Varan the Unbelievable*

Let's start with the positives, hmm? Varan is a good looking monster who can live on land, swim underwater, and glide through the air like a two hundred fifty foot tall squirrel. That is the unqualified good. The unqualified *bad* is that there are at least two versions of this movie, and the more widely available one is pretty lifeless. I have, up to this point, heaped praise on pretty much every movie we have talked about. I just can't do that for *Varan*. I've heard several other people who discuss this sort of movie refer to it as a film "for completists only". Well, this podcast is called "Record ALL Monsters", not "Record Only the Very Good, or, At Worst, Stupid and Entertaining Monsters" so here we are.

Varan attacks Haneda International Airport

Varan's origins as a movie really do explain why it turned out so dull, though. After *Rodan* had been so successful in the US, in no small part due to its television advertising campaign, an American production company approached Toho for a joint production to release a new Giant Monster Movie straight to television over three thirty minute episodes. Different sources name different studios as the genesis for this idea, but from what I can tell, it seems to have been American Broadcasting-Paramount Theaters[42]. The timing works out, and Kaiju Youtube super-star Up From the Depths arrived at the same conclusion, as did the good folks over at Wikizilla, so I think I'll go with that, too. AB-PT had been formed in a merger of the American Broadcasting Company and United Paramount Theaters, as an effort from the two companies to bring Hollywood quality filmmaking to TV[43].

Producer Tomoyuki Tanaka decided that since this film was being produced for television, it wasn't necessary to film in color, which had been done for *Rodan*, nor was it necessary to use their new TOHO SCOPE widescreen process, as they had done for their alien invasion flick, *The Mysterians* in which the giant robot MOGERA debuted, before being seen again more than 30 years later in *Godzilla vs Spacegodzilla*. No, this was a movie for American TV audiences, and as such the focus was on the monster more than anything.

And, as I've already said, Varan is a really cool looking monster. Ever since the original *Godzilla*, Toho seemed to like unveiling a little twist during the monster's rampage. In *Godzilla*, it was the atomic breath. In *Godzilla Raids Again*, the death of Anguirus during the monsters' fight, and in *Rodan*, the revelation that there are actually TWO flying monsters. Here, Varan lifts its arms like Rocky Balboa at the entrance of the Philadelphia Museum of Art, and unfurls some flying squirrel-like wing membranes, jumps into the air, and floats away. This moment would be referenced by Guillermo del Toro 55 years later in *Pacific Rim*,

---

[42] *Master of Monsters*, pg. 55
[43] "Ambitious ABC Planning Initiated Under New Merged Ownership" (PDF). BROADCASTING TELECASTING. Vol. 44, no. 7. February 16, 1953. pp. 27–29. Retrieved April 8, 2015

when the kaiju Otachi takes off into the night skies over Hong Kong while battling Gypsy Danger. If that sounds like a whole lot of nonsense to you, how did you find this book? Welcome, pull up a chair. Let's watch some movies.

Shortly after filming had begun, the US backers of *Varan* pulled out, and Tanaka decided to release it as a theatrical film in Japan[44], much to the annoyance of director Ishiro Honda, who was already feeling restless in his role as Toho's go to Monster Movie Guy. All of the film shot after Tanaka's decision was shot on proper, widescreen cameras, and the footage that had been shot previously was cropped to fit into the cinematic ratio.

So let's briefly meet producer Tomoyuki Tanaka, one of the Four Fathers of Godzilla. There isn't as much information on him that is easily available as there is for say, Ishiro Honda, who we've already talked about, or Eiji Tsuburaya, who I will gush about real soon, I promise. Tanaka was a producer at Toho beginning in 1940, and came up with the idea for the movie *Godzilla* in early 1954. He and the studio had been in negotiations with the

Tomoyuki Tanaka produced every Godzilla movie from 1954-1995

Indonesian government on a movie about Indonesia after Japanese occupation, but popular sentiment in the country was very against the Japanese at the time, so negotiations fell through, and Tanaka and his crew were denied entry visas[45].

On his return trip, Tanaka recalled a news story about a tuna trawler being contaminated by radiation fallout from nuclear testing, and he also recalled *The Beast From 20,000 Fathoms*.[46] This is a pretty well known story, and I feel a little silly rehashing it here, but Tanaka was a titan of the genre, producing every single Toho monster movie from *Godzilla* in 1954 to *Rebirth of Mothra II* in 1997[47]. He also served as the Studio's chairman through much of that time[48]. To not discuss him at all would be a gross oversight, and with *Varan* being a rare misstep for him in terms of quality seemed like a natural place to bring him up.

Even though I call *Varan* a misstep, his decision couldn't have been an easy one, and the film serves as an example of his ability to think on his feet when something doesn't go to plan. Just like he had done in creating Godzilla 4 years prior, he made the best of a bad situation and made something that could work. You've got to admire that kind of attitude.

---

[44] *Master of Monsters*, pg. 55
[45] *Master of Monsters*, pg. 34
[46] *Master of Monsters*, pg. 34
[47] Tomoyuki Tanaka. https://www.tohokingdom.com/people/tomoyuki_tanaka.htm. Accessed 24 Aug. 2023.
[48] "

Just quickly, *Varan* was brought to the US in 1962 with a new human storyline built around the monster footage, and this is where we get the title *Varan the Unbelievable*. The flying scene is cut from this version. If the Japanese version of the film had been unremarkable, the US version was just as much. By then, the genre had moved on to the highest marquee value fight in its entire history. Seems a lot of things about this one are un-something. One more thing it is is "Unessential." But, then again, at least the monster is cool.

Chapter 8: *The Giant Behemoth*

Here's another movie, like *Varan* and *The Giant Claw*, that came along just a little too late. *The Giant Behemoth* came out in 1958 under the title *Behemoth the Sea Monster* in England and the next year in the US. Five years after *The Beast from 20,000 Fathoms* introduced the idea of a radioactive dinosaur attacking a major city, four years after *Godzilla* gave the monster an atomic death ray, 3 years after *Godzilla Raids Again* pit two monsters against each other, and two years after *Rodan* showed us a Giant Monster in Full Color. So, you can see how a black and white, single monster rampage flick could look a little dated even in such a short time since the genre really got going in 1953, even if this monster did have its own atomic death ray.

All that's not to say that *The Giant Behemoth* is bad. The film barely seems to have any reputation at all, and what I had heard before watching it almost always dismissed it as a cheap rehash of *Beast from 20,000 Fathoms*. And it is. But it rehashes it very well. It does this in part because this is the second radioactive dinosaur movie from director Eugene Lourie. And he's not our only serial offender here, as Willis O'Brien steps back into our narrative here providing stop motion effects at a fraction of the cost of his protege and *Beast From 20,000 Fathoms* animator Ray Harryhausen. We've already talked about Obie, but I'll remind you not to touch those level gauges once again, he's coming back in another few chapters and we'll see what he's been doing all this time when we get there.

The US (left) and UK (right) posters for The Giant Behemoth

Let's get personal. When I was in high school, I bought a DVD set of *Beast From 20,000 Fathoms* and the atomic ant movie *THEM!* from a local bookstore, which I watched when nobody else was home one day. I loved both movies, but as a long time fan of Godzilla and dinosaurs, *Beast* spoke to me much more loudly, so I looked it up on one of my favorite genre movie review sites, One Thousand Misspent Hours And Counting. Following various links, I discovered that not only did Eugene Lourie direct *Beast* and *Behemoth,* but that he also went on to direct another Giant Monster Movie, *Gorgo*.

He only directed 4 movies, (the three mentioned, and *The Colossus of New York* in the year before *Behemoth*) and it fascinated me that three quarters of his output was devoted to radioactive dinosaurs. Although Gorgo's not radioactive. We'll get to that. It further fascinated me that *Behemoth* is the only one of these films for which he has an on-screen writing credit, co-writing the screenplay here. What makes someone return to the same idea twice? This struck me as different from Ishiro Honda directing 8 of the original Godzilla movies, since he was under a studio contract, and all 3 of Lourie's Monster Movies were independently produced. He only directed the 4 films, all between 1953 and 1961, less than a decade, before returning to primarily working in art and design for films, even receiving an Oscar nomination in 1969 for the visual effects on *Krakatoa: East of Java*[49].

I got no closer to finding out why Lourie returned to this well so many times, but my guess would be that the people making these movies sought him out as a director because of his success with *Beast From 20,000 Fathoms*, because the little bit of information and the one quote I could find indicated that he wasn't too happy to be involved with the genre, sadly reducing his terror beasts to "comic strip monsters"[50]. I think his Monster Movies are pretty good as a body of work, and they've brought me a lot of joy. The effects are good in all of them, and you can see Lourie had a talent working with miniatures. The human stories are also fairly compelling in each film. *The Giant Behemoth* deserves special praise for its characters behaving realistically. The scientists are brought in by fishermen who disappear when they're no longer relevant, and they turn to scientists in different fields when their own expertise is inadequate. No Buckaroo Banzai-esque, multi-disciplined weirdos, just a couple marine biologists, one of which deals with how radioactive waste affects sea life. That's another nice change of pace. We're not talking about nuclear bombs and warfare here, but nuclear waste. The movie is definitely derivative over all, but it keeps itself fresh with little changes like this, and rewards you if you're paying attention.

I just want to touch on one more thing, and that is the film's monster, an invented dinosaur called a Paleosaurus. Not to be confused with the very real *palaeosaurus*, a prosauropod from late triassic England. As previously mentioned, this monster has a death ray, not unlike Godzilla's atomic breath, but at the same time, very different. It's represented on screen by a rippling pulse emanating from the creature's body. Our marine biologist protagonists posit that this is a result of the animal's radioactive mutation working in tandem with its natural bioelectricity, like an eel. And like a real life electric eel, we eventually see it using it to navigate as it swims under water.

Dinosaurs make good monsters because we know so little about them, and can ascribe any number of fantastic abilities to them. I said in the *King Kong* chapter that I don't personally consider *The Lost World* to be a Giant Monster Movie because its monsters are realistically portrayed dinosaurs. Well, for their time, anyway, they're realistic. But dinosaurs strike us as monstrous over all because we know so little about them. It's a little like the story about the three blind men and the elephant. The one who touches the trunk thinks an elephant is a kind of snake. The one who touches the leg thinks it's a kind of tree. The one who touches the tail decides it's a kind of rope. They begin to fight over who's right based on their limited information[51]. This may not seem to be related to how dinosaurs are monsters, but bear with me. The men begin to fight to defend what they believe to be true, what they believe they *know*. There we are again, face to face with the *unknown*. That's what makes us think of something as a monster. We know the dinosaurs existed, but we don't know what color they were, how they moved, what they sounded like. Sure we can make guesses, even really good guesses founded on the evidence we have, but we're still only seeing part of the elephant. It's up to us how we accept that knowledge, or even if we do. Do we accept how

---

[49] https://www.oscars.org/oscars/ceremonies/1970
[50] I would eventually do more research on Lourie that would go deeper into his feelings about his Giant Monster Movies, which you can find in a later essay in this very book on the movie *Gorgo*.
[51] E. Bruce Goldstein (2010). *Encyclopedia of Perception*. SAGE Publications. p. 492. ISBN 978-1-4129-4081-8.

little we know with wonder and curiosity? Or with fear and anger? When we choose the latter, do we create monsters where there are none? Or maybe even become monsters ourselves? Who can say. Not me!

A Quick Look at *DINOSAURUS!*

To start with, I didn't grow up with this movie. I first encountered it on TV, late one night when I was about 20 years old. And what I saw was a little Hispanic boy and a caveman riding a brontosaurus through a tropical jungle. I sat through the rest of the movie, my eyes wide with wonder and bleary with fatigue, to the point that I actually thought that I dreamed this movie.

Years later, I discovered that I had NOT dreamed this movie. Amazon continually recommended the Blu-ray to me. I didn't connect the dots until I stumbled upon it on TV again, and this time I was alert enough to notice the little thing in the corner of the screen saying, "You're watching DINOSAURUS! on GetTV" and then it was like a bomb went off in my brain.

So now, let's talk about *Dinosaurus!*, a movie whose title ends with an exclamation point. In what I think is supposed to be an island in the Mexican Caribbean, some white guys find a frozen T-rex and Brontosaurus in an icy channel beneath the sea and also a caveman, but one of the local tough guys named Mike Hacker and has a German-kinda sounding accent hides it for himself to make money somehow? Anyway, all three prehistoric creatures get revived when they're struck

The climax of Dinosaurus!

by lightning and the T-rex eats a drunk Irishman in a scene that I think was an influence on Jurassic Park's lawyer's death.

The most important thing about this movie is that the caveman and a little Hispanic boy named Julio become best friends over bananas and a glass of milk. They then go for a ride on the back of the brontosaurus. Nothing else matters.

Ok, that's not entirely true, the other important thing is we have an old friend returning to this movie behind the scenes in the person of Marcel Delgado, who, though uncredited in the film itself, created the dinosaur models in only three weeks, after the studio told him he had six and then said, excuse me, Marcel, where are my Dinosaurs? It's nice to see his work again, but the truth is, you've seen his work everywhere! Not only did he build the creatures from movies we've talked about like *King Kong* and *The Lost World*, but he did miniature work on *The Wizard of Oz*, *War of the Worlds*, Disney's *20,000 Leagues Under the Sea*, *It's a Mad, Mad, Mad, Mad, Mad, Mad World*, and *Fantastic Voyage*. In 1949, he built the armature for Mighty Joe Young, just like he did with King Kong and his monstrous menagerie of Skull Island Residents. Just a few years after *Dinosaurus!*, Delgado built the bird props for Alfred Hitchcok's *The Birds* and as well as various special effects props for *Mary Poppins*. I already spoke at length in our *King Kong* episode about why Delgado's involvement in that film meant so much to me, but it's nice to see that he was a part of my life for longer than I'd even imagined.

The dinosaurs here aren't his best work, but they look pretty cool, all things considered, and the movie is a lot of fun, if a little iffy on its portrayal of the various ethnicities that populate the island. In addition to that, there are definitely scenes that you just know stayed in Steven Speilberg's mind because they seem to show up again in *Jurassic Park*, including the T-rex chasing and flipping over a jeep. All in all, I recommend this movie, even if it sits just slightly outside our normal purview.

Chapter 9: *Konga*

Who doesn't love a good giant monkey movie? Now, *Konga* is not a "good" giant monkey movie, but it is one of my favorites. There's so much ridiculous stuff happening and that audio clip we just heard sums it up nicely. The only thing I'd add is that there's also an old school mad scientist in this movie. *Konga* is the first of **four** Giant Monster Movies that we'll be talking about from 1961, two of which, including this one, are from England. I call this the First Kaiju Boom, and it represents Giant Monster Movies becoming a full blown phenomenon. Ironically, while Japan only had one entry in 1961, beginning the next year with *King Kong vs Godzilla,* that nation, and Toho studios specifically, would dominate the genre.

Konga is unique among Giant Monster Movies of this era because it embraces a science fiction and horror movie trope that we haven't seen a whole lot of up to this point, the Mad Scientist. *Konga* is extremely derivative, just look at its name, but it brings a sort of outlandish creativity in the face of a deadly self seriousness that I just adore. In addition to that, while its plot could come from a Bela Lugosi starring Monogram cheapie from the 1940s, everything about the film's aesthetic is painfully early sixties, another great source of joy for me.

I usually try to refrain from just summarizing the movie in this section, but the details of *Konga*'s plot are too deliciously ludacris to pay no mention to, especially since my thesis on this film is that it is doing something truly unique in the history of Giant Monster Movies of this time by having an honest to goodness Mad Scientist. So here's a quick overview of what happens in *Konga:*

Konga and Decker take a stroll through jolly London

Botanist Charles Decker's plane crashes over Uganda and he is presumed dead. A year later, he returns to England with a pet chimp named Konga and secret knowledge from a native doctor that will allow him to grow certain plants, and maybe even complex living creatures like animals to outlandish sizes. Animals like Konga. His housekeeper/lab assistant/secret lover Margaret agrees to help so long as he marries her after the experiments are complete, he agrees to the conditions with no intention to honor them, as he is eying Sandra, one of his grad students to be his new housekeeper/lab assistant/secret lover. The dean of Decker's college refuses to give him funding for the outrageous experiment, so Decker has Konga kill him. And then he has him kill a few other people. When Margret discovers her intended replacement, who firmly rejects Decker's advances, she gives Konga a heaping helping of the growth serum and encourages Konga to kill his owner. He kills her instead, then goes on a King Kong style rampage holding Decker in his hand before being shot to death in front of Big Ben. Decker in no way resembles a doll during this scene, and ever since Konga got all big and murder-y, he has ceased to be a chimp and has become a man in a saggy gorilla suit. It's the stuff that dreams are made of, kids.

Up to *Konga,* there haven't been any actual mad scientists in our history of Giant Monster Movies. There have been shades of him in *Godzilla's* Dr. Serizawa and the Oxygen Destroyer, but he turned out to be a heroic character, less of a Dr. Frankenstein and more of a Frankenstein Jr. Except not a cartoon robot. The scientists in *Beast From 20,000 Fathoms, The Giant Claw,* and *The Giant Behemoth* never cross the line of "mildly eccentric" and into real madness. As a matter of fact, especially in *Behemoth,* they seem pretty reasonable given all that's going on. Dr. Deckard would have been played by Boris Karloff if this movie had been made fifteen or twenty years before, there's nothing reasonable about him. More than any movie we've seen yet, this is science run amok. I mean, science is running amok in all of these, but it is running EXTREMELY amok here, and that is because of our mad scientist.

In the American Giant Monster Movies, we see radiation and nuclear weapons treated as a monster-maker, but also as a savior. In *Beast, Behemoth,* and *The Giant Claw,* the monster is defeated by a radioactive bullet. There's more detail there, but that's essentially the fact. So The Mad Scientist would be counterproductive in this kind of narrative. Our view of scientific advancement needs to be bolstered and propagandized, having a heroic scientist instead of a mad one does just that. If you remember back in our episode on *Rodan,* we talked about Ishiro Honda's upbringing, and how he grew up respecting scientists and doctors in part because of his military medic brother. Since he had such a strong hand in shaping the genre in Japan and eventually around the world, the lack of mad scientists in his films makes sense. As a matter of fact, before Honda rewrote the screenplay for the original *Godzilla,* Serizawa *was* a mad scientist who lived in a gothic castle and dressed all in black.

Mad scientists come back around later, but for the most part, Giant Monster Movies are the home of heroic scientists. So *Konga's* a swing and a miss on that front, but I still want to recommend it for the sheer ridiculous spectacle. Just a word of warning, though, this film does feature depictions of both violence to animals, specifically, a house cat, and a relatively intense scene of attempted sexual assault. So avoid it if you need to, no judgment here, from me. About you skipping it. I judge both of the things I warned you about very harshly.

Chapter 10: *Reptilicus*

1961 was a busy year for Giant Monster Movies. In January, *Konga* came out in England. The next month, an even more ridiculous monster movie would come from the European mainland and the combined efforts of screen-writer Ib Melchior and producer/director Sidney W. Pink. Neither man was a stranger to exploitation films by 1961, and let's be clear, at the time of this movie's release, pretty much all genre movies were Exploitation movies. Foreign films were either destined for arthouse theaters or the exploitation circuit[52], the folks who frequented the former wouldn't have had much interest in Giant Monster Movies, so grindhouses and drive-ins it was.

Sidney W. Pink had made his name 9 years before by co-producing the first ever feature length color 3-D film, *Bwana Devil,* an 80-minute adventure film based on a real life tragedy. For most of 1898, from March to December, two man-eating lions killed and ate around 30 construction workers who were building a railroad bridge over the Tsavo River in Kenya[53]. The event was popularized in a book, *The Man-Eaters of Tsavo*, in 1908, which served as source material for Pink's film. *Bwana Devil* used a polarized 3-D process[54],[55], the predecessor of today's Real-D 3-D instead of the familiar anaglyph process that uses the red and blue lensed glasses, and kicked off a brief craze of 3-D films that ended in 1954.

In 1959, Pink produced writer and director Ib Melchior's *Angry Red Planet*, a bizarre and entertaining film that features a Spider-bat-monster and another cinematography gimmick called CineMagic, where they basically left the actors in negative so they would look cartoony and not clash too much with the cheap effects and then tinted it red[56]. This process was applied to all the scenes that took place on the surface of the planet Mars. Melchior had written the script from a story treatment handed to him by Pink at a party they were both attending. Pink would also write the story for *Reptilicus,* with Melchior again penning the script. This time, however, Pink would direct.

Ib Melchior had another Giant Monster feather in his cap. In 1957, he had written, along with Edwin Watson, the script for the ill-fated *Volcano Monsters* project, the first US attempt to import *Godzilla Raids Again.* He said in later interviews that he reused several of his *Volcano Monsters* ideas for *Reptilicus*[57], the movie we're talking about here, right now, in this book, based on the podcast *Record All Monsters*. You can sort of tell the ideas are older, since the movie does nothing really new, but it does a lot of things very strangely.

---

[52] Kalat, "Commentary", Godzilla
[53] Patterson, J. H. (1908). *The Man-eaters of Tsavo and Other East African Adventures*. MacMillan and Co).
[54] *Make Your own Stereo Pictures* Julius B. Kaiser The Macmillan Company 1955 page 271 Archived 2011-02-26 at the Wayback Machine
[55] Richard Dyer MacCann (Aug 5, 1952). "Polaroid Spectacles Required For Feature Picture in Color: Hollywood Letter". The Christian Science Monitor. p. 5
[56] McGee, Mark (2016). *Faster and Furiouser: The Revised and Fattened Fable of American International Pictures*. McFarland, pp. 161-168.
[57] Homenick, B. (2017, May 18). The imagination of ib melchior! A conversation with the danish monster moviemaker! *Vantage Point Interviews*. https://vantagepointinterviews.com/2017/05/18/the-imagination-of-ib-melchior-a-conversation-with-the-danish-monster-movie-maker/

The monster regenerates from a frozen bit of tail found in the ground at a drilling site in Denmark. The tail chunk is taken to a university in Copenhagen where, through a series of hijinks, it is unfrozen, grows into a full giant snake monster with itty-bitty wings and legs. It's impervious to all conventional weaponry, spits deadly goo, and is eventually killed by shooting a poison bazooka round into its mouth. I guess the regeneration bit is new, but the thawed prehistoric monster spewing poison before dying from getting a magic bullet shot down its throat is an uneven blend of *Beast from 20,000 Fathoms, Godzilla,* and *The Giant Behemoth.* For all of its derivativeness, *Reptilicus* is still bizarre and wonderful. I was unable to obtain a copy, but the Danish version, directed by Poul Bang, whose name should always be yelled, is even bizarre-er and wonderful-er. It includes a non-diegetic musical number and an additional effects sequence in which the monster uses its itty-bitty wing-a-lings to fly. The proportions of the beast also change so that its wings look less useless and it's now got a big ol' head.

Reptilicus terrorizes Copenhagen with slime

Sid Pink cut the flying scene because he found it unconvincing. American International Pictures, or AIP, the company who had agreed to distribute *Reptilicus,* had more issues than just an unconvincing puppet. Pink had shot the English version using all but one of the same actors as Poul Bang's Danish cut, but with the actors reciting their lines phonetically in English. The strange sound that resulted was deemed unusable by the folks at AIP, who had to redub all of the lines to be discernible to American ears. Writer Ib Melchior is among the voice cast[58].

While it may sound like I'm a bit down on *Reptilicus,* much like *The Giant Claw*, it's a movie I really enjoy, even if not for the reasons its creators might have intended. It's good silly fun, and while it doesn't do anything new, it coasts on its charm and good looks. Yes, I said good looks. You'll have fun with this one.

---

[58] "The imagination of Ib Melchior"

Chapter 11: *Gorgo*[59]

There's a quote near the beginning of this movie where an Irish orphan speaks to one of our main characters, and tells him off for attempting to catch the titular monster and sell it to the highest bidder. He says "It's a terrible bad thing you're doing. A terrible thing." But it's not, unlike the subjects of our previous two chapters, a terrible, bad movie. While I've extolled the virtues of lunacy in recommending *Konga* and *Reptilicus,* I have no need to take that course of action with this feature, *Gorgo*. I can say with confidence that, after 1933's *King Kong* and 1954's *Godzilla*, this was the best movie I watched for this podcast's first season. It's entertaining and joyful, it plays its scenes of destruction straight for the most part, and, in a key way, points to the future of the genre.

Vincent Winters as Sean, the real star of Gorgo

In terms of story, *Gorgo* is essentially a remake of *King Kong* set in Ireland and England, which I refuse to call the British Isles because my last name is Kelly. So what is it doing so new that it sets the tone of the genre going forward? It introduces a much derided element and admits a dirty secret of the genre, and the element and the secret are one and the same: CHILDREN. *Gorgo* is the first Giant Monster Movie in which a child is part of the main cast and this decision came in part because the film was being made with children explicitly in mind. Returning director Eugen Lourie, who I was able to find more information on thanks to VCI's excellent 2013 Blu-Ray of this film, recalls that after seeing *Beast From 20,000 Fathoms* with his daughter, she reprimanded him for killing the monster. That was his starting point when he was approached by The King Brothers about making *Gorgo*[60].

Frank, Maurice, and Herman Kozinsky were the sons of a fruit merchant who began producing slot machines in Los Angeles in the 1920s. Around 1940, they were charged with tax evasion[61]. They also got the idea that they could project movies onto screens in their slot machines, and set up a meeting with Cecil B. DeMille to see what could be arranged. According to Morris, they dropped out because DeMille, and I quote, "Had no class"[62]. The same year, they founded KB Productions, and in 1941, released their first film, *Paper Bullets*. In 1942, they changed their last name to King, and the company name to King Brothers Productions[63]. Three years later, they released their first major hit, *Dillinger,* an early biopic about the gangster John Dillinger. During the Red Scare, they frequently hired blacklisted

---

[59] It should be said, a version of this essay was printed in *Kaiju Ramen* #6. The version here is closer to the one that was read on *Record All Monsters*.
[60] *Ninth Wonder Of The World: The Making Of Gorgo*. Directed by Daniel Griffith, VCI Entertainment, 2013.
[61] Tax Evasion Laid to Three: Two Brothers and Sister Indicted After Inquiry Into CAMOA Member". Los Angeles Times. May 9, 1940. p. A1.
[62] THOMAS BRADY (Oct 12, 1941). "HITTING THE JACKPOT: The Kozinsky Brothers Muscled Into the Movies to Get Even With De Mille". The New York Times. p. X4.
[63] "RAISED EYEBROWS DEPARTMENT". The New York Times. Jan 11, 1942. p. X4.

writers[64], including Dalton Trumbo, who brought their studio an Academy Award with his screenplay for *The Brave One* in 1956.

The King Brothers had imported *Rodan* for US audiences in 1957, and had great success with it[65]. They realized that Giant Monsters were big business and set about making their own Giant Monster Movie from scratch. They approached Eugene Lourie, who would have just completed *The Giant Behemoth*. He wrote a basic story outline about pearl divers in the south pacific who encounter a giant monster when an underwater volcano very suddenly erupts. They take it to Tokyo for exhibition and its mother, who is ten times the size of the baby, comes directly to its rescue. The two return to the sea and there is no battle with the military or destruction. For fear of being too derivative of *Godzilla*, they moved the film's action to Paris, France. Lourie convinced the Kings that, since Paris was a hundred miles inland from the sea, London was a better choice for the mama monster's attack. They used the same suitmation techniques Eiji Tsuburaya had been using for more than half a decade in Japan, but placed hydraulics in the monster's head so that the eyes could blink, the mouth could open and the ears could waggle. The movie was finished in 1959, but The King Brothers had to shop it around to distributors until late 1960.[66]

With *Rodan*, The King Brothers knew they should market to children, running a tv based ad campaign for the film the week before its wide release that included a drawing contest where kids were encouraged to trace Rodan's outline while it was held still on screen[67]. Once again, with *Gorgo,* they knew what side their bread was buttered on. They got a comic book tie-in that included artwork by comics legend and spider-man co creator Steve Ditko[68]. And, like with *Rodan,* it worked. In January of 1961, *Gorgo* had its premier in Tokyo, before releasing in March in the US and October in the UK. It was such a success that some people claim it inspired Toho to revive their Godzilla series the next year, but even though there hadn't been a new Godzilla movie in six years at that point, Toho had been making successful and popular sci-fi and Giant Monster Movies during that time, and their offering for 1961 would be another bold step forward.

While the film's producers had altered numerous things about Lourie's initial draft, like changing the pearl divers to treasure hunters and adding encounters with the military for Gorgo's mother, one thing was left unchanged: The monsters live and return to the sea with the smoldering city scape behind them as the sun rises and our child protagonist sheds a joyful tear, looking on and smiling. That's right, there's a kid in this movie. While there had been several important child characters in 1954's *THEM!*, it was pretty rare to see kids in these movies. In Japan they were seen as general audience fare, but in America, they were pretty much aimed directly at children, or at the very least, teenagers, five sevenths of whom are legally no more adult than the tiniest of babies. The creative team behind *Gorgo* admitted who the movie was for from the very beginning, and by putting the child actor up front, in the face of all the action, and casting him as the lone voice of reason, were

---

[64] Matthew Bernstein (1999). *Controlling Hollywood: Censorship and Regulation in the Studio Era.* Rutgers University Press. pp. 215–. ISBN 978-0-8135-2707-9.
[65] Staff (May 30, 1958). "Toho's Science-Fiction Team Completes Another Thriller; Tint Entitled 'The H-Man'". Far East Film News. Tokyo, Japan: Rengo Film News Co., Ltd.: 15. OCLC 6166385.
[66] *Ninth Wonder Of The World: The Making Of Gorgo.*
[67] Staff (April 4, 1958). "Rodan". Far East Film News. Tokyo, Japan: Rengo Film News Co., Ltd.: 4. OCLC 6166385
[68] https://www.comics.org/series/1467/covers/

essentially saying, this is you, and this is for you. It's also telling that the monster is only a child as well. There's no question that *Gorgo* is for children. There's also no *problem* that *Gorgo* is for children.

As these movies progress, more and more of them will admit this dirty secret, and be judged harshly by the fandoms of the future for it. I can't get on that bandwagon. We'll discuss it in greater detail later, but I first encountered these movies as a young child. As a matter of fact, I was three years old the first time I saw a Godzilla movie. And it was one of the much derided, silly seventies movies that brought me to the party. As I got older I grew to appreciate the more serious films and the themes they carried, but that's never been what drew me to Giant Monster Movies, and it's never been what makes them work for me. Hell, it's very rarely what makes any of them work. What makes them work is whether or not we can become childlike enough to look up in awe and wonder, if we're comfortable enough with ourselves to let that happen. *Gorgo* works because it has no pretensions about what it is, and that makes it better than the sum of its derivative parts.

Gorgo's mother, Ogra, searches for her son

A Quick Look at *The Colossus of New York*

Still from the climax of The Colossus of New York

From time to time, there will be films that, for one reason or another, don't quite fit into our main narrative of the history of Giant Monster Movies, but like mysterious planets invisible from our position in this solar system, their influence is still felt on the heavenly bodies we can see. And by heavenly bodies, I of course mean Giant Monster Movies.

Now that we've looked at the 3 Giant Monster Movies directed by Eugen Lourie, there's only one more movie in his filmography as a director, 1958's *The Colossus of New York,* and we're gonna take a quick look at it just for the sake of completion. As previously discussed, Lourie's directorial output is an outlier to his overall career in film, and with the movie we're examining today, we have the outlier of the outliers, his sole film that is not about a giant dinosaur monster stomping cities.

Colossus of New York feels to me like an extended episode of *The Twilight Zone,* and this may be due in part to the presence of composer Van Cleave, who would go on to compose for around thirty episodes of the fabled anthology series. Interestingly, this score is performed solely on the piano, as orchestras were on strike at the time. The sparse instrumentation, combined with footage occasionally sped up to keep the runtime down to the preferred 70 minutes for a B-movie on a double like this was, gives some of the movie's horror sequences a feeling similar to silent films especially Fritz Lang's *Metropolis,* as this story deals with many of the same themes about humanity, empathy, love, and progress.

This movie centers on the death of a brilliant humanitarian and scientist, Dr. Jeremy Spensser. His father, another scientist, transfers his son's brain into the body of a monstrous, Frankenstein-esque robot, hoping to keep Jeremy alive in order to continue his research. But once Jeremy is revived, he has to be convinced by his father to continue living and working, and is aware that he is slowly losing his humanity. At the same time, his brother is moving in on Spensser's wife.

Director Eugene Lourie in 1952

Of particular note is the Colossus itself, an 8 foot-tall costume that took 7 foot tall actor and stunt-man Ed Wolff 40 minutes to get in or out of. Notably, Wolff had played the Robot in the 1949 serial *The Phantom Creeps* alongside Bela Lugosi. His performance here apparently includes some underwater stunt work, which I can't imagine was fun or comfortable, but looks amazing.

Overall, this movie is good, if a little rushed and simple. That puts Eugene Lourie at four and four in my book, and I recommend all four of his directorial efforts. If I had to rank them, I would say *Gorgo* is my favorite. The *Beast from 20,000 Fathoms* would be next, followed by this and *The Giant Behemoth*, but separated by the thinnest of margins. In the end, I say check this out, it's better than I expected.

Chapter 12: *Mothra*

In 1958, Toho had made a mediocre Giant Monster Movie called *Varan The Unbelievable* that had initially been commissioned by the American TV production company, AB-PT, who promptly went out of business and left Toho holding the bag. They finished the movie and released it to theaters, making back their money, but they didn't really consider it an artistic success. They were impressed, however, with the humorous but appropriate dialogue with which screenwriter Shinichi Sekizawa peppered the fairly standard monster movie's script[69]. He had been hired to write for Toho after penning an alien invasion flick for rival Beehive Studios in 1956. After writing *Varan*, Sekizawa wrote two more sci-fi films for Toho, 1959's *Battle in Outer Space,* an exciting and lively alien invasion movie where much of the action takes place on Earth's moon, and *The Secret of the Telegian,* a horror-revenge movie about a teleporting man killing soldiers who left him for dead during the war. *Telegian,* coincidently, is the first time we're seeing future Godzilla director Jun Fukuda, as it was his directorial debut[70].

Screenwriter Shinichi Sekizawa

But let's get back to Shinichi Sekizawa. While his screenplay was adapted from a serialized short story called *Mothra and Her Luminous Fairies,* written by Shinichiro Nakamura, Takehido Fukunaga, and Yoshi Hotta,[71] Sekizawa truly put his stamp on it. The *Luminous Fairies* story has four fairies, an explicitly political message, and according to Steve Ryfle and Ed Godziszewski's commentary on Mill Creek's recent Bu-Ray release, no cohesion, due to its having three authors[72]. Sekizawa streamlined the story overall, cutting the number of fairies down to two, saving the political drama for the last act, and, most stunningly of all, introducing a *human* villain in Jerry Ito's Charles Nelson. While human hubris, egoism, and general bone headedness had all contributed to the characters' woes in previous Japanese Kaiju movies and in Giant Monster Movies in general, the *monsters* were always the villains; the movies were about stopping the monsters. Even in *Gorgo* from earlier the same year, the film is framed to make us expect the monster to rampage after being captured and put on display ala *King Kong*, before subverting our expectations and revealing his mother on a rescue mission. The inciting incident in *Mothra* immediately results in a threat; if Nelson takes the fairies from their island, Mothra will come and save them, and no one in the way will be spared.

In July of 1961, *Mothra* does many of the same things that *Gorgo* did back in March, but doesn't bother with all of the explanations or attempts to ground us in reality, and this is part of the charm of Sekizawa's writing. He understands fairy tales well, and introduces the rules of that genre into the Giant Monster Movie effortlessly. And like the best fairy tales, we are

---

[69] LeMay, John. *The Big Book of Japanese Giant Monster Movies: Showa Completion (1954-1989).* 2nd ed., 2017.
[70] *Showa Completion,* pg
[71] *A Life in Film*
[72] Ryfle, Steve and Godziszewski, Ed, "Commentary", *Mothra*, Mill Creek, Directed by Ishiro Honda (Japan, Toho Studios, 1954, 1956, 2011) Blu-ray

expected to accept the unusual aspects of the story as they come and simply roll with the weird stuff. Not only that, but by making the hero a monster and the villain a human, he allows us to openly root for the monster, just like we've all been secretly doing all along.

Mothra arrives to save her priestesses

And this is *Mothra*'s greatest significance, it centers the monster as the hero while still recognizing that it is a force of nature, a god with a lowercase "g". It gives them an almost religious role. Think about ancient stories of heroes and saints; as conduits of whatever attribute of God is supposed to be on display in the story, they act *upon* the narrative, exerting their will on the human characters, who can either accept and facilitate it, or oppose it and face the consequences. Whatever you believe, Mothra is coming to punish Nelson and anyone else who stands in the way of justice, which is only the restoration of that which is owed. The beautiful Song of Mothra sung by her fairies in Nelson's revue is their prayer for not only their own salvation, but the punishment of the wicked. He may as well ask them to sing that sooner or later God's gonna cut him down.

Sekizawa handles these heavy themes with a light touch that makes for an extremely fun and entertaining movie. With his addition to the team of special effect filmmakers at Toho, Sekizawa provided an ally to Eiji Tsuburaya, who I swear I will talk about in depth. Believe me, I really want to talk about Eiji Tsuburaya. His light scripts gave the monsters more well defined personalities, something Tsuburaya had been wanting to do, and would do in his own work with his TV production

Pop duo Emi and Yumi Ito as The Shobijin

company. The future of the series would come to embrace Sekizawa's vision, and he became its primary writer, eventually penning the screenplays or stories for ten of the fifteen movies in the original Godzilla series, and several episodes of Ultraman.

I'd be remiss if I failed to mention the gorgeous score in this movie, which was NOT composed by the Maestro of Monster Music, Akira Ifukube, but by Yuji Koseki, who had already written music for the pop duo The Peanuts, AKA Emi and Yumi Ito, who were playing Mothra's fairies, heretofore referred to as The Shobijin, a name coined by Sekizawa meaning "little beauties". While Koseki's work on *Mothra* is gorgeous and suits the film perfectly, Ifukube had already created the powerful and iconic theme for Godzilla, as well as another beautiful score for the otherwise mediocre *Varan the Unbelievable*. Oh look at that. We've come full circle.

Tomoyuki Tanaka, Ishiro Honda, Shinichi Sekizawa, Akira Ifukube, and Eiji Tsuburaya were now all in place to make what would become the highest grossing film of the original Godzilla series, and one of the most famous movies of all time.

Chapter 13: *King Kong vs Godzilla*

Ok, you can remove the level gauges; it's time to play with Willis O'Brien once again. When last we saw him, he had completed work on Eugene Lourie's second Monster Opus, *The Giant Behemoth*, but we're gonna go back a little further and discuss a tragedy in his life that can't be ignored. In 1915 Obie married a woman named Hazel Ruth Collette, and had two children with her, sons William and Willis Jr. Their marriage, like Obie's working relationship with *Ghost of Slumber Mountain* producer Herbert M. Dawley, was troubled from the start. O'Brien was, by most accounts, not a very good husband or father. He drank, had affairs, and spent most of his free time either at boxing rings or race tracks.

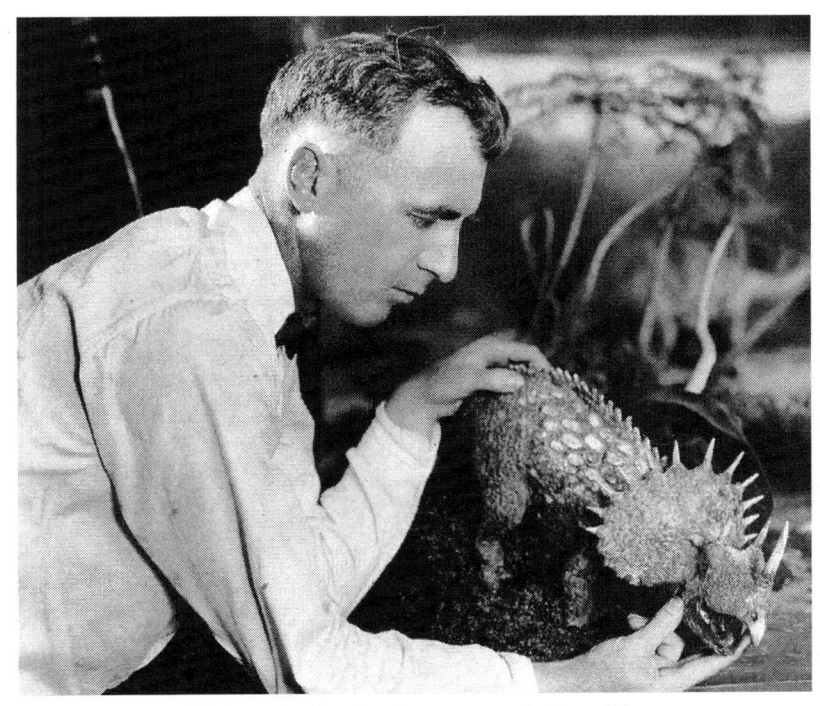

His wife, justifiably frustrated, publicly accused him of impregnating and then abandoning one of his female collaborators, and in 1922, attempted to kill both herself and their oldest son William by flipping over a canoe they were riding in. 8 years later, they would divorce, and Ruth would be diagnosed with tuberculosis and cancer. William also developed TB, and went blind in both eyes as a result. Despite her unstable behavior, the boys remained in Ruth's custody.

Willis O'Brien animating the styracosaurus for Son of Kong

In 1933, during the production of the lackluster *Son of Kong*, O'Brien brought his sons to visit the film's set, showed them the miniatures, and he began to rebuild his relationship with the boys after 3 years of neglect. When he returned them to Ruth, the two fought about child support.

I'll stop here to give a word of warning about domestic violence toward children, and self harm. I'll keep it as short as I can. Please skip the following paragraph if that is something you do not want to read about.

On October sixth of 1933, Hazel Ruth Collette shot and killed both of her sons, and shot herself in the chest as well. In doing so, she paradoxically extended her life by another year with this suicide attempt, as the bullet drained her tubular lung. She died in 1934, in the Los Angeles General Hospital Prison Ward. He remarried that year, to a woman named Darlene Prennette, and they stayed together the rest of his life.

O'Brien had a stroke of good luck in 1950, as he was awarded an Oscar for his special effects work on the previous year's *Mighty Joe Young,* which was also the commercial film debut of stop motion animator Ray Harryhausen, who we know from *Beast From 20,000 Fathoms,* wave as we pass by. The monster movie boom of the late 50's in America kept him busy on and off producing a dinosaur sequence for Irwin Allen's 1956 nature documentary *Animal World,* as well as work on 1957's *The Black Scorpion* and our old friend Eugene Lourie's *The Giant Behemoth*[73].

Here we go, back into the fun stuff. After a disappointing second team up with Irwin Allen, a 1960 remake of the earlier *The Lost World,* Obie was looking to get his career back on track. Allen had not allowed him to use any stop motion on *The Lost World*[74], instead gluing fins and other threatening appendages onto lizards and baby alligators. If returning to *The Lost World* hadn't worked, maybe revisiting King Kong would. So, O'Brien put together a pitch for a sequel, *King Kong vs Frankenstein,* where the grandson of Victor Frankenstein puts a beast called the Ginko together from dead African animals, and it has a boxing match with King Kong in San Francisco until they tumble off the Golden Gate Bridge together[75]. O'Brien's pitch got the attention of producer John Beck after shopping it around extensively and getting the permission of studio RKO to develop a project for Kong. RKO no longer produced their own movies, so Beck and O'Brien had to shop further.

The first thing Beck did was get a screenplay written, turning to George Yates, who had come up with the story to 1954's *THEM!,* as well as the screenplay for *It Came from Beneath the Sea, The Amazing Colossal Man, Earth vs The Flying Saucers,* and 1958's *Frankenstein 1970.* He then took Yates' screenplay around, finally landing at Toho, who were getting ready to celebrate the 30th anniversary of the company's founding[76]. What better way to celebrate than matching up the newly acquired original Giant Movie Monster who had inspired their own special effects wizard, Eiji Tsuburaya, who I will talk about in detail I PROMISE, to get involved in special effects, against their own Giant Monster star?

Toho producer Tomoyuki Tanaka had *Mothra* screenwriter Shinichi Sekizawa rewrite the screenplay to include Godzilla, and turned it into a salary man comedy. At director Ishiro Honda's request, the film would be a satire of people's obsession with TV. Back in the US, John Beck got a deal with Universal Pictures to be the sole distributor of the film in English speaking territories[77]. He had initially agreed to pay half of RKO's steep two hundred thousand dollar licensing fee for the right to use the Kong character, but didn't end up splitting the bill with Toho. As a result, they were saddled with the whole amount, which took up more than half of the film's reported production budget[78].

Beck left O'Brien behind, and like with *Ghost of Slumber Mountain*, he never saw a cent. Neither did *Kong*'s co-creator and co-director, Merian C. Cooper. He tried to sue John Beck,

---

[73]"The Kingmaker." The Guardian, 18 June 1999. The Guardian, https://www.theguardian.com/film/1999/jun/18/features1.
[74] "Willis H. O'Brien." Wikipedia, 17 Aug. 2023. Wikipedia, https://en.wikipedia.org/w/index.php?title=Willis_H._O%27Brien&oldid=1170856123.
[75] LeMay, John. *Kong Unmade: The Lost Films of Skull Island*. 1st ed., 2019.
[76]Morton, Ray (2005). *King Kong: The History of a Movie Icon from Fay Wray to Peter Jackson*. Applause Theatre & Cinema Books. ISBN 1557836698.
[77] Ryfle, Steve (1998). *Japan's Favorite Mon-Star: The Unauthorized Biography of "The Big G"*. ECW Press. ISBN 1-55022-348-8.
[78] "John Beck (Producer)." Wikipedia, 22 Sept. 2022. Wikipedia, https://en.wikipedia.org/w/index.php?title=John_Beck_(producer)&oldid=1111639299.

Universal, and Toho, but the case was dismissed, as Cooper was under the erroneous assumption that he was Kong's sole owner. That wasn't the only fallout caused by the American release of *King Kong vs. Godzilla*. Similar to how the original 1954 *Godzilla* was edited to have new scenes with Raymond Burr added, Beck commissioned scenes taking place in a United Nations newsroom, with an anchor commenting on the action periodically. These scenes add very little, but we get some fun, bad science out of it. Additionally, they replaced Akira Ifukube's score with stock music from Universal's library. And it's a damn shame, because it's one of his best scores.

Just one last thing, there's a rumor, first put forth by Famous Monsters of Filmland founder Forrest J. Ackerman in Spacemen Magazine issue #7, a companion magazine to his flagship book, Famous Monsters, that in the Japanese version of the movie, Godzilla wins the fight[79]. This isn't true. According to a recent post on Toho's website recapping the film, Kong was "Seemingly the victor", but the ending is ambiguous[80].

King Kong vs Godzilla was the highest earning and most attended film in the franchise until 1992, and it set the tone for Godzilla movies going forward. And we just got a rematch. After numerous delays, Legendary Pictures and Warner Brothers' *Godzilla vs Kong* was released on March 31st, 2021.

"EAT YOUR VEGETABLES!"

---

[79]. *Spaceman 07* Sept 1963. Accessed August 24, 2023. http://archive.org/details/Spaceman_07_Sept_1963.
[80] "KING KONG VS. GODZILLA." JFDB, https://jfdb.jp/en/title/7504. Accessed 24 Aug. 2023

Chapter 14: *Mothra vs Godzilla*

Come all without, come all within, you'll not see nothing like the mighty Thing. Unless you saw 1961's *Mothra.* Then you've seen something like the mighty thing. Because the Thing of 1964's *Godzilla vs the Thing,* as it was known in the US, is Mothra. Not *The Thing from Another World*, that already happened, and not John Carpenter's *The Thing*, either. It won't happen until 1982. No, not that *It!* That was in 1990, and they made a new version in 2017 with a sequel in 2019. First Base!

Enough waffling and Bob Dylan and outdated comedy references[81]. *Mothra vs Godzilla* has a reputation as one of the very best Godzilla movies, and it deserves that reputation. No, not THAT *IT!* Ok, ok, I'll stop. In all seriousness, this movie does a wonderful job of marrying the fairy tale tones of *Mothra* with some of the grimness of Godzilla's first two outings. Not too much, though, since according to Steve Ryfle and Ed Godziszewki's biography of Ishiro Honda, the production team was already beginning to respond to the audience for science fiction starting to skew younger, and the entire third act reflects this.

Speaking of that third act, it features some of the best effects work by the Father of Japanese Special Effects, my man Eiji Tsuburaya. That's right, it's finally time to talk about The Old Man, at least up to the War. Most of my information here comes from August Ragone's thoroughly researched and exceedingly rare book *Eiji Tsuburaya: Master Of Monsters: Defending the Earth with Ultraman, Godzilla and Friends in the Golden Age of Japanese Science Fiction Film*. Born in July of 1901, Tsuburaya was referred to as a "child craftsman" by a local newspaper due to the quality of his work making homemade model airplanes from wood[82]. Born Eichi, little Tsuburaya was always thinking about airplanes and flying. His dream, he said in a 1958 interview, was to fly around the world in an airplane he built himself[83]. This was spurred by the first successful airplane flights in Japan in 1910, and the next year, he had another formative childhood experience, when he saw a movie for the first time[84]. Tsuburaya then became obsessed with both airplanes and photographic projection. He even

American International's poster for Mothra vs Godzilla

---

[81] For you uncultured swine who didn't pick up on my hilarious and not at all obscure references, Bob Dylan wrote a song called *The Mighty Quinn* sometime in 1967 or '68, and just Google "Abbott and Costello 'Who's on First'"
[82] *Master of Monsters,* pg 18
[83] *Master of Monsters,* pg 18
[84] *Master of Monsters*, pg 21

claimed to have made cartoons for his own amusement using a toy movie camera, though his son Akira would later say this was just a part of his father's own self myth-making[85].

At the age of 14, Tsuburaya enrolled in the Nippon Flying School in Tokyo at what would become the Haneda International Airport. He was enrolled there from 1915 to 1917, when his instructor was killed due to engine trouble on a flight for newspaper photographers[86]. The school closed and 16 year old Tsuburaya went to engineering school and began working for a toy company to pay for his education. In 1919, during a business party at a tea house, Tsuburaya's co-workers got in a fight with employees of the Natural Color Motion Pictures Company. Tsuburaya avoided the confrontation and ran into one of the opposing party's employees, film director Yoshiro Edamasa[87]. Tsuburaya impressed him during a conversation about photography on the sidelines of the brawl, and Edamasa hired him to serve as his assistant cameraman. Tsuburaya continued to work at the studio through a merger and Edamasa's resignation to visit Hollywood up until December of 1922, when he was conscripted into the Imperial Army[88].

Eiji Tsuburaya in 1961

Honorably discharged after six months of service, Tsuburaya returned home, intending to run his family's general store, but decided to pursue his dream. He left the store with his uncle Ichiro and rejoined Kokukatsu Studios, which had purchased Natural Color Motion Pictures Company before Tsuburaya's military service[89]. He was invited to work at Kinugasa Motion Picture League in Kyoto and worked as their chief cameraman and an uncredited assistant director. He also innovated with camera equipment, creating a wooden crane for wide, sweeping camera movements. By this time, Kinugasa was absorbed into Shochiku Studios. In 1929, while Tsuburaya was working with his wooden crane, a part of it collapsed on him. A young woman touring the studio with her friends rushed to his aid, and would visit him daily while he recovered. Ms. Masano Araki married Tsuburaya in February of the next year. The nineteen thirties were off to a great start for Tsuburaya, and in 1933, he came to the same crossroads all monster makers seemingly reach at one point or another. In 1933, Eiji Tsuburaya was one of millions of people who saw *King Kong*.

In December of that same year, Tsuburaya published an article detailing how *Kong*'s effects were accomplished. He had figured Willis O'Brien's stop motion techniques out by watching his own personal 35 millimeter print of the film one frame at a time. This led to his then

---

[85] *Master of Monsters*, pg 23
[86] *Master of Monsters*, pg 21
[87] *Master of Monsters*, pg 21
[88] *Master of Monsters*, pg 22
[89] *Master of Monsters*, pg 23

current studio, Nikkatsu, to allow him to experiment with various special effects techniques. They grew impatient with his constant tinkering and perfectionism, and he quit the studio. He found work elsewhere quickly, and by the end of 1934, was chief cameraman at JO Studios, where he built a truck mounted, iron version of his wooden camera crane.

In 1937, Tsuburaya joined the recently formed Toho studios at the behest of executive production manager Iwao Mori[90]. He was reluctant at first, since it involved a change of focus. Mori wanted Tsuburaya specifically because of his innovations in special effects, and had him head up that newly formed department. In 1939, he began making flight training films for the government, producing spectacular footage and earning a certification for acrobatic flying. His bosses at Toho were more impressed with the former, and it resulted in more and better assignments[91]. That brings us back to World War II. And for now, we'll leave him there, but we'll rejoin him shortly.
There's too much to go over all at once, but I did want to touch a little bit on American International's bizarre marketing campaign for *Mothra vs Godzilla*, the movie we are supposedly here to talk about.

The first thing I wanna note about the American version of this movie, is it contains a spectacular effects sequence[92] wherein the US Navy bombards Godzilla on the beach. It's one of 3 similar sequences in the film, but together, these scenes sell the outright indestructibility of Godzilla, and the problem the Japanese people face if Mothra will not come and help them. After his comedic wrestling antics in *King Kong vs Godzilla*, The King of the Monsters is once again a walking terror.

There is a deep sense of justice in this film, but also of mercy; a concern for the innocent to be preserved from the punishment meant for the wicked. But what level of culpability do we bear for the transgressions of our neighbors, countrymen, race, and all of humanity? Sekizawa's seemingly simple, fairy tale script, much like a real fairy tale, has much on its mind.

In bringing the movie to America, AIP kept this text intact, but bungled a pretty important aspect of *Mothra vs Godzilla:* they tried to write out Mothra! Note that the Japanese title which is now Toho's preferred international title, bills the large lepidopteran above Godzilla, while AIP released it as *Godzilla vs The Thing,* obscuring Mothra behind giant question marks and disclaimers on their posters, and cutting away with cryptic references in trailers, *"what is the THING?"* This decision is often questioned by commentators, since Mothra had been an established character with her own successful film just three years earlier, why wouldn't audiences want to see her fight Godzilla? I love Mothra, and most fans of Godzilla I know do too, but that wasn't always the case. I used to think Mothra was lame, especially when I was a kid. I remember renting this movie when I was five or six and rolling my eyes at the Mothra larva's victory. I didn't understand it, and I don't think whoever made the decision to hide Mothra in the advertising did either. Well, at least as a worst case scenario. Maybe they thought their largely juvenile audience wouldn't be enticed by a big ol' butterfly as much as a giant radioactive dinosaur.

---

[90] *Master of Monsters*, pg 27
[91] *Master of Monsters*, pg 28
[92] This particular scene is not in the Japanese version.

This is a gorgeous film, both in terms of its cinematography and its message, and even if you do think the idea of Godzilla fighting a big fluffy bug is a little silly, well, isn't all of it? Why draw the line there? Enjoy yourself, maybe reflect a little. The Japanese version of this film ends with the characters asking each other how they can thank Mothra for her help, and coming to the conclusion that the only thing they can really do is do their best to make the world a better place. How can you be mad at that?

Chapter 15: *Ghidorah the Three-Headed Monster*

This movie, for good or for ill, is really the beginning of what most people think of as a Godzilla movie. For me, this is a very good thing. In the ten years since his debut, Godzilla has already softened considerably as a character, going from walking nuclear bomb in his first film to a more satirical and comedic take on his first incarnation, and then in *Mothra vs Godzilla*, a more general symbol of humanity's sins against nature and each other. Here, we see Godzilla begin his transformation into the hero of his own series. This decision was probably inevitable, but it was and is a controversial one, and the film's creative staff were split over it.

King Ghidorah lays waste to Japan

Ishiro Honda, according to Steve Ryfle and Ed Godziszewski's biography was not happy with the overall direction that the film took with its monsters, saying "I used the Peanuts as Mothra's interpreters, but even that was something I had to force myself to do." and "The Producer liked how it turned out. It was a big success.[93]" Special Effects Director Eiji Tsuburaya was happy with the new direction, as he was already beginning to realize the influence his work had on children[94]. This change is brought on because we get a new monster, an alien monster from Venus, or Mars if you're watching the American version, called King Ghidorah, who would go on to be considered Godzilla's greatest enemy.

Ghidorah is a spectacular creation, a golden, three headed space dragon with two tails, who cries out a different high pitched chirp from each head and shoots lightning-like gravity beams from his mouths. He was designed by Tsuburaya apprentice and future Special Effects Director in his own right, Akira Watanabe. According to August Ragone's book on Tsuburaya, Watanabe's influences were primarily Chinese dragons and the folkloric, eight-headed Japanese dragon, Yamata No Orochi[95]. Tsuburaya wanted the monster painted bright red, but he and his crew eventually decided that gold would be the most impressive color on-screen[96].

Ghidorah the Three-Headed Monster was the second Godzilla film of 1964, having been rushed into production when Toho's "New Year Blockbuster", Akira Kurosawa's *Red Beard*

---

[93] *A Life in Film*, pg 215
[94] *Master of Monsters*, pg 90
[95] *Master of Monsters*, pg 90
[96] *Master of Monsters*, pg 90

ran into some trouble and was delayed. Something needed to fill the slot[97]. This would be the only time two live action Godzilla movies would be produced in the same year.

The big innovation here is the fact that there are three monsters who had each starred in their own films meeting each other. True, Godzilla had fought Mothra earlier that year, but the mere fact that all of Toho's headlining giant monsters, except for Varan, were in this one movie was definitely impressive and surprising, but it wasn't totally unheard of. In 1943, Universal Pictures put two of its most popular monster franchises together in *Frankenstein Meets the Wolf Man*, and established that these movies shared a very loose continuity. From there, they piled on Dracula for 1944's *House of Frankenstein,* and 1945's *House of Dracula*, which had almost no continuity.

Cinematic universes are all the rage, nowadays, thanks to the success of Disney and Marvel's *Avengers* series of films. The approach they take is hyper focused on making sure the details from film to film line up with each other, but the Universal Horror Cycle and Godzilla's Showa Era films are much less scrupulous in this regard. We have the same actors playing different roles from film to film, details and locations changing in between sequels, and it's all done with a straight face. These crossovers were little treats, and might have almost played out as surprises if the films hadn't been marketed on the number of monsters appearing in them.

Godzilla, Rodan, and Mothra had each starred in their own film before appearing together in Ghidorah the Three-Headed Monster

In John LeMay's *The Lost Films' Big Book of Japanese Monster Movies,* he speculates that *Ghidorah* grew from the concept of having a straight versus film between Godzilla and Rodan, and that Honda and company went above and beyond in bringing in Mothra and also introducing a new monster in King Ghidorah[98]. This concept of adding more and more monsters would hit its peak in 1968 with *Destroy All Monsters*, which included almost every monster in the Toho stable up to that point, 11 in total. But we're not talking about that one yet. We're talking about how *Ghidorah the Three-Headed Monster* laid the groundwork for the rest of the series, from its highest highs and down to its lowest lows.

But for the time being, this film has the most spectacle from one of Toho's monster flicks, and in the Godzilla franchise in particular. We've discussed 3 Godzilla movies in a row, but

---

[97] *A Life in Film*, pg 215
[98] LeMay, John, and Ted Johnson. *The Big Book of Japanese Giant Monster Movies: The Lost Films.* 1st ed. pg. 62

he's gonna take a little bit of a break, and we'll meet a new monster next time, who is also an old monster, who gets a uniquely Japanese spin.

Chapter 16: *Frankenstein Conquers the World*

In the background of almost every movie that we've discussed, there has been a ghost. We've named it on a few occasions when it was unavoidable, but there has been a general attempt to keep the tone here light, and to maintain a relatively fun and lighthearted atmosphere. Today, that ghost will be front and center. That ghost is World War II, and the bombings of Hiroshima and Nagasaki, and Hiroshima is where this film begins.

After *Godzilla* debuted in 1954, the general tone of Toho's Monster Movies remained grave, but lightened considerably from their first effort. This tonal shift was completed by 1961's *Mothra*, and by 1962's *King Kong vs Godzilla*, more or less finalized. These were fun, family oriented movies now, and would remain so. Despite these strides toward a more family friendly and fantastical, wonderstruck tone, *Frankenstein Conquers the World* is a more serious and dark minded film. In those terms, it almost feels like a step backwards from the upbeat and triumphant *Ghidorah, the Three-Headed Monster,* but it is too good a film, too sincere and thoughtful, to really be a step back.

Baragon and Frankenstein fight for the fate of the world! Or something.

More than anything, in terms of the genre's evolution, *Frankenstein Conquers the World* is a deeply weird film, and that comes from a couple of things. Firstly, this is an evolution of the Willis O'Brien *King Kong vs Prometheus* story that Toho purchased from John Beck at the start of the decade. After the success of *King Kong vs Godzilla,* and not wanting to pay further licensing fees for the giant gorilla, Toho accepted a spec script from American writer Jerry Sohl, who would go on to write for the original *Star Trek* series, called *Frankenstein vs Godzilla*[99]. Things get a little messy from here. Harry G. Saperstein, an executive with American studio UPA, had been working on a deal with Toho to import and distribute Godzilla movies in the US. It's been speculated that his writer Reuben Bercovitch came up with a considerable portion of the story, and in the American and International versions, he's credited along with Takeshi Kimura as screenwriter. Sohl receives a story credit along with *Frankenstein* author Mary Shelley. Kaoru Mabuchi is the only credited writer of the Japanese version, and according to John LeMay's *Big Book of Japanese Monster Movies: Showa Completion*, is responsible for replacing Godzilla with the new and beloved monster Baragon[100].

---

[99] *A Life in Film* pg. 224
[100] *Showa Completion*, pg 97

Secondly, this movie stars American TV actor Nick Adams. He's comfortable and happy with his Japanese co-stars, but there's more confusion here. Saperstein and UPA had discussed sending actors to Japan to increase appeal to their American audiences, but Adams may have already been in Japan for Toho by the time UPA reached their deal[101]. He appeared in two more movies for the studio, including Godzilla's rematch with King Ghidorah in *Invasion of Astro-Monster* later the same year.

And that's just the behind the scenes weirdness. The film itself deals with unusual things, even in a genre known for its weirdness. In a lot of ways, I feel like this movie, with its heroic, size changing, humanoid monster fighting a big dinosaur at about half the scale of Godzilla, is a predecessor to Ultraman. Just a moody and depressed predecessor. Speaking of Ultraman, let's rejoin his creator, Eiji Tsuburaya, as World War II rages on.

Tsuburaya and Toho found themselves making propaganda movies for the Japanese government in the War, notably for Tsuburaya, was *The War at Sea from Hawaii to Malaya* in 1942[102]. Tsuburaya and his team's work on the film's Pearl Harbor sequence was so realistic, that it has often been confused for actual footage shot by Japanese pilots during the attack. The tide of the war began to turn, and eventually, in March of 1945, Tokyo was bombed, and Tsuburaya and his family were forced to take refuge in a public bomb shelter during the air raids. He distracted his three sons by telling them fairy tales[103]. The tragic bombings of Hiroshima and Nagasaki followed, and Japan surrendered on September 2nd that same year. In a strange and remarkable coincidence, I find myself writing this exactly seventy five years later on September 2nd, 2020.

In 1946, Tsuburaya was accused by occupying American officers of taking part in an espionage ring due to the detailed miniatures from *the War at Sea*, and he was effectively blacklisted from the Japanese film industry. He was let go from Toho. Undeterred, he and his oldest son Hajime opened their Tsuburaya Visual Effects Laboratory, and worked as private contractors in small capacities for various studios. Once the US occupation ended in 1952, Tsuburaya was able to resume working at Toho, and for the first time, he would collaborate with director Ishiro Honda and producer Tomoyuki Tanaka. Once again, the stage was set for great things. And once again, we'll leave Tsuburaya for the time being, but this time with friends, all on the brink of creating the film that would define their careers and lives for most of the world.

Frankenstein Conquers the World's frank dealings with World War II are unusual for a film from its time and place, especially as it admits that the Japanese were allied with the Nazis, and that this was not a good thing. It's also interesting that its main human character is an American who is working with radiation poisoning victims who grew up in Hiroshima. None of the human characters in this film are innocent, and it takes a much more direct and cynical approach to this than the previous years *Mothra vs Godzilla,* which admitted the same thing, but decided that there is enough good in humanity to make it worth saving. This film simply asks the question, and leaves it open ended; What makes us human? And what makes something monstrous?

---

[101] *A Life in Film* pg. 222-223
[102] *Master of Monsters*, pg 28
[103] *Master of Monsters*, pg 29

Chapter 17: *Gamera*

In 1963, *King Kong vs Godzilla* changed everything for Giant Monster Movies. And now, Daiei Studios wanted in on the action. So, in 1964, they began work on their first monster epic: *Giant Horde Beast Nezura*. Not what you were expecting, huh? *Giant Horde Beast Nezura* was written, miniature sets were produced, six foot giant rat props were made, and hundreds of live rats were gathered to begin shooting the effects sequences. A publicity campaign was launched in which people were encouraged to bring rats to the studio for 50 yen a head. This was the seed of a big, itchy problem. Most of the rats were white, but special effects director Yonesaburo Tsukiji wanted black rats. So they dyed them black. So the rats licked the dye out of their fur. *sigh* fine. What else can go wrong?

So much, just so much more could go wrong. The rats wouldn't move under the electric lights of the studio, so they tried using low light and high sensitivity lenses, but that didn't work. Finally, they decided to send a mild electric current through the miniature sets to get the rats going. Fleas began to infest the set, then the studio. Then they started to eat each other. That was enough. No more giant rat movie. They had won and Daiei had lost[104].

Part of the problem here was that the studio was in a bit of financial trouble, and they were stuck with this elaborate miniature city set. They couldn't let it go to waste, so they pivoted, and started work on *Gamera, the Giant Monster*.

Noriaki Yuasa directed all but one of the original 8 Gamera films

Let's talk about Gamera. He's a turtle with big ol' tusks who breathes fire and flies by shooting flames out of his shell's limb holes, a word I made up just now. You love it. The story goes that either Yonejiro Saito or Masaichi Nagata, both producers at Daiei, was flying back to Tokyo when he saw a cloud that resembled a turtle. Now that *Nezura* wasn't happening, maybe a giant turtle movie could put those miniatures to use. Helming the new film was sophomore director Noriaki Yuasa, who had directed a musical comedy the previous year, and had also been involved in *Nezura*'s production. He wound up directing many of the special effects sequences too. Yuasa wrote the script with Nisan Takahashi, who was credited alone on the finished film, though Yuasa had the clearer vision of what Gamera should be: A giant monster Franchise aimed directly and explicitly at children.

Like many western viewers and fans of the Gamera movies, I was introduced to the character through the *Mystery Science Theater 3000* episodes that featured five of the films being mocked by Joel and the Bots. I thought the movies seemed like fun, even without the humorous commentary. So I found Mill Creek's *50 Sci-Fi Classics* box set at my local Target

---

[104] *The Lost Films,* pgs 65-66

and went to town. I believe four Gamera movies were on that set, but there's no way of knowing. I watched them all in my bedroom on a portable DVD player, something well out of style even at the time.

What struck me the most, and still is very striking to me, is the sincerity of these films. Sure, they began as a cash grab, and remained in that spirit, but Noriaki Yuasa clearly loved what he was doing, and while the only Showa era Gamera film he didn't direct is absolutely the best one, it's not as much fun. Well, it's more fun than *Gamera Super Monster*, but I'm getting ahead of myself. These films are fun, even when they're bad, and that feels like a direct result of someone knowing what kind of movies they were making and who they were making them for.

Gammera The Invincible

This particular movie never sinks to the depths of something like *Konga* or, Godzilla forbid, *The Giant Claw*, but it's a pretty basic set up. The really unique thing here is the film's child protagonist, Toshio, who is obsessed with turtles, and is like Sean from *Gorgo* on steroids from a story perspective. Whereas *Gorgo* needs Sean as its voice of reason, Toshio contributes very little to the story in *Gamera*. That's not necessarily a bad thing though, and was probably key to *Gamera's* success. This kid barges into military tribunals demanding they not hurt Gamera because he had saved his life and "all turtles are good". Of course, this ignores that Gamera created the situation from which Toshio needs to be saved. He's not quite the friend of all children yet.

Gamera, like so many movies we have discussed, is derivative. Obviously of Godzilla, yes, but it also recreates the lighthouse set up from *The Beast from 20,000 Fathoms*, and *Gorgo* is another clear inspiration, with its focus on a child protagonist. And, even though it was the last black and white daikaiju eiga, the monochrome cinematography hides any shortcomings in the monster suit and effects. *Gamera* seems like it would have come along too late, doing nothing new 12 years after the genre began in earnest, but it took Japan by storm, and ended Daiei's financial woes for the time being. A sequel was planned and given a bigger budget and shot in color. We'll cover that soon enough.

The last thing I wanna talk about is the name Gamera itself. I find this information very interesting, and it has to do with Japanese Monster Naming conventions. Godzilla's name comes from smashing two Japanese words together, "gorira", which means "gorilla", and "kujira", which means "whale". Even though Toho's next few monster's names were inspired by real life animals, Rodan[105] is an abbreviation of pteranodon, Anguirus of ankylosaurus, and Varan derived from the scientific name for a monitor lizard, Mothra begins a trend following after Godzilla's name, using the last syllable, "ra" to indicate size and power. Think how in the west we use "-zilla" to indicate something is monstrous, hog-zilla, bride-zilla, et cetera. "Ra" came to mean the same thing, more or less. Gamera can be loosely translated as "turtle-zilla", since the Japanese word for turtle is "kame", which Daiei modified to begin with a "g" so that their giant monster wasn't named "camera", which is the same word in English and Japanese[106]. Special thanks to Will Laughlin of braineater dot com, where I initially discovered this info years ago.

Gamera would be the only real challenger to Godzilla and his franchise's popularity, but at this point in our story, their rivalry has only just begun.

---

[105] "Radon" in Japanese.
[106] http://www.braineater.com/gamera.html

Chapter 18: *Invasion of Astro-Monster*

Today's film is among the first Godzilla movies I saw as a young boy. Rewatching it for the show, I was surprised it held my attention then. This film has the least screen time for Godzilla in the entire franchise as of this writing. Out of the 94 minute runtime, The Big G is on screen for 5 minutes and forty five seconds. 6% of the movie is Godzilla footage[107]. But it has some of the most

The aliens "borrow" Godzilla and Rodan

effective and memorable imagery of the whole series in my opinion. One of my first thoughts when Godzilla is brought up is when the Xilliens lift him out of the lake in a bubble, and pull Rodan out of a mountain the same way. There's also the part where Rodan throws Godzilla at Ghidorah, and they all tumble down the side of a cliff and into the ocean together. This movie, for my money, has some of the best monster action.

On the downside of things, finding this movie at the video store was an ordeal. It was one of my favorites to rent, but it seemed to have a different title whenever I was looking for it. I distinctly remember a VHS copy that called it *Godzilla vs Monster X,* though I can't find anyone else corroborating that title. I do know that *Gamera vs Jiger* was initially called *Gamera vs Monster X*[108] when it aired on US TV, but I don't remember our Hollywood Video having any Gamera movies besides 1995's *Gamera: Guardian of the Universe*. Most often, I found this movie under the title *Godzilla vs Monster Zero*. The old Simitar VHS cover is the one I remember getting the most often, with a very t-rex-y looking Godzilla fighting Ghidorah's three heads, entangled all in them against a purple, marbled field inside of a little gold box on a black background. Sometimes, they had Paramount's older VHS release.

They had re-released those tapes with gorgeous illustrated covers, presenting the titles of each movie in a vaguely Asian font. I never rented a tape with this *Monster Zero* cover art, as the store I went to as a kid only had the Simitar release and the old Paramount tape, which just had a still of Godzilla and Ghidorah fighting on Planet X. All this for a movie originally released in the US as *Monster Zero,* plain and simple. Now if you were to go into the entertainment section of a Walmart or Target and ask for *Godzilla vs Monster Zero* today you would be met with confused looks and exclamations of puzzlement and not just because you won't typically find Godzilla movies at either establishment. No, even if you typed it into

---

[107]https://www.unusualhorror.com/post/godzilla-screen-time
[108] Pellegrini, Mark. "Gamera vs. Monster X (1970) Review • AIPT," November 2, 2015. https://aiptcomics.com/2015/11/02/gamera-vs-monster-x-1970-review/.

Amazon, a query for *Godzilla vs Monster Zero* would only bring up old VHS tapes like the ones I already described.

In 2007, Classic Media, the same distribution company that brought us digital home video releases of the stop-motion animated Rankin-Bass Holiday Specials, released a glorious DVD of the film that contained both Henry Saperstein's US version and Ishiro Honda's with an excellent commentary on the former by Stuart Galbraith IV. This disc was released under Toho's preferred international title, *Invasion of Astro-Monster*. Interestingly, when the film was initially released in the US, it was distributed only to American military bases under a closer title than Saperestein's *Monster Zero*, as *Invasion of the Astros*. Insert baseball joke here.

This confusion over international titles is another bizarre point of light from these movies that provides me with great joy. Especially for the German versions. For example, in Germany, *Invasion of Astro-Monster* was called *Command from the Dark*. *Frankenstein Conquers the World* was called *Frankenstein: The Terror with the Face of an Ape*. Their titles would only get weirder and weirder overtime, with later entries like *Godzilla vs The Sea Monster* becoming *Frankenstein and the Monster from the Sea*, and *Terror of Mechagodzilla* becoming *Konga, Godzilla, and King Kong: The Devil's Brood*[109]. No wonder Toho began making distributors use the international titles!

Kumi Mizuno (left) and Nick Adams (right) in Invasion of Astro-Monster

The biggest *positive*[110] innovation for the Giant Monster Movie genre that *Invasion of Astro-Monster* has to offer is its humanoid alien invaders crossing over into a kaiju movie. At this point in the genre's history, it's a fresh turn for the story to take. Aliens using giant monsters as a vanguard of invasion? It hadn't been done quite like this before. And while this would become a heavily repeated trope in the series and genre at large, right now it's fresh, shiny, and new. The other innovation is not a good sign in terms of things to come, and that is the use of stock footage in the special effects sequences to fill out the fights and save a buck. City smashing scenes were borrowed from *Ghidorah the Three Headed Monster* and the original *Rodan*.

There's good and bad on the horizon for Godzilla, and we're saying sayonara to him for this season of RECORD ALL MONSTERS, but he'll be back, and there are still a handful of

---

[109] *"Terror of Mechagodzilla."* Accessed August 24, 2023. https://www.tohokingdom.com/movies/terror_of_mechagodzilla.htm.
[110] For many people I have talked to, this is the beginning of the end for the Godzilla series. As you will see, I heartily disagree.

73

movies left before we wrap up the season in earnest so we will too. This movie is kind of the finale for the King of the Monster's Golden Age, and I feel good leaving him on a high note.

Chapter 19: *The Magic Serpent*

Fun fact: I love folk and fairy tales[111]. They're my favorite literary genre. I have so many books both of and about folk and fairy tales from around the world that they have their own dedicated, free standing bookshelf. And as you have probably guessed from this show's mere existence, I also love Monster Movies. So, back in November of 2016, while I was driving home listening to Kyle Yount's Kaijucast, looking forward to the Bill Miller[112]'s chopped barbecue sandwiches I'd just picked up, the movie they were discussing sounded like a dream come true! It was called *The Magic Serpent*, and was adapted from a Japanese folk tale called *The Tale of Gallant Jiraiya*. Its story sounded like a cross between *Clash of the Titans* and *Star Wars*. I just had to find and watch this movie.

The monsters of The Magic Serpent

That would prove more difficult than I could have possibly anticipated. Sure, as a lifelong Godzilla fan I knew it was challenging to find these movies sometimes. I knew that the same people who held the American distribution rights now weren't the same people who held them when the movies were initially released. Some had entered the public domain in this country, or their ownership was so vague that they may as well be in the public domain. I expected to find it on some no name distributor's "Creature Double Feature" DVD in a dollar movie bin at Walgreens or CVS, packaged with one of AIP's TV versions of Gamera, or *Monster From a Prehistoric Planet*. Would that I were so lucky.

As of this writing, it has been just shy of four years since I heard that episode of Kaijucast, and lo, these many years have I searched for a quality version to set myself before. There was a difficult to watch version of AIP's dub on youtube with extremely poor picture quality, and another version that was much better looking, but undubbed and unsubbed. On Amazon and Ebay, even the VHS went for more than I was willing or sometimes able to pay. What was a poor boy to do?

---

[111] I really do!
[112] It's a San Antonio based fast food barbecue chain. I love it, but it is not the best representation of Texas style BBQ if you're visiting from out of state. Look for a mom and pop place or, failing that, something you saw on the Food Network.

Well, he could start a podcast talking about Monster Movies and put *The Magic Serpent* in the line-up so that he can tell himself that he *has* to spend that money because he's scheduled to talk about the movie! So here I am, with an imported DVD with English subtitles, watching *The Magic Serpent* and eating kettle corn. My own hero's journey at an end. But what challenges await on the horizon? One challenge has felled me already. A movie I sought to view as a double feature with *The Magic Serpent*, that was easily available not that long ago, but is now as hard to find as *Godzilla 1985*. *Daimajin*.

Even a used copy of this trilogy, all released in 1966, just after *The Magic Serpent,* and in 2012, Mill Creek put out a blu-ray set that I foolishly never picked up while it was just around fifteen bucks. These films were made by Daiei, the same studio responsible for the Gamera films, and… Unfortunately, that's all I can really tell you, because I haven't seen them[113]. I intended to watch *The Magic Serpent* as a double feature with *Daimajin*, using them as a point and counterpoint about Giant Monsters in the context of fantasy films, almost as an extension of the ideas in *Mothra,* but alas, it was not to be. So we'll look at this episode as a stand-in for this little tributary the genre briefly took for a year in the mid-sixties, at the start of the second Kaiju Boom.

1966 saw the theatrical release of *seven* Giant Monster Movies, as well as the premieres of Eiji Tsuburaya's TV projects *Ultra Q* and *Ultraman,* and his child focused monster show, *Friendly Monster Booska*. The next year would see another 5 theatrically released Japanese movies, including two from major studios Nikkatsu and Sochiku, and a South Korean Giant Monster movie to boot. Kaiju ruled on TV too, as Tsuburays's third Ultra series, *Ultraseven*, debuted just ten days before my favorite tokusatsu TV show, *Johnny Sokko and His Flying Robot*, known simply as *Giant Robo* in Japan.

We'll be riding this high through to the beginning of next season, and it's hard not to look ahead with excitement and trepidation at what is to come. For now, I'm happy to finally get to watch this movie, which was everything I hoped it would be. Even if the monster action is minimal, It's probably more than there was in our last episode's movie, even if it's not as good. The suits do look pretty nice, if highly stylized, but I don't have a problem with that. I recommend this movie, if you can find it.

---

[113] I have since seen them thanks to Arrow Video's 2021 Blu-Ray box set. They're covered here in a special section.

A Quick Look at the *Daimajin* Trilogy

I wanted to present this quick look at Daimajin. It's going to be a little different from how we normally do a quick look since it's covering three movies. What happened here is, I sat down and watched *Daimajin*, then *Return of Daimajin*, then *Wrath of Daimajin*, and I recorded a quick little rundown of what I thought after each film. These are those transcripts, minimally edited for clarity.

Daimajin

Okay, so I've just finished *Daimajin*. It was very good. Really very good. A couple of things that stood out to me. This is, again, kind of a *Clash of the Titans*-ish story: the deposed son of a lord who was assassinated, coming back to reclaim his title. He has a sister this time, and she's really the driving force of the narrative. Her pleas for mercy on the monster or for her brother to the monster, who is- one aspect of it seems a dual aspect god who lives above the village and either protects or destroys it based on its whims. And that monster is Daimajin, who seems to be one side of the god Shino. It reminded me a lot of *The Magic Serpent*. It is a chambara film first and foremost. There's no ninjas in this. There's samurai, and I really enjoyed it. And I'm curious to see *Return of Daimajin*.

Daimajin in his debut feature

One thing I do want to say real quick is this has a score by Akira Ifukube, who is most famous for his work on the Godzilla movies. It's undoubtedly Ifukube, and this score just sounds like what you think of- my main issue with Ifukube, who is a great composer, and I can never come up to his level in terms of any music I could write, but I find him a bit repetitive. And his *Daimajin* music, while powerful, about halfway through, he starts repeating the themes again. And it's not so much in the way of a leitmotif until the end, but just good. All good. This whole thing is good. So now we're going to watch *Return of Daimajin*.

Return of Daimajin

Okay, so I just finished *Return of Daimajin* and I liked it a lot. It's basically a remake of the first one, but it's more spectacular. The effect sequences are better. There's still just the one big one at the end, but it's more spectacular. And while Daimajin himself is- well the theology behind him is much clearer this time. There's no like, oh, this god keeps this god in check

77

and they live in the mountain. And while that stuff is cool, it's much more interesting to me that it's just Daimajin. Our god, he lives on this island and you don't want to piss him off. And it also, as opposed to the ten plus years that happened in the first movie, this one, it's just like a few days.

So the differences aside, it is pretty similar. Of course the differences aside, it's pretty similar, what am Italking about? But I did like it and I probably would throw this one on, of the two so far, more often because again, it is more spectacular. It's a good one to have on just like, as a lead up to doing the dishes. It's about 10 minutes shorter than the first one, but I'm about to watch *Wrath of Daimajin*. The third one, this is probably the one I'm most excited about just because it's supposed to be the most different of the three. So let's find out.

Wrath of Daimajin

One thing I liked more about it was its focus on common people. The first two, the heroes are deposed aristocrats. And this one, the heroes are four peasant boys whose fathers and older brothers have been kidnapped to mine sulfur. For our evil lord, he's probably the most over the top, but we don't spend as much time with him as we do with the other evil lords in the series. Also a note on that, all three evil lords have a symbol that's very close to the Rebel Alliance symbol from the Star Wars movies, and I can't help but thinking that had to have been an influence. It's a little different in each one, but in the second one specifically, it looks a lot like it. And this movie would have been on TV in the late sixties. The first two movies would have been on TV in the late sixties. Third one didn't get a US release for a long time until it came out on video and they used the international dub there instead of AIP doing their own, which AIP released the first two straight to TV in the late sixties, sixty seven or eight, I want to say, but this one was my favorite. It's got great, beautiful, snowy sets.

The story is again, because it's focused on the peasants- I find it to be the most compelling story of the three. It's almost like- there's very little connection. There's no connection between all three movies except the Daimajin is in them. So I almost feel like the Daiei studios gave three different directors the same concept and they each had a different take on it. It's almost like variations on a myth. Like in variations on Cinderella. I come back to Cinderella a lot. That oh, in the Scottish version, she becomes a scullery maid and leaves her ring in the prince's porridge. And in the French version, she leaves her glass slipper behind. And then one version, her fairy godmother is the ghost of her mom in a haunted tree and stuff like that.

These little variations, it's essentially the same story. The people are oppressed. They pray to a mostly wrathful god who sees justice in their cause and swoops in to save them. Literally. In this one, he swoops in to save them. Daimajin is predecessed in *Wrath of Daimajin* by a hawk. And I think that's a pretty cool touch. I have ornithophobia. I'm very scared of birds, but I had a warning. I knew that there was a bird, a very violent bird in this movie. And it is a violent bird, make no mistake. But it makes it feel more fleshed out. It makes it feel more- the mythology with it feels more real. While I'll still probably throw on *Return of Daimajin* more often because it's the lightest of the three, this one is my favorite. It's kind of like if 80s Spielberg made a children's kaiju movie set in feudal Japan.

This is also the only movie, I think, where no one gets crucified in this series. There are two crucifixions. In the first one, well, Diamajin has a great sense of ironic justice. And the bad guys in the first two movies try to crucify the heroes and Daimajin crucifies them, mirroring the way they wanted to kill their opponents. So that was very fun. Interesting, not only that, in the first one, Daimajin pins his victim to the cross with a spike that they had earlier used to try and destroy him that was nailed into his head while he was a statue. I recommend all three of these movies. I know most people won't agree with me about *Wrath of Daimajin* being the best one, but in my opinion, it is. Most people seem to like the first one best of all, though, we all seem to agree that the second one is weakest. But if you like that one best, more power to you.Yeah. Daimajin. Check it out.

It's interesting. He does evolve a little over the course of the series from just purely wrathful, having to be begged to stop his revenge. In the first movie, after he kills the bad guy, he keeps killing people and he has to be persuaded to stop. And in this one, after he kills the bad guy, he stops himself and acknowledges the kids and then disappears. Now, the very interesting thing about this one is that people who die stay dead. I almost didn't expect it

Chapter 20: *Gamera vs Barugon*

At this stage in their development, it's a little hard to talk about the Gamera movies. There was no clear direction for the newly formed film series to go, and the first film's director Noriaki Yuasa had been at odds with the studio during the production of the 1965 film[114]. He had wanted to gear *Gamera the Giant Monster* more toward children, but they had created a kind of tonal dissonance by pulling against his instincts and trying to make a more adult film. Now that it had been a tremendous success, the executives at Daei had decided to give *Gamera* a prestige sequel.

The first step they took was to demote Yuasa from the director's chair to only working as the special effects director[115], a task he had done while also helming the film's drama scenes on the first film. They brought in Shigeo Tanaka to direct the more adult oriented *Gamera vs The Ice Men from Outer Space.* He had been directing since 1931, and I can find very little information on his earlier features, but he went on to direct many of the *Woman Gambler* series of films, which starred this movie's lead actress, Kyoko Enami.

Now, obviously, *Gamera vs the Ice Men from Outer Space* isn't the movie we wound up getting, but that film, according to John LeMay's *Big Book of Japanese Giant Monster Movies: The Lost Films,* would have featured Gamera escaping from the Z-Plan rocket to find Earth being frozen by men from outer space, trying to take it over. Gamera presents them with a problem, so they throw their own giant monster at him, a huge Ice Monster[116]. Screenwriter Niisan Takahashi kept the plot about freezing the earth, giving that power to the newly created monster Barugon.

Barugon attacks with his rainbow ray

If you're new to the genre of Giant Monster Movies, and have been reading these chapters in order, you may be saying, now wait a minute, cowboy, hold your horses, we talked about Baragon being in *Frankenstein Conquers the World* a year before this movie, four chapters ago! And you are right! Have a cookie. We did talk about Baragon then, this is a wholly original, quadrupedal, horn-faced dinosaur monster. The key difference is that this guy breathes ice instead of a weird pink laser and doesn't have adorable elephant ears. And his name is Bear-roo-gon, not Bear-uh-gon. How could you possibly confuse them? I can't find a very good source for this, and it seems to be backward speculation on

---

[114] Ragone, August, and Jason Varney. *Commentary: Gamera vs Barugon.* Shout! Factory, 2010.
[115] Ragone & Varney. *Commentary: Gamera vs Barugon.*
[116] Ragone & Varney. *Commentary: Gamera vs Barugon.*

their part, but Gojipedia states that Baragon gets his name from the Japanese word for rose, bara, due to the scales on his back resembling the flower's petals[117], and an abbreviation of the English word dragon. The generally more reliable Wikizilla is silent on this matter. Now Barugon, this film's antagonist monster, takes his name from an aboriginal word for crocodile and the same abbreviation of dragon[118]. That's according to August Ragone and Jason Varney's excellent commentary on Shout Factory's DVD of the film, where much of my information on this episode is coming from. So, who can even say if there was even any copying going on? Not me!

But I digress. The budget on this film was almost four times as much as the previous film's[119], so it was shot in widescreen and in color. There are few remnants of the solely and explicitly adult film Daiei initially intended to make outside of a generally darker tone to the story and more violence between the human characters, and indeed, it is the more compelling of the two films. This puts it in a very strange position for a Gamera movie. This is the kaiju series, it seems, people most often visit in order to poke fun at or just turn their brain off and just watch men in monster suits wrestle in miniature cities while they do the dishes or play with their toys. This film is better than that, though, and reflects its increased budget despite its rushed production. This movie came out in April of 1966, less than five months after the first Gamera!

So what do you do with a Gamera movie that's too good for a Gamera movie? This is a question that no one would really tackle with another serious Gamera movie for 30 more years[120]. While *Gamera vs Barugon* wasn't a flop by any means, its increased budget meant it had to make even more money than its extremely successful predecessor, and it didn't. I have heard from many different sources, books[121], commentaries[122], that children ran wild in the theater in between monster scenes. This is a hundred and one minute movie, and kids watching it would have already sat through the first *Daimajin,* as these two films were released together on a double bill[123], which is itself eighty four minutes long, and also very deliberately paced.

By 1966, Giant Monster Movies were becoming more and more blatantly for children, and children weren't here to watch grown men fight over jungle treasure or diamonds. They wanted to see monsters messing each other up, dangit, and Noriaki Yuasa delivered on his end as special effects director. While his monsters are a little more cartoony than Tsuburaya's, they're still pretty effective, especially in this film. The monster fights are filled with Eastmancolor green and purple monster blood, and the long standing pattern of Gamera losing one fight and then coming back to finish the job during the finale after the human characters have proven incapable of doing so is established here.

---

[117] "Baragon (FvB)." *Gojipedia*, https://godzilla.fandom.com/wiki/Baragon_(FvB). Accessed 1 Sept. 2023.
[118] Ragone & Varney. *Commentary: Gamera vs Barugon*.
[119] Ragone & Varney. *Commentary: Gamera vs Barugon*.
[120] Shusuke Kaneko's Gamera Trilogy began in 1995 and ended in 1999. The films are very different from the original series and highly praised. I, of course, have very mixed feelings about them.
[121] *Showa Completion*, Pg 131
[122] Ragone & Varney. *Commentary: Gamera vs Barugon*.
[123] Ragone & Varney. *Commentary: Gamera vs Barugon*.

So, like with its predecessor, Daiei checked the receipts and learned and adapted, keeping what worked and tossing out what didn't. We'll see Gamera in his next adventure early in season 2 of RECORD ALL MONSTERS, and see how the disparate elements of this film and the previous year's titanic terrapin outing came together under Yuasa to create something truly unique that would shift the course of the genre like nothing since 1962 had done. At last Godzilla had a worthy opponent in terms of cultural influence and box office dominance, and the fight would get ugly and desperate for both of them in the next decade. But these are the good times, artistically and financially, for the Giant Monster Movie genre, and in our next chapter, which was our first season's finale, we'll discuss what many consider to be the pinnacle of the art form. We'll see you and what you think about it then.

Chapter 21: *War of the Gargantuas*

As we come to the end of this first season of the show, we approach one of the films that is considered a high watermark for the series and has fans as diverse and famous as Guillermo del Toro, Quentin Tarantino, Brad Pitt, and Tim Burton, just to name a few. It's an appropriate finale, as it closes out what many consider the Golden Age of Toho's Giant Monster Movies as the Kaiju Boom forced productions to get faster and cheaper in order to remain competitive. Let's catch up with Eiji Tsuburaya, and bring him up to today's movie before we look at its themes.

When last we left our hero, Tsuburaya had begun work on 1954's original *Godzilla* film. We've already talked about producer Tomoyuki Tanaka coming up with the idea for the film after his project about post-war Indonesia fell through due to broad anti-Japanese sentiment there, by blending the real life tragedy of the Lucky Dragon #5 tuna trawler with the story of *Beast From 20,000 Fathoms*. Tsuburaya submitted an old pitch for a giant octopus movie he had written 3 years earlier, and Tanaka took that with his own story outline to pulp sci-fi writer Shigeru Kayama[124]. Then Tanaka reached out to *Eagle of the Pacific* director Ishiro Honda, who we have talked about up to this point in his career as well, due to the strength of his partnership with Tsuburaya on their previous film. Honda found Kayama's tale lacking, and filled it in with human drama with his writing partner Takeo Murata. Much of the "monster as nuclear war" allegory comes from their treatment[125]. Things were beginning to take shape.

War of the Gargantuas was released on a double feature in 1970 in the US with Invasion of Astro-Monster

Tsuburaya desired very much to bring the as yet undesigned monster to life through stop motion, but Tanaka deemed it too time consuming[126]. Tsuburaya then determined that his team's strength with miniatures would lend itself very well to filming the monster as a man in a costume. The race to design was on. The first to take a crack at it was Wasuke Abe, a manga artist who had worked with Shigeru Kayama before. His mushroom cloud-headed giant was rejected, but he was retained to help storyboard the effects sequences, which would assist Tsuburaya and Honda in figuring out which shots could be achieved without wasting any time or money[127]. It was production designer Akira Watanabe who came up with the now iconic design, pulling together traits from a t-rex, iguanodon, and stegosaurus,

---

[124] *Master of Monsters,* pg 34
[125] *A Life in Film,* pg 231-234
[126] *Master of Monsters,* pg 35
[127] *A Life in Film,* pg 89

83

based off of a LIFE magazine paleoart pictorial feature[128]. After approving a clay model, Tsuburaya had his team begin building the suit.

The first suit was a complete failure. A wire frame covered with cloth and then hot rubber shaped like a monster proved inflexible. Nobody could move in it, so it was cut in half, and used for shots of the feet and tail from the waist down[129]. A second, lighter suit was made, and stuntmen and actors Haruo Nakajima and Katzumi Tezuka alternated to give the other breaks[130]. As previously discussed, they played Godzilla and Anguirus, respectively, in the film's sequel the next year.

Tsuburaya finished the effects photography in 62 brutal days[131]. Haruo Nakajima lost 20 pounds from the difficult and dangerous role as Godzilla[132]. But an Icon was born. Now, 12 years later, a lot has changed for Tsuburaya. He had his own production company once again, having formed it in order to gain the capital to purchase an optical printer, which is how Godzilla's atomic breath and other beam weapons were achieved from *King Kong Vs. Godzilla* on[133]. Part of this deal gave Tsuburaya the chance to produce his own television show for the Tokyo Broadcasting System, who had helped him purchase the optical printer in exchange for a program[134]. That program, *Ultra Q,* as well as its more famous spin-off series, will get some attention here eventually, but movies are the order of the day.

Russ Tamblyn in War of the Gargantuas

So, now that we're all caught up to the present day of 1966, let's talk about *War of the Gargantuas*. First of all, this movie is a sequel to the previous year's *Frankenstein Conquers the World.* You wouldn't know it from the American version, which is still very good, but the Japanese version is very upfront about it, even calling the film *Frankenstein's Monsters: Sanda and Gaira*[135]. If their names were Sandra and Gaia, this would be a very different movie. Another change is our American leading man, no longer portrayed by Nick Adams, and indeed, a different character, *West Side Story*'s Russ Tamblyn gives a low energy performance, and has none of the zest or enthusiasm Nick Adams brought to *Frankenstein Conquers the World.* His line readings are flat and his tie is too short. I'm not sure which annoys me more. As a matter of fact, according to the Steve Ryfle and Ed Godziszewski biography of Ishiro Honda, he was disliked by the Japanese cast and crew due to his attitude. Assistant director Seiji Tani

---

[128] *Master of Monsters,* pg 38-39
[129] *Master of Monsters,* pg 39
[130] *Master of Monsters,* pg 39
[131] *Master of Monsters,* pg 42
[132] *Master of Monsters,* pg 42
[133] *Master of Monsters,* pg 76
[134] *Master of Monsters,* pgs 82-83
[135] *A Life in Film,* pg 232

recalled: "Honda-san had to hold back and bear so much during that one. [Tamblyn] was such an asshole. He was exactly like that character he played [in *West Side Story*]. Like a hoodlum turned actor. Raw, very selfish, rebellious, and disobedient... What a punk. He pissed me off.... Afterwards we complained, 'Why the hell did they bring over a guy like that'"[136] Hard words. US co-producer Henry G. Saperstein echoed the sentiment in a 1994 interview, saying, "Tamblyn was a royal pain in the ass."[137]

But the heart of this movie, like every movie we've discussed on this show, lies with its monsters, who tell a tale as old as humanity itself, brother against brother. See, even though these characters have different names and, with the exception of Kumi Mizuno, are played by different actors, it's implied through the dialogue that the two warring gargantuas grew from pieces of the feral Frankenstein boy from *Frankenstein Conquers the World*. And their relationship is truly tragic, almost Shakespearian in its drama. After 5 years apart, they are reunited while the military attacks the green, evil Gargantua, Gaira. He is saved by the brown, good, Gargantua, Sanda. Gaira is played by Godzilla himself, Haruo Nakajima, while Sanda is played by Hiroshi Sekita[138]. The two men would spar with one another two more times on screen, Nakajima as Godzilla and Sekita as Ebirah in *Ebirah, Horror of the Deep* later that year, and Nakajima as King Kong with Sekita as Gorosaurus and Mechani-Kong in the next year's *King Kong Escapes*. Sekita would reprise the role of Gorosaurus in *Destroy all Monsters* in 1968 while also playing Anguirus in some scenes[139]. He would retire after playing a bat man in 1969's *Latitude Zero*.[140]

The Gargantua brothers recover from a military attack

The conflict between Gaira and Sanda begins when Sanda discovers the remains of his brother's human victims, their clothes that he spits out like the shells of sunflower seeds. The brown Gargantua picks up a tree and begins hitting Gaira, and the two fight for the rest of the movie. The battle is savage, with choreography more brutal than anything in a monster movie since *Godzilla Raids Again*. Even Gamera's battle with Barugon in that film, while incredibly bloody, isn't as animalistic and desperate as *The War of the Gargantuas*. The two

---

[136] *A Life in Film*, pg 231
[137] *A Life in Film*, pg 231
[138] *Showa Completion*, pg 116
[139] *Master of Monsters*, pg 165
[140] *Monsters Are Attacking Tokyo*, pg 131

brothers fight while the military tries to bring them down, but this is really more of a minor annoyance to them at this time. Even though we've seen the damage these new maser cannons can do to the monsters, Gaira and Sanda see only each other, and their hatred seethes between the two of them as blow after blow rains down between the two giants. Eventually, their fight leads them to sea, where they are swallowed up as a new island is born out of a volcanic eruption, killing them both.

War of the Gargantuas has always felt to me like something of a swan song for the genre's golden age. The adult oriented, brooding monster on the loose films of the fifties had given way to the family friendly sci-fi spectacles of the early sixties. And now the tide was already turning toward the child focused monster brawls that would come to define these movies in the cultural subconscious. Daiei had seen the writing on the wall and was already shifting gears with the Gamera franchise, and the next Godzilla film would be deemed unimportant enough that both Eiji Tsuburaya and Ishiro Honda would be pulled away to work on other projects. The sun was setting on the golden age, but once the sun goes down, you can either tremble in fear of the darkness, or throw a big goofy bonfire party, and that's what we have to look forward to when we come back for season two of RECORD ALL MONSTERS.

Chapter 22: *Ebirah, Horror of the Deep*

I promised you a big goofy bonfire when we got back, but how does a dance marathon sound to kick off this season? Well, even before that, our story today begins with a big monkey, THE big monkey, really. Our story begins with Rankin/Bass' *The King Kong Show*, which aired 25 episodes from 1966 to 1969 on ABC. Rankin/Bass, then Videocraft Entertainment, was already pretty famous for their "Animagic" stop motion television specials, 1964's *Rudolph the Red Nosed Reindeer* in particular, but they also produced traditional hand-drawn animation through partners at Japan's Toei Studios[141].

Popular on both sides of the Pacific, Rankin/Bass approached Toho for a live action tie-in film. Toho put our man Shinichi Sekizawa on the script, and he came up with something very reminiscent of a Saturday morning cartoon. A young man from a rural area comes to the city to look for a boat, intending to look for his shipwrecked brother, who is believed dead. He joins up with two other young guys he meets at a dance marathon where the prize is a yacht, and they go down to the shipyard and look at some boats. Ah, boats. I love boats. I know next to nothing about them, I just think they're neat[142]. The three young men climb aboard one yacht they think looks very nice, and run into Akira Takarada.

Not a lot of talk about monsters yet, huh? That's what Rankin/Bass thought too. While the script has a lighter tone, it takes about 15 minutes for our first glimpse of a monster, and that's nothing more than the claw of our mysterious adversary, the kaiju Ebirah, whose name can be very loosely translated as "shrimp-zilla". None of this was in *The King Kong Show*. Neither was the terrorist organization Red Bamboo. Rankin/Bass nixed the treatment, and commissioned a new script[143]. Not wanting *this* script to go to waste, it was allegedly repurposed as today's film[144], *Godzilla vs the Sea Monster,* or *Ebirah, Horror of the Deep* if ya nasty.

With their Big Dogs of Honda, Tsuburaya, and Ifukube working on other projects, Toho put new blood into the creative roles of this film once the script was finished. This included director of the *Young Guy* series, Jun Fukuda, who went on to direct four more films in the Godzilla series, effects director Sadamasa Arikawa, Tsuburaya's protege, who had worked on episodes of Ultra Q and Ultraman as an effects director, and as Tsuburaya's assistant director on nearly every Toho sci-fi movie up to this point[145]. Finally, Akira Ifukube was replaced by Masaru Sato, and his score here is indicative of what Tomoyuki Tanaka was trying to do with this film, that is, something completely different. Specifically, appeal to teenagers[146].

Sato had scored a Godzilla film before, but he wasn't quite in his element on *Godzilla Raids Again.* Here, Sato is quite himself, using elements of jazz, surf rock, and traditional island music, all of which would be used again as he scored 3 more Godzilla films after this,

---

[141] *The Animagic World of Rankin/Bass*. Directed by Constantine Nasr, 2018.
[142] It's true!
[143] Kalat, David. *A Critical History and Filmography of Toho's Godzilla Series*. Second edition, Reprint, McFarland & Company, Inc., Publishers, 2017, pg 95
[144] *A Critical History,* pg 95
[145] *Master of Monsters,* pg 145
[146] *Master of Monsters,* pg 144

creating some of my all-time favorite musical cues in the franchises' history. Sato's radically different approach to scoring complements Fukuda's dynamic directorial style. Whereas Ishiro Honda had an almost documentary style, Fukuda takes his cues from the action films of the day, while making the most of the island locales created for the film.

Arikawa's work diverges less from his predecessor's than Fukuda and Sato's, but it does differentiate itself nonetheless. Part of this is due to Haruo Nakajima remaining inside the Godzilla suit. Nakajima had played Godzilla for 12 years at this point, and as such had an established way of portraying the character. Even when he does something outside of what we might consider "normal" behavior for Godzilla, it's grounded in the history of his portrayal of Godzilla. So while his interest in our female lead is an obvious leftover from this script's days as *The King Kong Show The Movie*, we've seen Nakajima's Godzilla do popular dances and curse up a storm while negotiating battle terms with Mothra in the past two years, so why couldn't this be just another new facet of the character?

Nakajima also choreographed the fight scenes with Hiroshi Sekita, who played the aforementioned Ebirah, and you might remember was the good, brown Gargantua Sanda in *War of the Gargantuas* earlier in 1966. They even filmed underwater, breathing from oxygen tanks off screen between takes[147].

Godzilla and Ebirah

With fresh talent on their flagship science fiction franchise, Toho and Tomoyuki Tanaka thought they had found a way to keep Godzilla relevant for the rest of the decade, and while *Ebirah* would sell fewer tickets that *Invasion of Astro-Monster,* it's lower budget would make up the difference, ensuring that Fukuda, Arikawa, and Sato would return for the series' next installment. But what about the Old Guard? They were already hard at work on something King-sized with Rankin/Bass.

---

[147] *Master of Monsters,* pg 140

Chapter 23: *Gamera vs Gyaos*

Gamera movies had a problem. Noriaki Yuasa had a solution. For those of you who don't remember, the previous Gamera film, *Gamera vs Barugon*, had been a full blown A-picture for Daiei studios. Director of the first Gamera Film, Noriaki Yuasa, was bumped down to effects director, with experienced journeyman Shigeo Tanaka taking over on the adult oriented, big budget sequel. As successful as the original *Gamera* had been, that success was largely due to the film's appeal with children, who were bored senseless by the grown-up sequel. It was observed that they ran through the aisles of the theaters, hung out at the concession stand, and only really watched the monster scenes. So, Daiei had a problem, and Noriaki Yuasa had a solution.

That solution was to make the movies explicitly for children, and the first step in that process was having series screenwriter Niisan Takahashi follow the structure of a children's picture book: have the monsters introduced early, along with all of the characters and conflict, and let the rest of the story play out from there[148]. According to Stuart Galbraith IV's commentary on Arrow Video's recent blu-ray set, where most of my information comes from for this chapter, Yuasa wanted this film to be targeted squarely at kids, as suited his own sensibilities. It was what he wanted for the Gamera films from the very beginning.

Let's talk about the monsters. Of course, we have Gamera, portrayed by suit actor Teruo Aragaki, who had played Gamera in *Vs Barugon* and would play him again the next year in *Gamera vs Viras,* and also cross over into the Godzilla franchise, playing Rodan in *Destroy All Monsters* the same year[149]. The same suit was used for today's film as *Vs Barugon,* with the eyes modified to look friendlier than they had in the monster's previous two outings. It's an appropriate choice, as this begins Gamera's transition to being the "Friend of All Children". Why, it even includes a scene where Gamera deliberately saves a jovial boy with chubby cheeks named Eiichi from the other title monster, gives him a ride on his back, returns him to his friends, waiting at an amusement park, on top of a ferris wheel. When the man retrieving Eiichi can't reach him, he gestures Gamera closer to the ride, and the Titanic Terrapin obediently complies.

The villainous and vampiric Gyaos

Less is known about the suit-actor who portrayed this movie's antagonist monster, Gyaos, not even his name. Once again according to Galbraith, he cameos alongside Aragaki in one scene where the highway construction that drives this film's conflict is being discussed[150].

---
[148] Galbraith, Stewart IV. *Commentary: Gamera vs Gyaos*. Arrow Video, 2020.
[149] *Commentary: Gamera vs Gyaos*
[150] *Commentary: Gamera vs Gyaos*

The monster Gyaos himself was partially inspired by the success of Toho's duology of *Frankenstein Conquers the World* and *War of the Gargantuas* and their use of the Frankenstein monster. If he could get a daikaiju sized update, why not Dracula? So Daiei's Vampire Bat monster was conceived and initially named "Bambaiya"[151], which I love.

While this movie is very fast paced and action heavy it still features the obligatory "scientists discuss how to stop the monsters with the military" scenes. Yuasa was not a fan. "That's the grown up part of the story, that's boring. Telling you honestly, I really hate it. Since the original Godzilla, it's almost like a kind of rule, to have scenes like these. Scientists and military men coming together to explain everything. That's why I included it, but the truth is, these people are useless."[152] he said once. He'd much rather have the monster's weaknesses revealed through the plain and simple observational logic of a child, as is done in this and every following Gamera movie. These are the days of the Kennies, in their baseball caps and windbreakers, interrupting governmental proceedings in the shortest of shorts, cutting through bureaucracy and red tape with the logical cry of "Gyaos seemed to hate the sunlight. Maybe he's a vampire? Let's make some fake blood and get him dizzy enough to stay out until morning!"

I don't mind the Kennies as much as other fans of these movies do, and I think the use of Eiichi here is actually pretty good. The young actor, Naoyuki Abe, was thought by many studio hangers on to be director Yuasa's son, though the two were not related[153]. Indeed, Abe himself made this observation repeatedly on set. He's a decent actor as far as I can tell, and plays the role of "child friend of monster" with a wonderful kind of combination of frustration at being a kid, and confidence. Like a tiny Old Testament prophet, frustrated at the lack of faith around him, but confident in Gamera's power. Additionally, he's breaking with tradition here and wearing long pants.

Naoyuki Abe as Eiichi

One of the long standing issues people seem to have with kids in these movies, and even kids in action oriented children's media is that kids don't want to be the sidekick, they want to be the superhero! Who wants to be Robin when you can be Batman?! Who wants to be Eiichi when you can be Gamera?! Well, what if I were to tell you that Eiichi *IS* Gamera? Is your mind blown? No, Eiichi isn't physically a Gamera, but they are constantly linked to one another through the language of film, especially in a scene where our child protagonist imagines Gamera healing under the sea, and fades back to Eiichi sleeping at home. The film encourages kids to see themselves as Eiichi, yes, but also to see themselves as Gamera!

---

[151] *Showa Completion 1954-1989*, pgs 130-132
[152] *Commentary: Gamera vs Gyaos*
[153] *Commentary: Gamera vs Gyaos*

All of this is really just to say that in 1967, the Gamera series hit its stride when studio big wigs finally listened to Noriaki Yuasa, the man with a clear vision.

One more note, this film was released straight to TV in America by American International Pictures Television, in the fall of 1968 as *Return of the Giant Monsters* in their "Young Adult Theater" syndication package[154]. In 1985, almost 20 years later, TV producer Sandy Frank acquired the rights to the Gamera movies, and using their international dubs, released them under their international titles on VHS in 1987[155]. These are the versions you saw on Mystery Science Theater 3000, and their dubs are much worse.

So now that Gamera is Gamera, let's dive into the rest of 1967's Kaiju boom. Everything was quite terrestrial for today's movie, but neXt we'll get downright out of this world....

---

[154] "The Classic Horror Film Board-1960s American International Television - Sci Fi Packages." *The Classic Horror Film Board*, 10 Apr. 2013, https://www.tapatalk.com/groups/monsterkidclassichorrorforum/1960s-american-international-television-sci-fi-pac-t49287.html.
[155] LeMay, John. *The Big Book of Japanese Giant Monster Movies: The Lost Cuts - Editing Japanese Monsters Volume 1: U.S. Edits 1956-2000.* 1st ed., Bicep Books, 2021, pgs. 507-508

Chapter 24: *The X From Outer Space*

This is a film I am fairly confident it is impossible to talk about with any kind of intelligence. On the one hand, it's very silly, with one of the worst giant monster designs ever, maybe, one of the most meandering plots, and a weird love triangle that never really resolves itself. On the other hand, it's extremely stylish, has wonderful miniature sets, and a joyfully bizarre score. Either hand, though, could be considered good, depending on what you're looking for in a late 60s kaiju movie. If you're just looking for a monster movie, *The X from Outer Space* is probably not for you. Oh it has a monster, and it is a movie, but it doesn't appear until about 50 minutes into this less than 90 minute feature. No, if you want to enjoy this one, you'll need to come in prepared to look at a weird time capsule of 1960s sci-fi aesthetics, and a botched attempt at a cash in.

You see, we're now deep in the heart of the Second Kaiju Boom. Godzilla and Toho studios had already proven that these movies were big business, Gamera and Daiei proved that there was enough room in the market for competitors, and Ultraman was proving that there was enough demand for monsters that people would get them anywhere they could. Sochiku, one of Japan's oldest and most respected movie studios, decided that they qualified as anywhere, so they took it upon themselves to cash-in and make their own Giant Monster Movie[156]. They had no thought of letting the fact that they had never made one before stop them, not with all that money to be made!

The approach taken by Sochiku interests me, because in a year when the juvenile-ification of the genre had begun in earnest with *Gappa, the Triphibian Monster, Gamera vs Gyaos,* and even the Godzilla series introducing a baby monster in *Son of Godzilla*, the screenwriters of *The X From Outer Space* seemingly decided to look to the previous year's *Invasion of Astro-Monster* as primary inspiration, which was also big on a near-future, shiny fabric, space mods aesthetic and romantic melodrama, and light on monster action. I guess that means we've got to talk about our monster, the infamous Guilala.

Guilala is born from a space egg that somehow gets attached to the AAB-Gamma, a manned spacecraft investigating a UFO that has exploded some unmanned probes, because that makes so much sense. Before we even get to that, though, the ship's doctor gets sick, and the crew is forced to land on the moon base, where the captain's girlfriend, Michiko, is waiting. This complicates things for the crew's biologist, Lisa, who is in love with the captain. But if you were to watch the movie on mute, once they land on the moon and hang out in the lunar base's cocktail bar, you'd think Lisa was in love with Michiko, and that Captain Sano was the third wheel, jealously watching from the sidelines.

At any rate, we finally see the monster after some more moon love triangle stuff, and the UFO passes by the ship once again, this time depositing the egg. On returning to Earth, Captain Sano, his girlfriend, and *her* girlfriend, all go out for drinks, leaving the egg in a containment unit, which fails. The egg reacts with our oxygen rich atmosphere and, voila! Instant Kaiju and a goofy looking one at that. Its head looks like a cross between a chicken and a pierogi with antennas, and thighs that foreshadow the Heisei era Godzillas. I just watched this movie and I can't remember if he actually made a sound like squeaky mattress

---

[156] *Showa Completion,* pg 134

Oh no! *snickers* It's Guilala!

springs with every step or not, but it would not be out of place. Its roar sounds like they slowed down and distorted a guy going "rawr", and it had shoulders with natural pads that look like something Lady Gaga would wear.

A lot of people are down on this movie, and I can't really blame them. If you're expecting anything like a Giant Monster Movie, you'll be disappointed, but if you're a fan of retro-future aesthetics, subtextually sapphic love triangles, bossa nova music, or questionable morals about not dating outside your nationality, this movie is for you. I fall somewhere in the middle, and I try to treat this movie like I treat an oatmeal raisin cookie. It is what it is, you can't be upset that it isn't the chocolate chip cookie you imagined it was when you saw it on the table in the breakroom. You took a bite, and maybe it's not the cookie you wanted, but it is the cookie you have. It won't hurt anything to go ahead and finish it. Unless you're allergic to raisins, in which case I advise you to spit it out, call a doctor and maybe induce vomiting.

Chapter 25: *Gappa, the Triphibian Monster*

If *The X From Outer Space* is an oatmeal raisin cookie, April 1967's *Gappa the Triphibian Monster* is a sugar cookie. It's sweet and sentimental and one of the biggest signs that the Giant Monster Movie genre was becoming more and more intended for children, for it gives us a combination of the child focuses from previous kiddie oriented Monster flicks. We have the child protagonist of the Gamera franchise and the baby monster of *Gorgo* taking center stage, and while there is a fairly serious adult plot, like *The X From Outer Space,* its regressive moral and resolution negate the message it tries to peddle at the end of the film. The undercurrent, however, gives us something much more interesting to talk about.

The unfortunate moral is not the only problematic issue in the film. Like *Mothra, King Kong vs Godzilla*, and *Mothra vs Godzilla*, there is an uncomfortable amount of blackface in this film. And where these insensitive portrayals in the previously mentioned film are brief, one of our main characters is a native boy from the island home of our title kaiju. I suppose this is as good a segue into the story as we'll get, so let's take a look.

A publishing mogul decides to open an exotic theme park on an island in the South Pacific, and while collecting flora and fauna, the expedition finds a monster egg, which they take from the island and back to Tokyo despite the native's objections. It hatches, revealing a man-sized, beaked, winged, bipedal dinosaur monster, which is called Gappa by the natives. Pretty much as soon as the expedition returns to Japan, the baby's parents destroy the island village while seeking it out, and then head to Japan to continue the hunt.

It sounds a bit like *Gorgo*, but the initial set up is closer in practice to *King Kong vs Godzilla* before it begins taking cues from the British monster movie. Although, it isn't actually taking cues from *Gorgo,* because according to an interview with screenwriters Iwao Yamazaki and Ryuzo Nakanishi with Stuart Galbraith IV in his seminal book *Monsters are Attacking Tokyo,* they weren't even aware of the earlier film's existence[157]. *Gappa* was one of five giant monster films considered by the studio, and won out to actually be produced over the other four.

Like Sochiku when they set about to make *The X from Outer Space*, Nikkatsu studios' intentions in making their kaiju cash-in was purely financial, but with an added wrinkle: it was a little bit of a scam on the Japanese government! You see, the government was giving loans to movie studios to make Kaiju movies for export, as they were just as popular overseas as they were in Japan. Nikkatsu was on the verge of bankruptcy due to excessive real estate purchases, and used their loan to pay off many of those debts, reserving very little of the money to actually make the film[158]. It turned out pretty good, all things considered.

Despite its many problematic aspects, shady origins, and tiny budget, *Gappa* is a mostly wholesome, entertaining kid's movie. Much of this is due to special effects director Akira Watanabe, who worked with Toho effects maestro Eiji Tsuburaya on the earlier Godzilla films as an art director and creature designer, even creating the iconic villain King Ghidorah. Watanabe uses all of his skill to stretch the budget, and makes the scenes of city stomping

---

[157] *Monsters Are Attacking Tokyo,* pg 110
[158] *Showa Completion,* pg 137

especially fun to watch. It's interesting to note that, according to John LeMay's *Big Book of Japanese Monster Movies,* the creatures in this film were initially possible designs for Ultraman![159]

When this movie came stateside, it was part of American International Television's 15 New Science Fiction Movies Package, which also included *Mothra Vs. Godzilla, Daimajin,* and *Gamera vs Barugon.*[160] They left in the international dub produced in Tokyo, which is charming in its own right, despite being a source of ridicule for many English speaking audiences.

The reunited Gappa family leave for home

As a children's film, this movie succeeds pretty well, despite telling young girls to stay at home and "wash diapers" and parading a young Japanese boy around in blackface. As a money making scheme, despite its success in Japan, it being picked up straight to TV in the US kind of torpedoed Nikkatsu's plans. They began making violent, soft core pornography just to stay afloat in the seventies[161], and while these films have gained a cult reputation of their own over the decades, they were not enough to do more than keep the studio gasping along to their bankruptcy in 1993.

I hope you're able to enjoy this film for what it is, and I'll once again remind you of its objectively wrong choice to portray the islanders through blackface makeup, and encourage you to be open to the film's surprisingly progressive, anti-colonial messaging. *Gappa* is a triphibian monster, and at home in a number of environments as such. However, it is most at home in its home.

---

[159] *Showa Completion,* pg 137
[160] "The Classic Horror Film Board-1960s American International Television - Sci Fi Packages.", 10 Apr. 2013
[161] *Showa Completion,* pg 138

A Quick Look at *The King Kong Show*

When we discussed *Godzilla vs the Sea Monster*, I brought up Rankin/Bass' animated series *The King Kong Show*. Since we'll be discussing the movie version in the next chapter, I thought now would be a good time to look at the series itself, and how it came to be.

We'll start with some history on the company itself. Arthur Rankin Jr had been an art director for the American Broadcasting Company in the 1940s, while Jules Bass worked in advertising in New York City. In late 1960, they founded VideoCraft Entertainment and produced the animated TV series *The New Adventures of Pinocchio*. The show is bizarre, beginning as a fairly traditional retelling of Carlo Collodi's children's novel, only narrated by Geppeto. By the end of the first 5 minute episode, Pinocchio has signed a fraudulent Hollywood contract and robbed a bank, before being set right by his cricket, named Cricket. The episode I found had a British accented train engine named Herald in it.

King Kong and his friend Bobby Bond

The New Adventures of Pinocchio was a stop motion animated series, in the style of the later Videocraft Holiday classic *Rudolph the Red Nosed Reindeer*. Rankin and Bass called this process "animagic", a portmanteau of the words "animation" and "magic". It was a kind of blend between traditional stop motion and Puppetoons as produced by George Pal if you remember from our biography of Ray Harryhausen in the chapter on *The Beast from 20,000 Fathoms*, Puppetoons was animated by the use of wooden figures carved into certain positions being swapped out between frames to give them the appearance of movement. Animagic used interchangeable mouths, hands, and feet on a wooden puppet. Enough about that, though. Let's talk about cartoon monkey monsters.

After a traditionally animated series based on Frank L. Baum's book series *The Wizard of Oz* the year after *The New Adventures of Pinocchio* first aired, Videocraft focused on holiday specials, beginning with 1964's *Rudolph the Red Nosed Reindeer*. Finally, in December of 1966, ABC began airing *King Kong* on Saturday mornings. While the series ran with two seven minute stories separated by a short cartoon called *Tom of THUMB* (**T**iny **H**uman **U**nderground **M**ilitary **B**ureau) about a tiny secret agent, it premiered in primetime with a full hour special.

The King Kong Show aired initially in ABC's 10 AM slot, after *Porky Pig* at 9:30 and before *The Beatles* at 10:30. Yes, those Beatles. Other show's in the line up included *The New Casper Cartoon Show*, *Milton the Monster*, a series about a Frankenstein style monster who lived in a house on Horror Hill with his two dads, Dr. Montgomery Weirdo and Count Kook. Milton was followed by *Bugs Bunny*, *Magilla Gorilla*, *Hoppity Hooper*, and finally *American Bandstand* at 1:30 PM.

The original MechniKong

Almost all of Videocraft's animation was done in Japan, and *The King Kong Show* was no exception. While *The New Adventures of Pinocchio* had been animated by Dentsu Studios, Rankin and Bass turned to Japan's Toei Animation studios, who we've heard of before in our *Magic Serpent* episode, and will hear from again when we reach the dawn of the sentai series, and probably a few things in between.

The King Kong Show aired for one more season on Saturdays, sandwiched between newcomers *Journey To The Center of the Earth* and *George of the Jungle*. It then aired in reruns on Sunday mornings in 1969. Special thanks to the website TVParty.com and Billy Ingram's exhaustive Saturday morning cartoon listings for that info. Check them out.

Like many cartoons of the era, *The King Kong Show* tells you everything you need to know in its theme song:

> *King Kong*
> *You know the name of King Kong.*
> *You know the fame of King Kong.*
> *Ten times as big as a man.*
>
> *One day, a boy, too young to know the danger,*
> *Made a friend of this giant fearsome stranger!*
> *And the life they led on their island home became a legend*
> *The legend of … King Kong.*[162]

The Bond family face off against Dr. Who

From there, Kong and the Bond family, along with good friend Captain Englehorne from the original film, fight the evil Dr. Who. More on him in the next chapter. For now, check the show out. Many episodes are on YouTube, as are episodes of *The New Adventures of Pinocchio* and *Tales of the Wizard of Oz*, all of which are worth taking a look at. In the description of this episode of the show, I also would recommend an episode of the podcast Ephemeral that discusses the studio's holiday specials, and YouTube videos by Quenton Reviews on some of their more out there projects.

---

[162] Lyrics by Jules Bass

Chapter 26: *King Kong Escapes*

A few chapters ago, we talked about *Godzilla vs the Sea Monster*, aka *Ebirah, Horror of the Deep*. Some of you may remember that that movie began life as *Operation Robinson Crusoe: King Kong vs Ebirah*, basically, *Toho Studios Presents: Rankin/Bass's The King Kong Show:The Movie*. Rankin/Bass, the producers of *The King Kong Show*, were disappointed with the lack of elements from their series present in that script so they had another one written, this time from a specific story treatment from Arthur Rankin Jr. himself. His involvement guaranteed a number of things carried over from the cartoon, including the villain, Dr. Who, and Kong's robotic double, Mechani-Kong.

Five years earlier, when Kong had fought Godzilla, that film was released as part of Toho's 30th Anniversary Celebration Series, and now, *King Kong Escapes,* or as it was called in Japan, *King Kong's Counter Attack*, was featured in Toho's 35th Anniversary Celebration. This was one reasons the film was important to our friend Eiji Tsuburaya, who was also thrilled to be working on his own King Kong Movie, with a chance to produce effects scenes from the original in his own way, with the techniques he'd developed with stop motion unavailable to him, and he does so spectacularly.

King Kong and MechaniKong

First of all, Kong looks better here than he did in 1962, with a slightly more together face, and now that he is played by Haruo Nakajima instead of Shoichi Hirose, who was nearly 45 at the time of his portrayal in *King Kong vs Godzilla*,[163] the big ape is more vibrant and emotive. The highlight for me, and I think possibly for Tsuburaya too, is Kong's fight with Gorosaurus, a big, bluish green Allosaurus type dinosaur, played by Hiroshi Sekita, who had sparred with Nakajima in the previous year's *War of the Gargantuas*[164]. Several aspects of the fight are lifted directly from Willis O'Brien's original Kong fight with the Meat-Eater on Skull Island, including Kong's finishing move, pulling Gorosaurus' jaws apart until he dies. Rankin/Bass and Toho executive Iwao Mori, who we met back in our episode on *Godzilla King of the Monsters,* wanted the dinosaur to bleed from his injured maw, but Tsuburaya,

---
[163] *Master of Monsters*, pg 62
[164] *Monsters Are Attacking Tokyo*, pg 131

famously adverse to bloodshed in his child focused entertainment, refused[165]. A compromise that I personally find more grisly was reached; Gorosaurus foams at the mouth in his death throes.

Of special note on the human side of things, are the two female lead performers, Linda Miller and Mie Hama as Lt. Susan Watson and Madame Piranha, respectively. Hideo Amamoto also deserves some recognition for his hammy turn as Dr. Who, in a performance worthy of Vincent Price, just short of mustache twirling, and probably only on account of his lack of mustache. The other actors range from "good" to "huh", with a friendly but bored looking Akira Takarada as Jiro Nomura, and a six foot length of two by four going by the name of Rhodes Reason in the ostensibly lead role of Commander Carl Nelson. The most noteworthy credit I have found for him outside of this film is "Rex Reason's Brother" in "Real Life"[166]. He's better than Russ Tamblyn though, and never talks down to or seems resentful of his Japanese co-stars, so he's got that going for him.

Newspaper ads for the double feature of King Kong Escapes and The Shakiest Gun in The West

The film was released as *King Kong's Counterattack* in Japan in July of 1967, and in June of 1968 as *King Kong Escapes* in the US, where it shared a marquee with *The Shakiest Gun in the West*,[167] which now in my head has resulted in this sketch:

Andy Griffith Theme Starts

Narrator: The King Kong Show! Starring- KING KONG

    With Bobby Bond

    Also Starring Don Knotts

Theme ends

---

[165] *Showa Completion,* pg 139
[166] This is a joke. I mean, he really is Rex Reason's brother, but the rest is a joke.
[167] *Showa Completion,* pg 141

I guess that's really all I have to say about *King Kong Escapes.* It's an enjoyable movie, and the last one Eiji Tsuburaya worked on directly as special effects director before being succeeded by Sadamasa Arikawa, his longtime assistant[168]. So, really there are two kings we are saying goodbye to, Kong, the King of Skull/Faro/Mondo Island, and Eiji Tsuburaya, King of Tokusatsu.

---

[168] *Master of Monsters,* pg 167

Chapter 27: *Yongary, Monster from the Deep*

Yongary is a strange bird, by which I mean it isn't a bird at all. It's a Giant Monster Movie, which is why we're discussing it here on Record All Monsters. If you came here looking for discussions on birds, you're definitely in the wrong place, I have ornithophobia. That's Greek for "fear of birds", or literally translated "I don't want things flying into my face and pecking my eyes out".

Uncomfortable bleeding from an orifice does come up later in this movie, though we'll cross that bridge when we get to it. This movie was produced quickly, with filming starting in April of 1967 and it being released in August of that same year, part of the 1967 Kaiju boom[169]. One thing that makes this movie stand out is that it is a South Korean Giant Monster Movie. There were actually two other Giant Monster Movies released by the Koreans in the 1960s, but all three of them are lost. I can hear you now, "but Robert" you're saying, "Robert, you handsome devil, if all three of those movies are lost, then what the heck are we even *talking* about today?" And you make a good point. First of all, flattery will get you nowhere with me. Second of all, the other two lost Korean Monster Movies will be covered in a special section in this book, and *third* of all, only AIP's TV version and 48 minutes of the original Korean language film exist[170].

It's curious that so much mystery surrounds what is a fairly by the numbers Giant Monster Movie, with a monster who is mostly memorable for looking like a rip off of pretty much all of its predecessors at once, with Godzilla's overall body shape and back plates, Gamera's tusks and fire breath, and Barugon and Baragon's nasal horn, which produces a beam weapon after this film's Kenny shines an itch ray at the monster while it sleeps. That brings us to this movie's real monster: Eicho.

Is it fair to call Eicho "The Evil Kenny"? I think so.

I have spoken out in defense of The Kennies on several occasions in the past, and will do so again in the future, but at the present moment, I must wash my hands of this "Eicho" and the crimes he has committed, including two counts of attempted manslaughter, one count of breaking and entering, one count of burglary, one count of larceny, one count of reckless damage and destruction, it goes on. While most Kennies have checked one or two of these boxes, I don't think any of them have ever screwed their castmates so thoroughly from the beginning of the movie all the way through to the finale and then get praised as the film's real hero.

Kenny- I mean Eicho- being the film's primary perspective character as well explicitly named its hero at the end does tell us something else about our beloved genre, though, and that's

---

[169] *Showa Completion,* pg 141
[170] Ryfle, Steve, and Kim Song-ho. *Commentary: Yongary, Monster from the Deep.* Kino Lorber, 2016.

the fact that even outside of Japan, and as early as 1967, these films were primarily seen not as adult oriented science fiction, not as broad family entertainment, but as having a special eye toward young boys in particular, and children in general. 1967 proved that this audience was, no matter what country you were in, the primary one for Giant Monster Movies, and their television counterparts. The 15th episode of Ultraman even touches on the subject, when a child's chalk drawing is brought to life by cosmic rays and the children get mad at our hero for fighting it, begging him not to hurt *their* monster[171].

An ad for the theatrical release of Yongary that never materialized.

This was the second to last Giant Monster Movie of 1967, and I feel bad having been so hard on it, as it is one I enjoy to an extent. It's silly and has a wonky charm to it, as well as some upsetting tonal whiplash in the form of our title character's ultimate demise. Apparently, he is shot into space offscreen and still alive in some more cribbing from *Gamera*, at least according to the lost Korean version[172], but he's just dead in the only version currently available, and his death, which I alluded to at the start of this essay, is deeply unpleasant and disturbing.

AIP released this one directly to TV, a sign of the market for these movies being oversaturated, perhaps, but thanks to the discovery of a widescreen version of the dub and posters and other promotional materials, our friend John LeMay suggests the possibility that they considered a theatrical release until fairly late in the game[173]. I personally had to work quite hard to see this movie for the first time, more than ten years ago, being refused a VHS copy at a second hand store, and YouTube was unable to host full movies at the time, so tracking down all the many parts it was uploaded in was not an easy task. I finally found a compilation DVD including several Gamera movies, *Gappa the Triphibian Monster, The Giant Gila Monster, Warning from Space,* and this film. I watched all of them while I was house sitting, and maybe that's why I find the film so charming. By the way, all of these movies now have gorgeous Blu-ray releases except for *The Giant Gila Monster*, so

---

[171] Sasaki. M. (Writer), & Jissoji, A. (Director). (10/23/1966). Terrifying Cosmic Rays [Ultraman]. Tsuburaya, E (Producer), Ultraman. Tsuburaya Productions.
[172] *Showa Completion,* pg 143
[173] *The Lost Cuts*, pgs 286 & 287

somebody get on that[174]. The Blu-ray for *Yongary* includes a fascinating commentary with Steve Ryfle and Korean film historian Kim Song-ho, which was a major source for this essay. Check it out if you want to, but it is pretty unessential viewing.

A Quick Look at Three Kaiju Films from Outside Japan

In last week's full episode on *Yongary, Monster From the Deep,* I briefly mentioned that it was one of 3 Korean Kaiju movies that were lost in one way or another. I thought now would be a good time to look at the other two, which are unavailable in any form, as well as a lost Kaiju movie from India that has come to my attention since writing the *Yongary* episode. We don't have a lot of time, so let's get right to it.

From left to right, the posters for Bulgasari, Gogola, *and* Space Monster Wangmagwi

Released in December of 1962, *Bulgasari* was the sole directorial credit of Myeong-je Kim, who otherwise had a prolific career as a cinematographer. The movie told the story of a martial artist in the waning days of the Goryeo period, placing this movie in the late 14th century. He's murdered by traitors in his school, but reeks his vengeance from beyond the grave when he is resurrected as Bulgasari, the iron eating monster of Korean Folklore.

Bulgasari was widely panned upon its release and, according to Korean Film site Cine21 dot com, "there was no doubt that historical dramas were the only spectacle, *Bulgasari* was immediately classified as a third-rate entertainment instead of being awarded the title of the first monster." The effects apparently caused audiences to laugh at, and I quote, "the string hanging from the dragon's head, or the unsteady gait of a blind Bulgasari". A disclaimer placed before subsequent screenings urging audiences to abandon common sense probably didn't help matters much.

---

[174] At the time I am editing this book for publication, a Blu-ray release is scheduled for September 26th, 2023 from boutique home video distributor Film Masters as a double-feature with *The Killer Shrews*.

All we have left of *Bulgasari* are some promotional materials: posters, a still image of the monster with its hands above its head, a newspaper review. The footprint left behind by *Bulgasari* is so small, that some even doubt it was even made at all. But I'd tend to believe the writers at Cine21 dot com. Also, since I can't find another place to insert this tidbit, Bulgasari is also the Korean word for "starfish". So there. Oh, and Bulgasari, with a b, is the preferred spelling and pronunciation of South Korea, as it is a more modern translation of the old word. North Korea still uses the old word, Pulgasari, but we'll cross that bridge when we get there.

Moving right along, our next missing monster movie comes not from Korea, but the West, that is, India. It's west of Korea! Look at a map! Take a geography course. Geeze. We have a tiny bit more info on 1966's *Gogola*, thanks to the survival of four songs from its soundtrack: Aaja Aaja Pyar Karen, Zara Kah Do Fizaon Se, Mohe La De Raja Machhariya Re, and Nacho Nacho Gogola (which I can only assume is some kind of crazy version of Duck, Duck, Goose). We also have a list of shots the Central Board of Film Certification objected to upon the film's release, in addition to the usual array of posters and still images.

This still is one of the only surviving elements from Gogola

According to an article by Rajesh Devraj, the script sent to the censors survived as well, and he gives us a summary of the movie based on it. According to Devraj, the movie begins with a musical number at a teen beach party, which is interrupted when our title monster rises from the ocean. Though the teens are initially disbelieved, authorities eventually take the fight to Gogola, and they do the usual song and dance. One of the beach girl's dad is a scientist, who develops a magic bullet weapon as is the tradition. In a scene not dissimilar to the climax of 1954's *Godzilla*, the girl's two rivals dive into the ocean to deploy the weapon. I'm skipping over some things. On to the next one!

Finally, we come to another tricky one. Like *Yongary*, *Space Monster Wangmagwi* both is and isn't lost. We know where it is, and it is even screened from time to time in South Korea, even as recently as 2019! However, the film's owners won't allow it to be released widely or on home video. The story is, according to most sources I've encountered, similar to *King Kong*, though it doesn't sound much like it to me. Space aliens intent on taking over the earth, send their giant monster Wangmagwi, which means King Devil if Google Translate is to be believed. During his attack on Seoul, he becomes infatuated with an airman's bride on the way to her wedding.

We have the usual stills and posters associated with lost movies of this time, but I'm so sad that the only reason we don't have this one is because it is being withheld. Some footage has been leaked online, presumably from somebody's home recording when it was aired on TV in the 80s[175]. I hope you learned something, I know I did.

A promotional still from SRS Cinema's new restoration of Space Monster Wangmagwi

---

[175] Since the time of this essay's writing, boutique home video distributor SRS Cinema has gotten the rights to release a home video version of the film in the US,

Chapter 28: *Son of Godzilla*

1967 had proved 2 things to the Godzilla creatives at Toho: 1- They were no longer the only studio that could make these things, and 2- These things were more and more becoming children's films. Their flagship Kaiju series had to address both of these issues, especially since it was planned as Toho's New Year Blockbuster at the end of the year. *Son of Godzilla* embraced it all, and is a very charming little film, if I may say so.

The success, as it were, of *Ebirah, Horror of the Deep*, had also convinced Tomoyuki Tanaka that the Godzilla franchise was in good hands with Jun Fukuda directing, Sadamasa Arikawa doing the special effects, and Masaru Sato composing, so they were kept on board. Now, with the next film skewing even younger than the previous year's teen focused island adventure, Tanaka came to series writer Shinichi Sekizawa with the idea of Godzilla having a son[176].

The initial draft of the film was darker, with the titular son of Godzilla being an adolescent with a destructive bent.[177]

The final son character was quite different, and has been the subject of much controversy in the American and English speaking world of Godzilla fandom. He is very "cute". I have that word in quotation marks here. My wife, Courtney, thinks he's very cute. Many people say he does not look like a baby Godzilla, that his features are too "squishy". I'm not sure what a baby Godzilla would actually look like, though, since Godzilla is a fictional monster. Minilla is as good a guess as any in my book.

Minilla, freshly hatched

Let's talk a little about that name, Minilla. First of all, I grew up knowing him as "Minya", from the *Godzilla's Revenge* dub. Second of all, it was decided on through a contest where over 8,000 fans submitted names that were entered into a raffle. Third of all, it is one of my favorite kinds of words, a portmanteau, a combination of "Miniature" and "Godzilla", which is why the pronunciation of "Minilla" is correct[178]. Minilla was played by Masao Fukazawa, a dwarf wrestler who performed under the name "Little Man Machan"[179], and he played the monster in all three of his Showa era appearances.

---

[176] *A Critical History*, pg 101
[177] *The Lost Films*, pg 88-89
[178] *Showa Completion*, pg 146
[179] *A Critical History*, pg 102

Godzilla was only played by our friend Haruo Nakajima during water scenes, using the suits from the previous two movies. The new suit, designed to be bigger in every way in order to emphasize the size difference between Godzilla and his adopted offspring, proved much too large for Nakajima, and so he was unable to do the land scenes. Toho turned to professional baseball player and actor Seiji Onaka to portray the monster monarch. Onaka was quite tall compared to Nakajima, and filled out the suit. This wasn't his first time in a Giant Monster Movie, but it was his first time in a suit. Previously, Onaka had appeared in various roles in *Rodan, The Human Vapor, King Kong vs Godzilla, Mothra vs Godzilla* and three episodes of *Friendly Monster Booska*. He would go on to make three more appearances in *Destroy All Monsters, Latitude Zero,* and *Space Amoeba*. His time as Godzilla was short lived, though, as he hurt his hand early on in production, and was replaced by Hiroshi Sekita, who had played the heroic brown gargantua Sanda in the previous year's *War of the Gargantuas*.[180]

The suit made for Son of Godzilla

The villainous monsters in this movie were not played by suit actors, but were essentially very elaborate marionettes, brought to life through wire work[181]. Kamacuras and Kumonga, a swarm of giant mantises and a giant spider, respectively, may seem like pretty basic creations, but they're really quite amazing feats of special effects work. The attention to detail present on them, including coarse, bristling hairs and frightening mouths are quite disturbing, and while the Kamacuras pose no problem for Godzilla, they nearly kill Minilla before the Big G can come to his rescue, and Kumonga proves dangerous to all the other monsters present on Sollegel Island, as well as the human characters.

Our lead character is a journalist, but not in the mold of Akira Takarada's Ichiro Sakai from *Mothra vs Godzilla*, or even Frankie Sakai's loveable but silly Bulldog from *Mothra*. Goro Maki as portrayed by Akira Kubo, who had played the dorky inventor boyfriend in 1965's *Invasion of Astro-Monster*, is a flamboyant and stubborn journalist who came to the island on a hunch, a correct hunch, that something newsworthy was happening there. He parachutes down in a bright red Hawaiian shirt, tells the scientists there to help him with his luggage, and then refuses to eat until he's allowed to help on their project. They're there conducting weather experiments on behalf of the UN. When one goes awry, it releases extreme heat and radiation, causing the already man-sized Gimantises to grow almost 10 times their previous size!

---

[180] *Showa Completion,* pg 174-175
[181] *A Critical History* pg. 102

Also of note is Beverly Maeda, our lead actress. A Japanese-American actress[182], she plays Riko, a young feral woman who was stranded on the island as a child. Her knowledge of how to survive among the monsters and extreme conditions allows the crew to complete their work just in time for the climactic battle where Godzilla and his son face Kumonga.

There were two English dubs for this one, an international one done by Frontier Enterprises at Toho's request, and one by Titan Productions for the Walter Reade Organization[183]. The latter was directed by and starred Speed Racer himself, Peter Fernandez, as Goro[184]. Unless you're in possession of the VHS tape, this dub is a lost version of the film. I, however, *do* have the VHS of this movie, and enjoy it regularly, as it's the one I grew up with.

This movie looks to be finding an audience again, as it seemed to be pretty well regarded initially, even though it sold fewer tickets than *Ebirah*. But when I first got on the internet to look at Godzilla stuff, it was quite derided. I always liked it, and it was one of the first Godzilla movies I owned my own copy of, if not THE first Godzilla movie I owned my own copy of. We'll get more into my nostalgia for Minilla later this season, but for now, check this one out. It's silly and fun and the effects are quite good, even if this Godzilla suit looks like somebody stuck his head in a coffee can for several days.

---

[182] *Showa Completion,* pg 146
[183] *The Lost Cuts,* pg 250, 274
[184] *The Lost Cuts,* pg 274

Chapter 29: *Gamera vs Viras*

In our episode on *Gamera vs Barugon*, I said it was hard to talk about the Gamera movies at that stage in their development because they weren't very established yet and hadn't had the time to settle in or experiment much. Well, now, four films into the Friend of All Children's series, it has become difficult to talk about them because it is already so reliant on formula.

1967's *Gamera vs Gyaos* had created the winning combination that the series would rework only once more before essentially making the same movie over, and over, and over, and over, and over again until they went bankrupt in 1971. The final ingredients are added here, an American friend of our child protagonist is added to appeal to AIP-TV's US audience[185], and anything resembling an adult as a main character is booted straight outta the movie. The only real authority figure of any consequence is our lead Masao's older sister, Mariko. Sure, Kojiro Hongo is on hand, but his role is nowhere near as important as it was in the previous 2 Gamera outings. Instead, Hongo spends his time being made to look like a fool by the boys, who are oh so clever and smart and good, you know. This would be his last Gamera movie for nearly 30 years.

There are some very nice touches throughout, though. While the film is overall much cheaper than any of the previous entries in the series, the effects are about on par with them, especially the scenes original to this film. Gamera's final fight with Viras gives us some bizarre and wonderful imagery. However, most of the effects footage is recycled, like a "Gamera's Greatest Hits" reel. It's integrated into the story as a flashback, so it doesn't feel too egregious. The second set of stock footage clips, when the aliens blackmail Gamera into attacking Tokyo, however, is just the black and white rampage from his first movie, still in black and white.

All of these things, for good or ill, would inform the entire genre going forward. The Godzilla series would make a whole film around stock footage the next year, and Gamera would be only a little less reliant on it in the future. However, the tone set by Gamera is one of goofy fun, and increasingly bloody and brutal monster fights, even if the violence was closer to something like *Itchy and Scratchy* than, oh, let's say, *Horrors of Malformed Men*, that is to say, it's cartoony. That doesn't mean it didn't distress kids to see their herptile hero impaled by a silver space squid. As a matter of fact, according to the first volume of John LeMay's *Big Book of Japanese Giant Monster Movies*, children screamed in terror at the prospect of Gamera dying before their very eyes.[186]

There is an anecdotal story that series director Noriaki Yuasa told, which I heard recounted on a DVD commentary, that one day while he was in a park, Yuasa was approached by a little girl who said she had a message from Eiji Tsuburaya. The message, she said, was to not have so much bloodshed in the Gamera movies. It frightens young children. Yuasa wasn't sure if the message was really from Tsuburaya, for whom he had a great deal of respect, and if it was, why didn't he call him at his office, or write to him in some official capacity. As such, he ignored the message, and the Gamera films continued to grow bloodier[187].

---

[185] *Showa Completion,* pg 151
[186] *Showa Completion,* pg 152
[187] Kalat, David. *Commentary: Gamera vs Guiron*. Arrow Video, 2020.

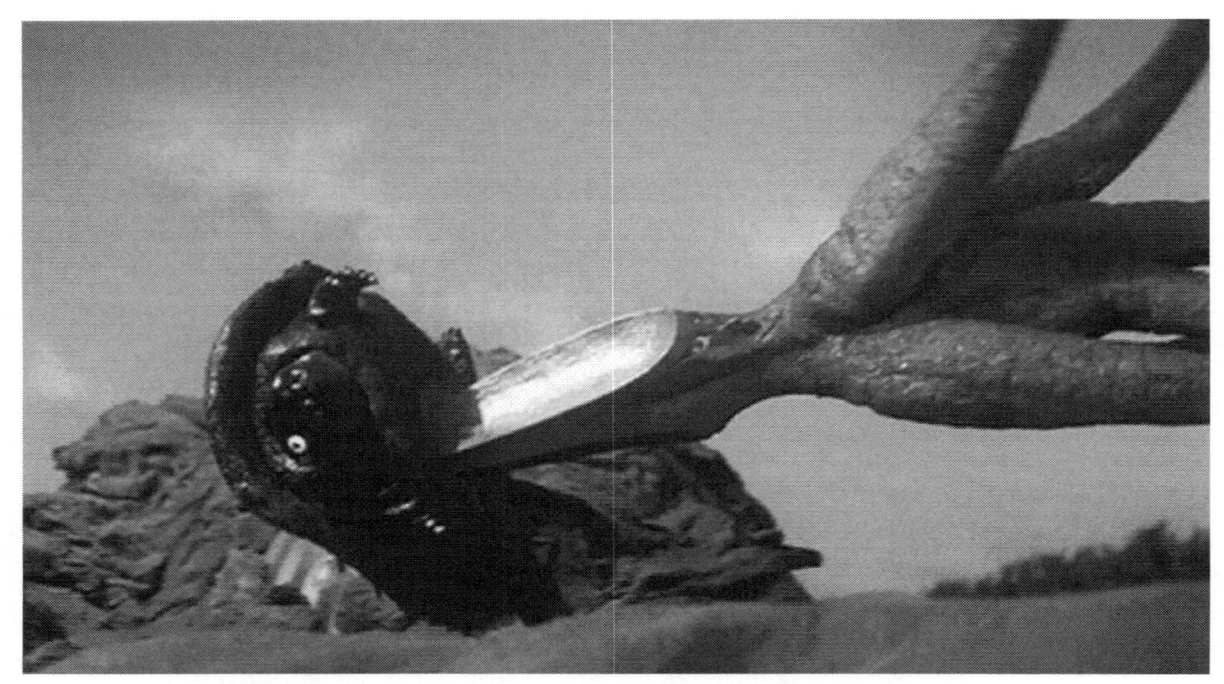

Under the impression that Gamera vs Viras would be the last film in the series, director Noriaki Yuasa cranked up the monster violence

This had been slated to be the last Gamera film by Daiei, which was part of why Yuasa ratcheted up the violence and drama, and he had initially been relieved to hear it. But as the production wrapped up, he found himself emotionally devastated, and broke down in tears after completing the final shot[188]. Gamera was something he had helped give birth to, and had proven his vision was the right one, the successful one, the one the audience wanted. His feelings remained decidedly mixed as the box office returns showed that he was right again, and the success of *Gamera vs Viras* ensured more Gamera films would come. In fact, Daiei requested Yuasa put out *two* Gamera films a year from then on, but he said it would be impossible[189]. However, there would be a Gamera film every year for the rest of the decade, right up until Daiei filed for bankruptcy.

---

[188] *Showa Completion*, pg 152
[189] *Showa Completion*, pg 152

Chapter 30: *Destroy All Monsters*

This is it, folks, this is THE Japanese Giant Monster Movie, and there are so many stories to tell here. First of all, here's mine. It was 1998, and the upcoming Godzilla blockbuster was on its way. As an awkward 6 year old who'd loved Godzilla as long as he could remember, the fact that the Gods of Popular Culture saw fit to belch forth an unbelievable wealth of Godzilla toys, books, and, yes, VHS tapes, meant I was in heaven, and that my friends finally knew a little bit of what I was talking about. Godzilla was real to them, and I was thrilled.

Something that did not thrill me, though, was how many Godzilla tapes were being rented when I went to Hollywood Video with my family. Fewer of my favorites were on the shelf because more people were interested in them. My problem was solved, sort of, when a new tape I'd never seen before was there one Friday after school. The cover was a glorious drawing of Godzilla, Minya, Rodan, Anguirus, and a floppy-eared triceratops dog I would later learn was named Baragon in the shadow of King Ghidorah who loomed over them. In crumbling stone letters, the title, DESTROY ALL MONSTERS.

Poster for Orion Video's slate of Giant Monster Movies

I knew it wasn't new, all the Godzilla movies were old, but it was new to me, and I was excited. Then I picked up the tape and read the back. It read, "Godzilla nukes New York! Mothra Blasts Beijing! Rodan levels Moscow! King Ghidorah tramples Tokyo! The greatest All-Star Monster Battle ever filmed! Under the command of alien invaders, an army of monsters attacks the world and mankind's only chance is to join behind the rallying cry 'DESTROY ALL MONSTERS'!" And THEN there were 1, 2, 3, 4, 5, 6...ELEVEN monster logos telling you who were in the movie! Wow. Wow wow wow wow wow. I rented it. OF COURSE I rented it. I specifically remember that I watched it at my grandparent's house, kneeling on their bed. That was the same place I had watched *Monster Zero* for the first time.

I didn't know it then, but *Destroy all Monsters* had had a rough road to American home video. AIP had purchased the distribution rights with the intention to release it to TV, but when they saw it, they decided it was good enough for theatrical distribution, and commissioned their own dub, and kept Toho's suggested international title. They did eventually release it to TV in 1978 as part of the "Fantastic Science-Fiction Theater" syndication package[190], and I'd like to thank Rob on the Classic Horror Film Boards for that info, as well as rvoyttbotts on the same message boards for pointing me in the right direction. The very next year, AIP was sold to

---

[190] "The Classic Horror Film Board-1960s American International Television - Sci Fi Packages.", 10 Apr. 2013

Filmways and studio head Samuel Z. Arkoff stepped down after the animation studio used the AIP library solely to sell syndication packages instead of producing new films and television under the brand[191]. Filmways was then bought by Orion Pictures and merged with them in 1982, bringing the AIP and AI-TV Library with them. This resulted in Orion releasing several AIP and AI-TV distributed Monster Movies together on VHS in 1989[192].

The rumor is that Orion intended to put *Destroy All Monsters* out on video in 1990, but no release ever materialized. This may be because Orion was in disastrous financial shape at the end of the 80s, and the rarity of the above mentioned VHS tapes today hints that they weren't exactly flying off the shelves; another wave of AIP Catalog VHS releases would be nothing but sunk cost for a studio now having to do all their home video releases through the much larger Columbia Pictures. Eventually, Orion went bankrupt and its assets were purchased by MGM[193]. By this time, *Destroy All Monsters* had also disappeared from TV airwaves, and was essentially a lost film in North America and the English speaking world.

That all changed in 1996 when the Sci-Fi Channel acquired both *Destroy All Monsters* and *Godzilla vs the Smog Monster* and began airing them regularly. Finally, in 1998, with Columbia Tri-Star's *Godzilla* looming on the horizon, and a veritable Kaiju Boom exploding in American pop-culture, anime focused distributor ADV released *Destroy All Monsters* on VHS and a little bit on DVD the following year. That brings us full circle to a five or six year old little Irish and Mexican boy in the Sci-Fi Aisle at Hollywood Video in central Texas at the turn of this century.

---

[191]"American International Pictures." *Wikipedia*, 11 Sept. 2023. *Wikipedia*, https://en.wikipedia.org/w/index.php?title=American_International_Pictures&oldid=1174858268.
[192] *Monster Movie Madness - Godzilla & Friends - VHS Promo Trailer. www.youtube.com*, https://www.youtube.com/watch?v=YXZyod9PSwA. Accessed 12 Sept. 2023.
[193] "Orion Pictures." *Wikipedia*, 11 Aug. 2023. *Wikipedia*, https://en.wikipedia.org/w/index.php?title=Orion_Pictures&oldid=1169758259.

I'll briefly touch on the behind the scenes info for this movie, because it seems to be fairly well known in most circles. This was intended to be the last Godzilla movie due to steadily declining ticket sales, but it proved to be such a huge success, especially among children, that Toho executive Tomoyuki Tanaka decided to greenlight another sequel for the following year[194]. Eiji Tsuburaya was terribly ill during filming, and was little more than an advisor to his assistant, Sadamasa Arikawa, who did most of the day to day work on the film. Tsuburaya was still credited as Special Effects director, largely out of respect[195]. Gorosaurus replaced Baragon at the last minute in the attack on Paris, not because, as has been largely believed until recently, the Baragon suit had not yet been repaired after being remodeled after its many uses on Ultraman, but because Arikawa and his team didn't want to damage the mechanics in his ears, which is why the shovel shaped head of Gorosaurus made more sense to attack the Arc de Triomphe from below ground[196].

This is one of my favorite Godzilla movies, now and then, because it is just fun and entertaining, and gets to the heart, I think, of what Godzilla is all about. If we can use our internal monsters to do good, help others, fend off attacks, and keep them wrangled on their own little island until we need them, the world would be a better place. Or maybe I just like watching 10 monsters curbstomp King Ghidorah for 10 minutes or so. It's a toss up, really.

---

[194] *A Critical History,* pg 106
[195] *A Critical History,* pg 106
[196] Ryfle, Steve, and Ed Godziszewski. *Commentary: Destroy All Monsters.* Tokyo Shock, 2011.

Chapter 31: *Gamera vs Guiron*

This is my favorite Gamera movie. It is silly, stupid, earnest, pretentious, joyful, violent, childish, childlike, and a hundred other wonderfully incompatible things. And, like our previous Gamera film, almost impossible to write at length about. The Gamera series is firmly entrenched in formula by this, its fifth entry.

All the ingredients are here:

To make a late 60s/early 70s Gamera movie, you will need:

- 1 Precocious Japanese boy
- 1 American friend of said Japanese boy
- 1 Japanese boy's sister
- 1 Ineffectual adult authority figure
- 1 Science fiction vehicle
- 1 Alien race intent on harming children specifically
- 1 monster controlled by said Alien race
- 1 Giant fire breathing turtle named Gamera

Gamera's opponent in his 5th film

Mix the boys, the sister, and the ineffectual adult authority figure together. Get your Gamera out, but you will not need it at this time, we just don't want the audience to forget he's here.

Separate the boys from the sister and the ineffectual authority figure, set aside with the science fiction vehicle. If you haven't already, get your Gamera out now.

Mix the boys with the Alien Monster. Apply Gamera now. Mix with the alien monster and separate boys. Mix the boys with the alien race. Remove Gamera, set aside for later. Season liberally with stock footage. Return to your Ineffectual Authority Figure and Sister. Let all ingredients rest for 10 minutes.

Mix your Gamera and Alien monster again now, this time having Gamera absolutely obliterate the Alien Monster. Let the boys help if at all possible. Destroy the aliens at the same time. Discard leftovers. Return boys, the sister, and the ineffectual authority figure to their original location. Put your Gamera away and say goodbye until you need him again.

Normally, for a Gamera movie, I'd break down where the monster's name came from, but that's what this episode's game is going to focus on, so sit tight, and we'll see you in Part II of this book.

Chapter 32: *The Mighty Gorga*

It's been a little while since we have stepped onto the sunny shores of the good ol' US of A. The last time we saw a movie produced by an American company was, well technically *Invasion of Astro-Monster* was co-produced by UPA[197], but the last one that was primarily an American production was last season's eleventh episode, *Gorgo,* and even that was an Irish/English/American co-production[198]. Look, the point is, while there were horror movies and Monster Movies coming out in America since 1962, very few of them were *Giant Monster Movie*s. And I'll be fair, we skipped some American movies last year. Movies like *Them, It Came from Beneath the Sea, Tarantula, The Black Scorpion, The Deadly Mantis,* and *The Giant Gila Monster.* I didn't cover them in part because most of those films' monsters are just, like, big animals. And four of them were big bugs, specifically. Yes, I know, scorpions and spiders aren't insects, but I didn't *say* insects, did I? So there.

My point is, as the Japanese monster movie evolved, the American monster movie stagnated. The atom age monsters of the 1950s were out, and the big thing was once again Gothic Horror. Remakes of the Universal Horror Classics began coming over from the UK's Hammer Studios, and AIP, one of the chief importers of Godzilla movies to America, was spending their production dollars at home on Gothic Horror vehicles based on the works of Edgar Allan Poe starring Vincent Price. Those are very good, by the way. You should watch them if you get the chance. Maybe it was one of the first instances of the Thirty-Year Nostalgia Cycle, but the classics were on people's minds through the 60s, and while Giant Monsters were being imported from the far east, they're not getting made at home in the late 1960s.

This brings us to a man named David L Hewitt. If you're a fan of early 60s B-Movies, you know his work. He wrote, produced, and/or directed some classic cheese. *The Time Travelers, The Wizard of Mars, Monsters Crash the Pajama Party,* and *Journey to the Center of Time.* So he had a pedigree, and it actually went back even further. In the 50s, he had worked as a spook-show magician and illusionist[199]. The first film mentioned, *The Time Travelers*, was made from an Ib Melchior script adapted from one Hewitt had sent to Famous Monsters of Filmland founder and editor Forrest J. Ackerman[200].

There's no doubt that today's film, *The Mighty Gorga*, was a labor of love for Hewitt. By 1969, when this movie was released, Hewitt had no real studio backing, and was making movies primarily for the regional drive-in circuit[201]. Somehow, *The Mighty Gorga* has survived from this obscure origin. I guess I've put it off long enough. Let's talk about this. It took me 2 tries to get through this movie, but only because I got very sleepy. Any bad movie fan worth his salt will find something to enjoy in this picture. It's got the basic set-up of a giant monkey movie, with a dash of *The Valley of Gwangi* thrown in for good measure. I can't tell the male

---

[197] *A Critical History*, pgs 82-87
[198] *Ninth Wonder Of The World: The Making Of Gorgo.*
[199] *David L. Hewitt.* http://www.tcm.com/tcmdb/person/85839%7C37034/David-L.-Hewitt. Accessed 12 Sept. 2023.
[200] *David L. Hewitt.* http://www.tcm.com/tcmdb/person/85839%7C37034/David-L.-Hewitt. Accessed 12 Sept. 2023.
[201] THE IMAGINATION OF IB MELCHIOR!

lead apart from the guy playing his brother, but it doesn't really matter, because we never see his brother again.

The main character, whose name I can neither remember or be bothered to look up, owns a circus which is being bled dry by a businessman of some kind who keeps luring away their top talent with money. Going off of a rumor his brother told him from the guy who sold them some lions one time, Main Character, MC from here on out, heads to "Africa" to look for a guy named Congo Jack who has a lead on a giant gorilla. Congo Jack has gone missing, so MC is met by his daughter April, whose name I DO remember for some reason. It might be because she's kinda cute. It might be because she had a strange African accent. Anyway, I looked the actress, Megan Timothy, up because Courtney and I wondered if she was Angela Lansbury's daughter and found the best piece of trivia about any actor ever: In the early 60s, while working as a waitress at the Playboy Club, she lit a customer's beard on fire while trying to light his cigarette, and then poured a glass of water on his head to put it out. This resulted in her being fired[202], but man, what a story Mark!

When we meet the Mighty Gorga, it's actually the very first scene of the movie. We get some great, spooky atmosphere as we see skulls tied to stakes with a live, horrified woman, screaming her head off as the worst gorilla suit we've seen on this show to date approaches her. The darkness kind of disguises how shoddy it is at the beginning of the movie, but when April and MC run into him in broad daylight, it is not good. Yet, at the same time, I love it. It looks like a cheap halloween gorilla mask being worn on top of a black fur coat with a chest piece sewn on. And it may be just that. There's a terrible, wonderful, goofy charm about it, and the presumably unintentionally googly eyes make it all the worse/better. It just depends on what you're looking for. Director Hewitt played Gorga himself, and I can't say I would have done anything differently.

Gorga's "famous" "fight" with a "t-rex"

There is, of course, also the famously bad T. rex fight. It's maybe 15 to 20 seconds long, and it features a T. rex hand puppet whose head is about the size of a dog's, some offscreen lizard hands fighting our title makeshift gorilla, who wins by mostly shoving the dinosaur's head downward out of the shot. Once he's succeeded, we're treated to some very labored, heavy breathing from Gorga. I love it. I love it so much. There are some special effects highlights, specifically a stop motion dragon guarding a treasure in a cave, but it doesn't interact with our characters

---

[202] "WILD RIDE OVERSEAS." *Chicago Tribune*, 19 May 1999, https://www.chicagotribune.com/news/ct-xpm-1999-05-19-9905190048-story.html.

because it was spliced in from a different movie. Specifically, the Italian Hercules movie *Hercules' Revenge,* known in the US as *Goliath and the Dragon*[203]. It's a much better movie.

Yeah. This movie is awful. But, like *The Giant Claw* before it, therein lies its virtue. This is something that somehow survived its birth on the regional California drive-in circuit, brought to us by Something Weird Video, who decided to release it on DVD as a double feature with the Ed Wood penned softcore porn parody of Hammer's *One Million BC, One Million AC/DC.* So if you choose to buy the DVD, be warned! The fact that it has survived for us to watch all these years, and that people like us are talking about it, is a small miracle, and I refuse to question it.

A Quick Look at *The Valley of Gwangi*

We've just looked at *The Mighty Gorga,* one of the only American made Giant Monster Movies of the late 1960s, and it wasn't very good. Now, y'all know me. Know how *I* make a livin'. I don't really consider "big animal" or "nature-run-amok" films to be Giant Monster Movies, so I don't cover them in full episodes. And dinosaur movies are usually both. But I do make a point of making sure the important and trend setting ones do get looked at, and we've got one of those today.

The Valley of Gwangi has its roots all the way back in our first episode's feature, *King Kong.* That film's special effects wizard and Record All Monsters alumnus, Willis O'Brien, had proposed a film called *The Valley of the Mists* to his bosses at RKO, in which a group of cowboys discover a living Allosaurus and make it the centerpiece of their wild west show. It escapes, wreaks havoc on the show's lions and goes on a rampage before being pushed off a cliff by one of the cowboys in a truck.

If any of that sounds familiar, it's because *Valley of the Mists* wound up getting split into a few projects over the next few decades. First, *Mighty Joe Young* used the image of cowboys roping an exotic animal for use in a show in 1949. It also used the fight with the show's lions. Next, in 1956, there was *The Beast of Hollow Mountain,* a Mexican/American co-production wherein an American rancher living in Mexico discovers an Allosaurus has been eating his cattle. Eventually, he and some ranch hands trick it into walking into a tar pit and the day is saved. While this movie's story has less to do with O'Brien's original story, it was the first to bring the cowboys vs dinosaurs battle to screen, and he's credited as a writer under the name El Toro Estrella, or, The Celestial Bull.

I have seen no direct evidence, but I do believe that the climatic bulldozer vs T. rex fight from *DINOSAURUS!* Was taken from O'Brien's *Mists* story. Finally, there's this film, *The Valley of Gwangi,* a movie I wish I had seen when I was younger. Yes, this movie is basically just cowboys vs dinosaurs. There's a little bit more going on though, and of course that must begin with another returning character, who we'll be seeing here for the last time for a little while: Ray Harryhausen.

---

[203] Bressan, David. *Prehistoric Monster Movie: The Mighty Gorga (1969).* http://historyofgeology.fieldofscience.com/2010/10/prehistoric-monster-movie-mighty-gorga.html. Accessed 12 Sept. 2023.

Harryhausen inherited a lot of O'Brien's projects, and he approached his producer Charles Schneer with two of his mentor's unfinished ideas. One was a *War Eagles*, where a disgraced US Airman discovers a lost civilization of Vikings who RIDE GIANT EAGLES AND CONVINCES THEM TO HELP HIM FIGHT NAZIS? Am I reading that right? Holy crap and hot damn! The other was *The Valley of the Mists*. Schneer thought there was little potential for a full script in the *War Eagles* concept- ARE YOU KIDDING ME? WHAT THE HELL CHARLES SCHNEER? HOW IS THERE *NOT* AN ENTIRE SCRIPT THERE? THAT WRITES ITSELF! AND YOU COULD EVEN USE FLIGHT OF THE VALKYRIES AND MAKE IT AN *ANTI* NAZI ANTHEM IN PEOPLE'S MINDS! YOU DONE GOOFED, CHUCK! YA DONE **GOOFED**. So they went ahead on *Mists,* now called *The Valley of Gwangi*.

As disappointed as I am that *War Eagles* never materialized, that isn't *Gwangi*'s fault. It's Charles Schneer's. Most of Schneer and Harryhausen's collaborations were funded and distributed by Columbia Pictures, but they were not interested in *Gwangi*. Their reasoning? Nobody wanted dinosaur movies anymore. Eventually the project landed at Warner Bros.- Seven Arts, and was one of the last films released before the company rebranded as Warner Bros. Inc., which may be among the reasons that they did very little to promote it.

Cowboys rope the title dinosaur in The Valley of Gwangi

Both Schneer and Harryhausen were unhappy with how Warner handled the release, and blamed them for the movie's box office failure, though Schneer eventually dismissed the film itself, saying, "it just didn't have the same appeal to me as our other pictures had." I was not there, of course, I am far too young and beautiful to have been traipsing about in August of 1969, so I can't speak to the effectiveness of the ad campaign or its proliferation. Even though I only saw this film for the first time earlier this year, I had seen scenes from it my entire life, and the trailer a few times. It was especially present in VHS trailer compilations with titles like *Godzilla, King Kong, and Highlights From Other Dinosaur Movies*, some of which you can find on Youtube, Amazon Prime, and other eclectic streaming services.

When I watched this movie for the first time, I was sitting with Courtney and felt myself reverting closer and closer to my 6 year old self with every scene. Cowboys and dinosaurs are two of the most primal and fascinating images for young kids, and I've loved both my whole life. To see them brought together in a movie that's so entertaining and light hearted was a long held childhood dream come true. Near the end of it, I turned to Courtney and said, "Do you know who would love this movie? Me."

Chapter 33: *Godzilla's Revenge (All Monsters Attack)*

All Monsters Attack, or as it was known until very recently in the English speaking world, *Godzilla's Revenge* may be the most controversial, despised, and looked down upon movie in the entirety of not just the Godzilla franchise, but in Giant Monster Moviedom as a whole. The Website Barry's Temple of Godzilla even went so far as to call it, "Without a doubt, the worst Godzilla film ever made."[204] I feel this reputation is far from deserved, so forgive me if I take a defensive tone; I have come here to chew bubblegum, and to champion this film. And brother, I'm all out of bubblegum.

We talked, way back at the beginning of season one, about Ishiro Honda and his wonder at the world, and his desire to tell stories about real people. I think of him a little bit like 80s and 90s Speilberg; there's an earnestness and optimism to a lot of his work. People, and monsters too, come together to make the world a safer and better place. In the movie *Gorath*, Honda depicts a future where the earth is threatened, not by a malevolent alien force, but by a star thrown out of its orbit by sheer chance. All the people of the earth come together to study how they can save the planet, and decide on building rockets at the South Pole to push earth out of its orbit until the rogue star has passed, and then return it to its original place in the solar system. Things go wrong, obstacles, including a cool walrus monster named Maguma, rear their ugly heads, but everyone is willing to sacrifice and work together to save the world as a whole, as humanity.

In *Destroy All Monsters* we saw the same thing; the people, and this time monsters, of the earth rally behind a common cause to save themselves and each other. It's more than humanity, more than monsterdom, at stake, it's the earth and everyone and everything on it, so everyone and everything on it has to fight back together as one. We see this theme throughout Honda's sci-fi works, all the way back to the original *Godzilla*, where Akiria Takarada's character Ogata convinces Akihiko Hirata's character Serizawa that he must put aside his fears for the sake of the world as a whole, for the sake of humanity. These ethos bleed out of Honda's foundational films at the beginning of the Godzilla series and into Jun Fukuda's previous two entries, making the heart of the entire franchise beat with the same kind of compassion and optimism that bubbles melancholily from 1954 to this very day.

What does that all have to do with this movie? The movie where the whiniest, tiniest Kenny pals around with the Son of Godzilla for 70 minutes and watches stock footage from the most child oriented Godzilla movies up till this one? Remember how I said that Ishiro Honda wanted to make movies about real people? Well, Toho wanted him to make movies about giant monsters[205]. Godzilla had been an allegory for many things, and had slowly morphed into a heroic, almost super hero-like character, and that transformation was not yet over. As we have observed over the course of this second season, the Giant Monster Movie genre had evolved squarely into kiddie matinee fare, with declining box office returns giving series producer Tomoyuki Tanaka reason to declare *Destroy All Monsters* the last of the series. The bigwigs across town at Daiei had decided the same thing about Gamera before his fourth outing was released. In both cases, the series was kept alive and continued for a few more films and into the seventies.

---

[204] *Barry's Temple of Godzilla - Godzilla's Revenge.* http://www.godzillatemple.com/movie10.htm. Accessed 7 Sept. 2023.
[205] *A Life in Film,* pg 253

Series screenwriter Shinichi Sekizawa returns and crafts a story that has many more layers than it is given credit for. Honda's desire to make films about people's everyday lives seems to be echoed by Sekizawa, as his focus here is a bullied child, and how that child escapes from not just his bullies, but his lonely and unstable homelife, into fantasy, the fantasy of Godzilla.

One of the many gripes people seem to have with this film is its reliance on stock footage, specifically, almost all of the fight scenes from both *Ebirah, Horror of the Deep* and *Son of Godzilla* show up here, only edited slightly to keep Minilla and irrelevant human characters out of frame. There's no disguising the origins of these clips, and one scene is even a shot for shot remake of one from *Son of Godzilla*. In order to defend this choice, it becomes necessary to take a closer look at our hero, Ichiro Miki, the King of the Kennies, played by Tomonori Yazaki. I'm very bad at guessing how old kids are, but I'd guess he's between eight and ten in this movie. That would make him between 6 and 8 when *Ebirah* and *Son* came out a few years earlier. *Destroy All Monsters* would have been very new, and he may not have been able to see it yet. He is, after all, a latchkey kid.

Ichiro's parents both work. His dad, played by Kenji Sahara, tells his coworker "The boy's alone a lot." in the English dub. He elaborates in the Japanese version, "He needs someone around, but my wife has to work. We're trying to save up, and move to where the air is clean. But when?" We never see his father away from work. He's a train conductor, and always in his dirty uniform. In two of his three scenes, he is speaking to his son through the window of his train cab. In his third, he is eating lunch with his coworker, and worrying out loud about Ichiro.

We're introduced to his mother, who unlike his father, is given no name, through a note she left for Ichiro. "Be sure to do your school work before you play. I left you some cake in the cupboard. I'll fix supper when I come home. Mother." The next time we see her, she is calling their neighbor from work so he can tell Ichiro she will not be coming home that night. More on her last appearance later.

We meet Ichiro walking home from school, talking to a girl his own age about monsters. She is uninterested. They're bulldozed on a grimy city stairwell by a boy named Gabera who is bigger than him, and surrounded by his own friends, who tease Ichiro as they push him aside. Smoke from trains, factories, and industrial chimneys choke the scene. Ichiro sneaks into an abandoned lot despite his companion's objections, and finds a vacuum tube. Gabera and his gang jump out of the tall grass, accuse him of stealing it, and take it from him.They tell him they'll only give it back if he honks the horn on a sign painter's nearby motorcycle. He dejectedly refuses. The little girl who had been walking home with Ichiro is picked up by her mother, who says nothing to the bullies as she walks by, but reprimands Ichiro for playing in the lot.

When Ichiro gets to his apartment building, he stops at the previously mentioned neighbor's apartment first, and takes his home's key out of a jack in the box. Ichiro's neighbor is the only adult whose full name is told to the audience in the English dub. Toymaker Shinpei Inami. Ichiro talks with him briefly about monsters and complains about how Gabera stole his vacuum tube. Inami tries to give the boy some advice that isn't very helpful. "Don't let him take it away! A bum like that will always try to put you down." Ichiro answers, "it sure is murder when you're so darn small", plays a little bit with some of Inami's new toys, then heads to his family's apartment. We will not spend much time here. Ichiro finds the note his mother left, eats his cake, and checks what's on TV. Inspired by Inami's toy computer, Ichiro pulls his own homemade toy computer, covered in volume knobs, crayon drawings of level indicators of all kinds, radio dials, and vacuum tubes, from its place in his toy cabinet next to a Maruson J-Tail Godzilla figure. He uses it to call Monster Island. "Calling Monster Island, Yes? You take a jet? You take a jet to get there?"

We hear the plane take off, and see Ichiro sitting alone in row after row of empty seats on board. He walks up to the cockpit and there are no pilots. Even in his dreams, Ichiro is alone. A voice calls the Monster Island Control Tower, and suddenly, Ichiro is on the ground during Godzilla's first battle with the Kamacuras from *Son of Godzilla*. After the fight plays out, he's among the monsters of Monster Island. He calls them by name as they appear in stock footage from *Destroy All Monsters* and *King Kong Escapes*. "There's bro-saurus! There's Manda. Anguirus! There's Kamacurus. Guy, Look at that!" In footage from *Ebirah*, the giant condor fight plays out just how you, and presumably Ichiro, remember it. He runs through the jungle, right into a Kamacuras, which chases him, and like Alice, he falls through a hole. Though he is safe from the big bug, now he is trapped. Slowly a rope or vine descends. Ichiro grabs hold, and half climbs, half is pulled out of the hole, where he sees his savior drop the other end of the vine. "Ai, it's Minya!"

Let's hit pause on the recap for a minute and look back on what has happened. A bullied little boy who watches TV at home by himself, who we've seen from his personal interactions and toys at home, is obsessed with Godzilla and has very few real friends. The only excitement we see from him is when he thinks Inami is playing monster sounds from his computer, and when he realizes he's on Monster Island in his dream. So, the stock footage is a storytelling tool. There are quite a few new effects scenes, directed by Ishiro Honda[206], and they're not bad. Even if the scenes were poor, that has not stopped Toho from sending out a monster movie. In *Godzilla Raids Again*, the camera was over-cranked, causing the fight scenes to play out at ridiculously high speed. They used the stock footage from recent Godzilla movies that had played on TV in Japan, because that is how Ichiro remembers Godzilla.

Where were we? "-Ai, it's Minya! -C'mon over here!" Right. Minilla. The Son of Godzilla. Let's talk about him. If you're a listener to the show, you know I am a defender of the little turd. I don't disagree with the criticism that he's ugly and that his voice in both the dub and Japanese version is annoying. Those are the same reasons I've avoided *Lupin III* all these years. Ha! Before I get into my defense of Minya, let me defend the US release title under which I, and many others first encountered it, *Godzilla's Revenge*. In my crowdsourcing research, this point came up a surprising amount[207]. Who is Godzilla getting revenge on? It's misleading. Blah blah blah. First of all, this talking point is stolen, often verbatim, from James Rolfe's *Cinemassacre Monster Madness Godzilla-thon* review of the film[208], which is largely

---

[206] *Showa Completion,* pg 177
[207] Poll conducted on March 26th, 2022 in the "Godzilla Fan Club" Facebook group and had 59 respondents.
[208] "Godzilla's Revenge (1969) - Episode 10." *Cinemassacre*, 29 Sept. 2008, https://cinemassacre.com/godzillas-revenge-1969-episode-10/.

dismissive and unable to look at the deeper subtexts of the film, mostly due to its length, clocking in at just over three minutes.

The fact is, it was never supposed to be called *Godzilla's Revenge*. The Japanese title was originally, *Gojira, Minira, Gabara: Ōru Kaijū Daishingeki*, which would translate quite literally to *Godzilla, Minilla, Gabara: All Monsters Attack*. Maron Films, the US distributor, wanted to emphasize the relationship between Ichiro and Minya when they released it in 1971, and so they called it *Minya: Son of Godzilla*[209]. They were unaware of the previous film, *Son of Godzilla*, but when it did come to their attention, they did not want potential audiences to confuse their new theatrical release with an almost 5 year old movie that had been released straight to TV, so they gave it a new name and a new advertising campaign, calling it *Godzilla's Revenge* and pairing it on a double bill with the Christopher Lee and Peter Cushing UK sci-fi picture *Island of the Burning Damned*. It was a last minute marketing decision, and bears no weight in regard to the quality of the film.

When we see Minya here for the first time, he waves Ichiro over, promising he won't hurt him. "-You won't? -Nooooo, Don't be afraid!" The same interaction humans always have when they encounter an angel in the Bible: be not afraid[210]. Whether it's intended in the text or not, from a Western perspective, this is a religious experience for Ichiro, a holy dream.They have a conversation like two kids on the playground. "-Why'd you come here? -I wanted to see you. And also your daddy, Godzilla. -Your folks'll get kinda worried, won't they?" The theme of Ichiro's loneliness is never touched lightly, it's being pounded like a drum for the entirety of the film. Their commiseration is cut short by the appearance of Minya's bully, also named Gabara. At this point, any questions about what this dream means in the context of the film should be answered. Ichiro is Minya and Minya is Ichiro. This makes the presence of footage from *Son of Godzilla* all the more important in the film; Minya spent the entirety of that film at the mercy of other monsters, and is often alone. Godzilla is always being pulled away from his business to protect his son. Hmmm. I wonder why that might resonate with a latchkey kid with two working parents who plays by himself after school for hours everyday?

Minya's weakness, helplessness, and whininess, which were often complained about by those surveyed in my Godzilla Facebook group inquiry, are absolutely essential to the character in this story, and to Ichiro, because once again, they are the same character in this film. To take an example from a series with no controversial elements that is beloved by everyone and nobody ever complains about, let's look at Luke Skywalker in the original *Star Wars* Trilogy. He is whiny, annoying, a little dumb, and pretty self centered. But he is also hopeful, resourceful, and humble. He is always willing to learn and change and grow, and we see him do just that over the course of the three films. It is important to establish these traits in our main characters here because when we see the film's ending, we see that Ichiro has grown and changed and learned? But how? Let's get back to the story.

When Gabara appears, Minya grabs his head and runs away, Ichiro calls out for his mother, and we cut to her first appearance in the film, where she talks with Inami, relaying the news that she has to work late to cover for a sick coworker. She won't be coming home that night.

---

[209] *Showa Completion*, pg 177
[210] Genesis 21:1-21; Daniel 10:8-19; Luke 1:11-13; Luke 2:1-12; Matthew 28:1-10; Acts 27:1-26

This is also the first we hear about a very important subplot; the police stop by her workplace to let the employees know that two bank robbers are at large in the area and have stolen 50 million yen. That would be roughly 400,000 American dollars today.

Inami goes to wake Ichiro up. The boy is confused and napping on the floor, wondering where he is and where did Minya go? In both the Japanese and English language versions, he asks Inami why he woke him up, that he was going to get to meet Godzilla. The toymaker breaks the news frankly and with little bedside manner. Ichiro is of course disappointed to hear that his mother has to work all night,

Inami wakes Ichiro from his dream of Monster Island

but Inami tries to cheer him up by telling him that they can have dinner together. And then he leaves too. Ichiro tries to go back to sleep, but gives up and goes to play outside again. As he leaves, we get a short look at the family's apartment. There is a small dinner table, an office desk and rolling chair where Ichiro has set his backpack. There's a child's drawing on the wall that I can't quite make out.

When Ichiro goes out to play, he runs into Gabara and his gang, fishing in a dirty stream with bamboo poles. They call him over and he runs away as cries of "Wimp" and "Baby" are hurled at his back. He returns to the abandoned lot from earlier, and this time goes into the empty building it is home to. The establishing shot of the building gives it an exhausted, worn out look. It bears a slight resemblance to a stern and tired face, neither smiling or frowning. The first of its four floors is boarded up and overgrown with vines and weeds. Once inside, Ichiro starts digging through the piles of building material and office supplies and finds two vacuum tubes, declaring that "Gabara won't get to take these!".

He climbs to the second floor and looks out the window. Gabara and his gang are on the way. Ichiro backs away from the window, but they're drawn from the building by the wail of police sirens, and the boys excitedly watch the car speed by before following it down the road. At almost the same time, the door falls off of a dusty old locker. Ichiro walks over to investigate. He finds a big, goofy pair of headphones and a driver's license directly below a hole in the ceiling. As he goes up the stairs, we see two men peeking out of another old locker. They quickly close the door as Ichiro's yellow baseball cap becomes visible in the stairwell. Before he can begin his search of the 3rd floor, more police sirens can be heard, and Ichiro runs down stairs. The two men stumble out of the locker, one dressed in a black suit and tie, the other in a green jacket and brown t-shirt, clutching a leather duffle bag to his chest. They're the bank robbers, and the little one in the green jacket is the owner of Ichiro's newly acquired drivers license. The one in the suit sends him to follow Ichiro home, and we learn that Inami is selling a car, sitting just outside the building, which the robber inspects as if he'd like to buy it while he stakes out the apartment.

As Ichiro and Inami have dinner, they talk about why Ichiro is sad. Not a lot, but he's worried he's a burden to his neighbor, who tells him not to worry about it. He can work for him as a play tester for all of his new toys. Ichiro shows much more enthusiasm for the food, and it makes his friend smile. From our perspective, we see that the prospect of joining the workforce is the only thing that has excited Ichiro besides monsters. The police stop by and warn Inami that he should make sure his car is locked and secured. The bank robbers are on foot and may try to steal a car. We cut back to them and see that they're having cigarettes for dinner, discussing where Ichiro lives. Once they finish smoking, they get up and head off to get the boy.

Minilla (or Minya in the dub) and Ichiro reunite

Ichiro has fallen asleep on the floor again, wearing his headphones, which he has now plugged into his homemade computer. We join once again on Monster Island. He calls for Minya and Gabara answers. He chases Ichiro, who manages to lose him in the jungle. Once on the other side, Ichiro meets up with Minya again, who's sitting down on a rock and eating a melon. A call back to *Son of Godzilla*. They start talking again, and this time Minya expresses his loneliness "Just sittin' by m'self bein' lonesome 'cause I got no friends." The subject turns to Godzilla again. And we get a great line of dialogue, one of my favorites in anything. "Godzilla says that I should learn to fight my own battles, y'know". Then, Godzilla calls Minya to watch the fight from *Ebirah, Horror of the Deep*. I have already explained the use of stock footage from a story perspective, but it bears repeating: these are the Godzilla movies Ichiro would have seen. This is how he remembers him. Budget may have been a reason behind the scenes, and Eiji Tsuburaya's worsening illness certainly was[211], but even within the story, the repeated footage has a purpose and is thematically relevant to the rest of the film.

We're about thirty minutes into the film now, and we'll spend the next ten minutes or so with Ichiro and Minya watching Godzilla fight. First he takes on Ebirah, followed by Kumonga in footage from *Son of Godzilla*. After that, Minya tries, unsuccessfully, to fight off Gabara, and then Godzilla takes on the Red Bamboo jets in more footage from *Ebirah*. Minya comments, when Ichiro points them out, "They sure are scary". In the Japanese version, he says "Humans are trying to invade our island again." When I was a kid, this really stuck in my mind. Minya is afraid, not just of other monsters but of humans, of us. And since Godzilla goes out to fight the jets, maybe he's afraid of them too. That always resounded with me. That scene is followed by a recreation of Godzilla teaching Minya to use his atomic breath, ala *Son of Godzilla,* only this is new footage, and they're firing their practice shots, not into the red water of Solgell Island, but on the destroyed fighter planes. As an adult, I may be reading too much into this, but it seems like a lesson in more than breath weapon usage. Godzilla has not only faced his fears, he has vanquished them. And he's done it before, and he'll do it again. So should you, Minya. So should you, Ichiro. So should you, Robert.

---

[211] *A Critical History*, pg 107

The order in which these scenes play out is important as well. We see Godzilla succeed twice, though, notably, Kumunga does briefly get the upper hand. As Ichiro puts it, "Godzilla's gone down". But Minya doesn't lose faith in his father. "It's ok". Then we see Minya fail in his fight with Gabara before the jet footage and teaching scene. It's also important that the teaching scene is NOT stock footage, even though it is nearly identical. The one major difference is what they are practicing on: the downed fighter jets. I've already explained the significance of that choice, and I do believe it is just that, an intentional choice. In this film, Godzilla teaches us that, like the humans in *Gorath*, you will face setbacks, you will fall and fail, but that's ok, as long as you are eventually able to get back up and move on.

A joyous Ichiro is then grabbed by a plant man. He wakes up, having been grabbed by the bank robbers, the besuited one brandishing a knife in his face. I always found it kind of funny that as they march him out of the room, they stop to put his shoes on. They turn out the lights, lock the door, and make off into the night. Shortly after, we see Inami leave his apartment and enter the cold, concrete hallway. He looks into Ichiro's door, knocks gently and calls the boy's name. No answer. Satisfied that he's probably asleep, he heads downstairs, and joins some policemen at a food stand. The owner, Inami, and the officers discuss what size bag would be able to hold 50 million yen.

Back at the robber's hideout, the one in the green jacket goes out to steal the car, while the one in the suit takes a swig from a liquor bottle and Ichiro, after covering the hole in the floor with newspapers, falls back asleep, rejoining Minya on Monster Island one last time. And it's just in time too. Minya is in a fight for his life with Gabara. Cornered against a cliff, the Son of Godzilla is trying desperately to fire a blast of atomic breath, but his smoke rings are all he can produce. Gabara shocks Minya with electricity from his hands, sending him to the ground. Ichiro, from the cliff above, pushes a boulder down onto his friend's tail, which startles a blast of radiation right out of his mouth and into Gabara's face. Godzilla arrives, and Minya runs to him, only to be rebuffed and told to finish the battle. Minya gives a roar and then runs headfirst back into the fray. When Gabara begins using his electrical powers again, Godzilla blasts an atomic beam at their feet, insisting on keeping the fight as fair as it could be. When Gabara turns around, Minya bites his arm, prompting a cheer of support from Ichiro. The bully throws Minya to the ground and turns to face Godzilla again. This buys the two friends some time to strategize.

Minya shrinks back down to Ichiro's size and they come up with a plan. As Gabara approaches the cliff where Ichiro and Minya are conspiring, he steps on the end of a log. Minya jumps down onto it and is back to his full size by the time he lands. This sends Gabara spinning through the air, landing flat on his face. Godzilla and Ichiro cheer for their boy, and Minya runs to embrace his father while Gabara shudders in disbelief on the ground. As father and son share a victory hug, Gabara bites into Godzilla's thigh. This earns him a few punches in the face, followed by a full blown beat down from the King of the Monsters, which Minya tries to join in. Godzilla emphasizes the "fight your own battles" lesson by keeping his son out of the brawl. This is Godzilla's fight now. Gabara has a few tricks up his sleeve, but Godzilla is always in the driver's seat, and he sends his opponent away limping. And now, at last, Minya makes the introductions between his friend and his father. It doesn't appear to be going well, as Godzilla reaches for Ichiro who calls out that he's Godzilla's friend. Don't hurt me, help me! And the bank robbers shake him awake.

They gag Ichiro and tie his hands together before carrying him and the bag of cash out to the waiting stolen car. As the robbers try to hotwire their getaway again, Minya appears to Ichiro and reminds him that "Godzilla says to fight our own battles and not be cowards". Ichiro wriggles his wrists free and bolts for the building. The besuited robber gives chase.

Throughout the following scene, we see Ichiro flashback to Minya's attacks and evasions in his battle with Gabara, and imitate them. He leads the robber in the green jacket to the newspaper covered hole in the floor, and hoses down the one in the suit with a fire extinguisher while recalling Minya breathing fire into Gabara's face. With the two men incapacitated, Ichiro runs out of the building and runs into Inami, who was heading back from the food stand when he saw his car running outside of the abandoned building. He finds the bag with the 50 million yen in it and helpfully exclaims, "Hey! That's not mine." He's called the police, who arrive just before Ichiro leaves the building. The robbers have chased Ichiro outside, and so are caught by the cops and carted away. Ichiro has his face buried in his neighbors chest through all of it. Once the bad guys are gone, Inami tells Ichiro "Let's go home", and in what is one of the series' most heartbreaking scenes, Ichiro answers: "But there's no one there..."

Who says Godzilla doesn't get any revenge in this movie?

The next morning, we see Ichiro and his mother sitting across from each other eating breakfast. She apologizes for what happened the night before and that she'll never work late again. Ichiro says not to worry about it, he knows they need the money and he can take care of himself. He finishes his food, puts on his cap and backpack, tells his mom bye, and heads out the door. His mother tells him to be careful as we hear the door shut. She collects the empty dishes on the table and starts to cry. This is the shot that Ishiro Honda wanted to end the movie on[212], and I think that speaks volumes about his intentions in making this movie. Ichiro is approached by a horde of reporters asking about his heroics the previous night. How did he do all of that alone? "I wasn't alone. Minya was with me!" More religious imagery. Inami takes over the interview and explains to the newsmen: "Minya's the son of Godzilla. The boy believes the monster is his friend and protector. Just like we grown ups look up to big heroes, this child is inspired by a monster." The religious imagery is reinforced in the Japanese version, where Inami explains that "Adults believe in gods, so why can't kids have their own gods too? Like Minilla?"

---

[212] Pusateri, Richard. *Commentary: Godzilla's Revenge*. Classic Media, 2007.

While walking to school with his friend, Ichiro is ambushed by Gabara and his gang. Ichiro tells him to get out of the way, and Gabara charges him. The ordeal the night before changed something in Ichiro, and this time he meets the attack head on, barreling head first into Gabara's stomach. The fight plays out in a series of still images, giving the scene a strobing, stumbling effect. This may have just been to avoid showing children fighting directly, the way they used to not show boxing on TV, but I think it also shows us how uncomfortable, maybe even unnatural, this turn of events is. It's taking everyone by surprise. Gabara has never had to make good on his threats because Ichiro does not fight back. Now he does. None of Gabara's cronies jump in to help, they just stand around stunned. Ichiro's friend does too. "All bullies are alike: you can't take it!" and Ichiro butts his head into Gabara's stomach one more time, knocking him back onto the ground. His gang nods grimly. The King is dead; Long live the King. Gabara rubs his elbow as Ichiro marches past him. Nobody helps him up. The sign painter from the day before is still at work, and now Ichiro goes and cheerfully honks the horn. The man yells at him to stop, loses his balance, and falls off the ladder, spilling paint all over his face.

Ichiro takes off down the road as the painter chases him, and the other kids head through a hole in the fence, laughing as they run away. Ichiro runs into the train yard and yells to his father, still driving an engine. "Whatever he says, I did it. And I'm sorry" before he runs away again. His father jumps out of the cab and stops the man. We can hear him apologizing as we see the other kids join Ichiro on the road. They all go together now, laughing and joking and running to school along the dirty river, under the smoke choked skyline, full of chimneys and factory buildings. Some hopeful music plays as the camera zooms out and "The End" comes onto the screen. This ending was what Honda came up with when his bosses told him he could not end the film on Ichiro's mother crying at the family table. This also tells us a lot about what Honda wanted to say with this film.

The world is often not a kind place, and that cycle repeats itself, over and over, as people who are hurt and experience trauma go on to traumatize others and hurt them. There are some conditions in the world that we cannot change as individuals, systems larger than ourselves that are geared toward keeping themselves alive and perpetuating the cycles that harm us. Like a Gabara, it picks on us because we are smaller. It overwhelms us with its powerful friends and takes our vacuum tubes. This is undeniable, and it can be a bleak and discouraging realization, but it can also be freeing. The worst case scenario is we join in with the same systems that oppress us, and turn its power onto others to protect ourselves. We don't know what happened to Ichiro after this movie. We don't even know what happened to the actor who played him[213]. But I think it is safe to say Ichiro did not learn all that he could have from his ordeal. It has to be said that there is a hint in his attempt to apologize that Ichiro has not turned bad, and this seems to be the accepted interpretation by other champions of the film, including Steve Ryfle, Ed Godziszewski[214], and most importantly, my sister Aubrey. However, despite the cheerful music, the ending is ambiguous, as Ichiro is swallowed up first by the endlessly large city, and then by the blackness of the film itself ending.

Overall, I think that many of the harshest points of this film's critics actually come out in its favor, from the stock footage and whininess of its protagonist, to its bizarrely heavy handed anti-bully messaging and slapstick comedy elements. I've explained most of my defenses as they came up in the synopsis, something I try to avoid on this show generally, but so many of its qualities have come under fire in the past fifty-odd years, there was really no way to defend them all without doing so. There are just a couple more points I would like to make before we wrap up this chapter.

Firstly, I have long had a theory that this film is held in such particularly low regard because Ichiro is too good of an audience surrogate. Many people I have spoken to over the course of my life share the same story with me when we talk about Giant Monster Movies. "I loved it as a kid, but nobody else liked it, I got made fun of, and I stopped watching them". This is common even among those who have rediscovered their fandom as adults, but still cannot accept that, at this point in its history, the Kiddie-Matinee Idol Godzilla is as storied and valid a representation of him as the walking radiation burn that first attacked Tokyo in 1954. Seeing Ichiro be bullied for his love of Godzilla, goofy, friendly, super-hero Godzilla, no less, is a cut too close to the heart for some. When we see what we consider negative aspects of ourselves portrayed in the media, it's easy, if almost unavoidable, to not take offense at being poorly represented. So if Ichiro, The King of the Kennies, is one of our most well known public representatives, it can definitely hurt to see him be cowed by his peers, ignored by his parents, and dismissed for his love of the thing we also love, in this case, Godzilla. By realizing that there is nothing wrong with this film, and that it is successful at everything it sets out to achieve, we should be able to realize that there is nothing inherently wrong with our love of something so quote-unquote childish. Minya is Ichiro, Ichiro is us, and we are all ok. We're not perfect, but we're fundamentally good, and we're ok.

Secondly, you can boil this whole film down to a very simple belief that I hold dearly, and maybe because I encountered this movie for the first time when I was about 5: Stories in general, and movies in particular, provide both a means of escape from everyday bleakness, loneliness, and worry, but also give us the tools we need to navigate life. Instruction has always been the purpose of stories, from campfire ghost tales and ancient fables, to Monster Movies and TV dramas. We learn about ourselves and each other from them, and, like Ichiro, dream about a world where everything can be couched in clearly divided lines of good guys and bad guys, heroes and villains, even if we know the real world is nowhere near as simple.

---

[213] *Interview: Ed Godziszewski - Regarding Ishiro Honda (2017).*
https://www.tohokingdom.com/interviews/ed_godziszewski_regarding_ishiro_honda_11-2017.html. Accessed 12 Sept. 2023.
[214] *Life in Film*, pg 257

I was always a weird kid. I was tall and very thin as a child, and got made fun of by my peers for it a lot. I also never did anything halfway. When I liked something, I *really* liked it. That was another cause for teasing. I was afraid to fight back because I was not very physically courageous, and felt ill equipped to put up my dukes or speak out in my own defense. No matter how many times my mom told me to tell the teachers or my dad told me to fight back, I knew that telling would just make the mean kids meaner and I was too fearful of pain or injury to retaliate. This movie, *Godzilla's Revenge,* gave me the courage to fight back for myself, and for those who actually weren't strong enough to push a bully back. And it really did stop a lot of it. Ichiro was right. All bullies are alike, they can't take it. I have always related to Ichiro, and I always will. I was him at one point. But just like Minya will someday, offscreen, become a powerful monster monarch like his father, I am a grown man now. I'm married, financially independent, and have enough free time to pursue my own interests. The future is not something we can really know until it happens, just like we don't know where Ichiro and Gabara go once the movie fades to black, but we can plan, we can hope, and we can dream.

There are two quotes I want to end on. The first is from Ishiro Honda himself. This film was a favorite of his among his Kaiju works, and while this statement isn't about the movie at hand today, it really sums up what I feel it's about. From a 1991 interview by James Bailey in the *Tokyo Journal*: "My nightmares are almost always about war - wandering the streets, searching for something that's lost forever. But it's possible for me to will myself to have pleasant dreams. For me, the most wonderful fragrance in the world is new film. You open the canister for the first time and breathe deeply. That night, the same wonderful fragrance fills your dreams. It's grand."[215]

The second quote is from one of my favorite spaghetti westerns, *The Mercenary,* starring Franco Nero and Tony Musante. The title character and a Mexican revolutionary part ways and dissolve their professional relationship because as Paco, the revolutionary says, "I have a dream of a free Mexico" before almost walking into an ambush by federales. They're gunned down by his ex-partner, who then utters the moral of that movie, as well as this one: "Keep dreaming, but with your eyes open!"

---

[215] *Ishirō Honda - Wikiquote.* https://en.wikiquote.org/wiki/Ishir%C5%8D_Honda. Accessed 13 Sept. 2023.

Chapter 34: *Gamera vs Jiger*

We haven't seen Gamera for a while, and the last time we did was my favorite Showa Gamera movie, *Gamera vs Guiron*. Today, we're talking about its immediate sequel, *Gamera vs Jiger*, or *Gamera vs Monster X*, as it was released to American television screens by AIP[216]. The conventional wisdom of the day argues that this is the best Showa Gamera movie, and, while it isn't my personal favorite, I can't deny that it strikes the best balance between Gamera kiddie matinee and a compelling story.

Part of the reason it works so well is that the Gamera formula is locked, loaded, and firing on all cylinders. We have the mostly ineffectual adults, the two best and smartest boys who ever lived, their sisters on the sidelines, and ample monster action throughout. There are, however, no alien invaders, and that might be another reason this movie works so well. The monster antagonist here is a free agent, not under anybody's control. Jiger just wants to jump around and destroy things, and Gamera is in her way. So is Expo '70.

So let's talk about Expo '70. It's important to this movie, and tells us quite a bit about what's coming up in the future. To start with, Expo '70 was a World's Fair held in Osaka, Japan from March 15th through September 13th. World's Fairs are international events where different countries from around the world show off some of their ideas for the future. The host country usually has a central pavilion as well as a signature structure[217], such as the Eiffel Tower in Paris, France, or the Sunsphere in Knoxville, Tennessee in the United States, which was famously knocked over in March of 1996. At least, I think it was. I saw it fall over in a documentary called *Bart on the Road*, which is available on Disney Plus[218].

The logo for Expo '70

The signature structure for Osaka and Expo '70 was the Tower of the Sun, which still stands to this day, and is seen in the movie we're discussing. It's widely believed that the Expo itself funded some aspects of the movie, since much of it was shot on the grounds during the 6 months of the fair and they told director Noriaki Yuasa he could not destroy any models of Expo related structures for the film[219].

We do get some nice city destruction from Jiger, who is a fascinating kaiju. She's explicitly said to be female, is quadrupedal, shoots darts from her face, deposits her young like a xenomorph parasite into Gamera with a stinger on the end of her tail, and can almost

---

[216] *Showa Completion,* pg 179
[217] "World's Fair." *Wikipedia*, 6 Sept. 2023. *Wikipedia*, https://en.wikipedia.org/w/index.php?title=World%27s_fair&oldid=1174114946.
[218] This is actually just a very good episode of *The Simpsons*, Season 7, Episode 20
[219] *Showa Completion,* pg 179

definitely fly. She also has some kind of sonic superpower that forces Gamera to protect himself by shoving telephone poles into his ears before murdering her with a giant whistle.

A couple of pages from the Expo '70 booklet promoting the Godzilla vs Gamera live show

Beyond this film, which was released just about a week after the Expo opened, Godzilla and Gamera also had a presence together in the form of a Godzilla vs Gamera stage show, from which only an event program, a few photos, and maybe a few seconds of video survive[220]. Yoshimitsu Banno, who had been an assistant director to Akira Kurosawa on four films, including *Throne of Blood* and *The Hidden Fortress*, would be selected to direct the following year's entry in the Godzilla series based on the overwhelmingly positive reactions to his directorial debut, *The Birth of the Japanese Islands*, which was made expressly for Expo '70[221].

This is the penultimate Gamera movie of the Showa era, kind of, but we'll cross that bridge when we get there. Although this movie was a huge success, the most profitable Gamera movie in the original series, as a matter of fact, Daei was still in deep financial trouble[222], and even a big hit like this couldn't keep them afloat.

---

[220] *Shout! Factory TV Presents Gamera Marathon + 26 Gamera Facts « SciFi Japan*. 4 Apr. 2019, https://web.archive.org/web/20190404102112/https://www.scifijapan.com/articles/2015/10/16/shout-factory-tv-presents-gamera-marathon-26-gamera-facts/.
[221] *A Critical History*, pg 118
[222] Holland, Edward L. *Commentary: Gamera vs Jiger*. Arrow Video, 2020.

Chapter 35: *Space Amoeba*

Space Amoeba, or *Yog, the Monster from Space,* sees the sun set on two of our history's biggest figures. Though he had been sick for most of the past two years and unable to work directly on *Destroy All Monsters* and *Godzilla's Revenge,* Eiji Tsuburaya had still been credited as the supervising effects director on those two films. And while we often think of *Destroy All Monsters* as the finale to Toho's Golden Age (which I think actually happened with *War of the Gargantuas,* but I digress), a case can be made for Today's film. Two days into the production, on January 25th, 1970, Eiji Tsuburaya passed away due to a heart attack while asleep in bed with his wife. He was posthumously awarded the Japanese Order of the Sacred Treasure for his cultural contributions 5 days later[223]. He is buried at Fuchu Catholic Cemetery in Fuchu Japan, where people still leave figures of his two most iconic creations, Ultraman and, of course Godzilla[224].

Tsuburaya's assistant, Sadamasa Arikawa, had been the effects director in practice for most of the past few years, though Tsuburaya had still been hard at work on the *Ultra* series of shows. Arikawa struggled with Toho's studio bosses since Tsuburaya was no longer there to advocate for their production needs, and Tomoyuki Tanaka was busy arranging Toho's contributions to Expo '70. Ishiro Honda was far too timid a man to make the demands on his behalf as well, so Arikawa's work is not at the level we know he was capable of from things like *Destroy All Monsters* and *Latitude Zero*. Arikawa was among a number of Toho employees who chose not to renew their contracts at the end of 1970 in protest of the studio brass refusing to add an "en memoriam" credit for Tsuburaya to *Space Amoeba*. I'd like to emphasize that this decision was not supported by Tomoyuki Tanaka or Ishiro Honda, both of whom were good friends with Tsuburaya[225].

Space Amoeba also marks the semi-retirement of Ishiro Honda. It was his last directorial feature for five years. Honda had long felt trapped by his mark as a monster maker, and there are ways in which it shows here. The script is a recycled one from 1966,[226] many ideas from it had already been used in earlier productions, such as *Destroy All Monsters, King Kong vs Godzilla,* and *Rodan*. It seems the general consensus around this film is that it is a failure of a swan song. In my opinion, it is not so much a dusk of Toho's Golden Age of Science Fiction, but a desperate, pleading fight, a last stand of sorts, to remind the audience, and maybe the filmmakers, of why these movies are worth watching.

Along with the array of issues discussed above, I feel this movie has some truly excellent qualities, among them, one of Akira Ifukube's best, most creative scores, even if there is some repetition and recycling of previous themes and motifs. Honda also gets wonderful performances out of the cast, which include veteran Toho Monster movie actors Akira Kubo as our hero, and Kenji Sahara in a surprisingly nuanced turn as a villain. We also have Haruo Nakajima playing both the giant squid Gezora and giant crab Ganime, while Haruyoshi Nakamura portrays one of my favorite Toho kaiju outside of the Godzilla canon, the giant turtle Kameba[227]. While the effects sequences and monster suits are far from

---

[223] *Master of Monsters,* pg 175
[224] *Master of Monsters,* pg 175
[225] *Showa Completion,* pg 185
[226] *Life in Film,* pg 259
[227] *Showa Completion,* pg 184

perfect, they're quite fun, and Gezora in particular has become a kind of icon for the bizarre nature of Japanese movie monsters.

Honda also chose not to renew his contract with Toho after the completion of this film, and did not even quit himself, instead asking his wife, Kimi, to do it for him[228]. They sold their home and moved to a smaller one, in which they were quite happy. After about a year, Honda returned to directing, but this time in television, directing the premier and finale of the first *Ultra* series after Tsuburaya's death, *Return of Ultraman*[229]. In addition to his work for Tsuburaya, Honda began editing classic Godzilla films for the child focused Champion Festival, held throughout the year when Japanese children were out of school. Champion Festival screenings consisted of a full day of monster movie programming, with classic Toho features edited to appeal to children, leading up to the headlining film, usually a new Godzilla flick. *Space Amoeba* headlined at the Festival for Summer 1970[230].

Soon, we will have to look at the continuing battle of the Giant Monster Movie industry to remain relevant, but in our next chapter, I want to digress a little bit and talk about something very near and very dear to my heart. In our next chapter, we're going to be talking about *Voyage into Space,* or, as I like to call it, *Johnny Sokko and His Flying Robot: The Movie.*

---

[228] *Life in Film*, 261
[229] *Life in Film*, pg 263
[230] "Toho Champion Festival." *Toho Kingdom*, 15 Dec. 2013, https://www.tohokingdom.com/blog/toho-champion-festival/.

Chapter 36: *Voyage into Space*

Voyage into Space is a movie that is very near and dear to my heart, and my decision to cover it on this show breaks some rules. But I made the rules, so I can break them when I want. The rules it specifically breaks are rule 2: Films must be theatrically released. And rule 3: Must, at least partially, contain material original to the film. But, I love it, and it represents something very important to our little history here, as TV was slowly but surely killing the Giant Monster Movie in cinemas. To begin with, we need to look at two trends in Japanese media of the day that we haven't talked much about before: Manga and Mechas.

For those of you who are unfamiliar with the art form, the term manga comes from the Japanese words "man" and "ga", which mean, respectively, fanciful and drawings. While the practice of telling stories through drawings is as old as drawing itself, the specific tropes and conventions of manga are usually considered to have been typified in the post World War II period, showing influences from earlier Disney cartoons of the era and older Japanese art styles. The art style we typically think of as manga or anime in the west was typified by Osamu Tezuka, who created, among many, many, many others, *Mighty Atom*, better known in the US as *Astro Boy*, in 1952.

A cover for the manga version of Giant Robo

Later in the same decade, another manga-ka, or writer/artist, named Mituteru Yokoyama created a series about a little boy who came into possession of a giant, pointy-nosed robot that obeyed his commands that he used to fight crime called *Tetsujin 28-go*. It reached a similar level of popularity as Tezuka's *Astro Boy*[231], and was likewise adapted into an anime that was dubbed and imported to the US and other English speaking territories as *Gigantor*.

This brings us to the year 1966, just before the Second Kaiju Boom really and truly exploded. *Ultra Q* was in the books and *Ultraman* was set to do the same. Toei Studios, behind last season's feature *The Magic Serpent*, decided they needed a show to compete with the Tsuburaya produced giant. Studio brass turned to their TV producer Tohru Hirayama to work his magic in that particular arena. Hirayama had produced the live action show *Li'l Devil*, based of the popular manga *Akuma-kun* by Shigeru Mizuki, in which the title character is a little boy acts as a kind of paranormal pied piper, as well as *Red Shadow: the Masked Ninja*, based off the manga by *Gigantor* creator Yokoyama[232]. Naturally, Hirayama turned to Yokoyama's work again, and wanted to adapt *Gigantor* into live action. After some production meetings, it was decided that instead of simply adapting *Gigantor*, which was already a popular anime, to adapt the concept[233].

---

[231] Ragone, August. *A Boy and His Giant Robo: The Making of Johnny Sokko and His Flying Robot.* SHOUT! Factory, 2013, pg 3
[232] *A Boy and His Giant Robo*, pg 3
[233] *A Boy and His Giant Robo*, pg 4-5

Hirayama took the new idea to manga-ka Yokoyama, and together they fleshed out the story: A young boy in an Interpol type agency fighting against an international organized crime syndicate accidently assumes control of their secret weapon, a nuclear powered giant robot, called GR-1 in the manga, and simply Giant Robot in the TV show. The show and comic ran concurrently, though they took different approaches to the same concept. In the manga, the boy and his robot are primarily fighting the bad guys' other two giant robots, the aquatic GR-2, and the flying GR-3, both of which GR-1 would have to be modified in order to effectively combat[234]. In the show, the bad guys commanded an impressive stable of giant monsters for Giant Robot to Megaton Punch in the face. I don't have to tell you which version I prefer.

Giant Robot vs Emperor Guillotine

I had a hard time finding details about the adaptation from *Giant Robo*, the Japanese version of the series, to *Johnny Sokko and His Flying Robot*, the one I'm familiar with. What I can tell you, though, is that the show freakin' rocks. It's about a ten year old kid with a gun and a giant robot who fights space gangsters with his gun and giant monsters with his giant robot. It's formulaic action television at its finest, which is why the fact that it has a surprisingly emotional ending seems to hit people so hard.

American International Pictures' TV wing, American International Television, or AI-TV, distributed the show through syndication in 1968 and 69, where it was popular and successful enough to have 5 episodes, the first two, two with some pretty good monster action, and the finale, edited together into today's movie. The complete series is available on DVD from Shout! Factory in North America, and the movie has a gorgeous blu-ray from Scorpion Releasing. This is one I desperately urge you to seek out in either form. Everything that is good about Giant Monster stuff from this era is featured prominently throughout. You just can't go wrong with *Johnny Sokko and His Flying Robot: The Movie*.

---

[234] *A Boy and His Giant Robo,* pg 5

Chapter 37: *Gamera vs Zigra*

We've said goodbye, at least temporarily, to several key figures in our continuing story this season. Ishiro Honda has retired, Eiji Tsuburaya has died, and Sadamasa Arikawa has left the industry. We've also said goodbye to some one-off monsters. Goodbye, Giant Claw, goodbye, Giant Behemoth, adios mis amigos, Gorgo and Reptilicus. Konga, Gorga, Frankenstein and his Gargantuan progeny. Guilala, Gappa, Yongary, and even the stars of our last week's episode, were one and done monsters for decades. As successful as the genre was, outside of the Godzilla and Gamera serieses, none of these myriad imitators had been able to launch a big screen franchise. One by one, the pillars are falling, and now only two remain. Today, one of them topples.

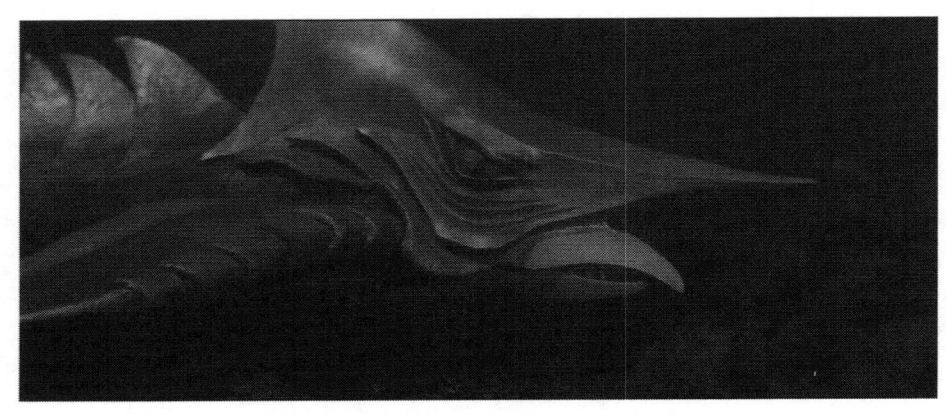

Gamera vs Zigra is the last Gamera film in the original Showa era continuity. Daiei and Noriaki Yuasa were able to crank it out between the release of *Gamera vs Jiger* and when the studio filed for bankruptcy. It hits all of the expected notes, does the song and dance, and does it all cheaper and worse than any previous Gamera movie. While they were never what anybody would call high art, even by the genre's often low standards, this is a huge downgrade from the previous film. The fights are ok, the kids are younger than they've ever been, and SeaWorld was not as generous a production partner as AIP and Expo '70 had been[235].

Zigra, the antagonist of the 1971 Gamera outing

The fallout of Daiei's bankruptcy was far reaching, and no one was hit harder than Gamera series writer Niisan Takahashi. Daiei owed him a considerable amount of money, 3 million yen by his own accounting[236]. Takahashi was unable to collect unemployment since he had never joined the Screenwriter's Union. Eventually, executives from the defunct studio told him he had the rights to Gamera. This was adequate compensation to him for a time. He wrote an original Gamera novel just before the Gamera Heisei series kicked off[237]. Takahashi was not consulted by Daiei's new owning and parent company, Kadokawa, who said that since their Daiei was not the same Daiei that made the deal with him, they were under no obligation to consult or pay Takahashi. The details aren't quite clear, but it was agreed that he would receive royalties from the new films and screenings of the old ones[238]. Takahashi passed away in 2015.

---

[235] Rhoads, Sean, and Brooke McCorkle. *Commentary: Gamera vs Zigra*. Arrow Video, 2020.
[236] Homenick, Brett. "THE MAN WHO MADE GAMERA ROAR! Screenwriter Niisan Takahashi on Creating Japan's Remarkable Flying Turtle!" *Vantage Point Interviews*, 9 Sept. 2020, https://vantagepointinterviews.com/2020/09/09/the-man-who-made-gamera-roar-screenwriter-niisan-takahashi-on-creating-japans-remarkable-flying-turtle/.
[237] THE MAN WHO MADE GAMERA ROAR!
[238] THE MAN WHO MADE GAMERA ROAR!

Noriaki Yuasa, someone who's name I used to have to look up every time I wrote about a Gamera movie in season 1, is now a little bit of a hero to me. After this film, he primarily worked in TV, including directing episodes of *Ultraman 80*. We will see him again next season, but for now, I want to say farewell to the man whose vision of a series of Giant Monster movies for Children, for good or for ill, indelibly changed the trajectory of the genre. Gamera began as a surprise hit cash grab on the Godzilla series, and for a time, surpassed the Kaiju King in popularity and box office returns, before going out with a whimper. Even though this chapter of the Gamera story closes on a downswing, these films do something I think the Godzilla films of the Showa era never actually did: They had set a particular tone, and stuck to it perfectly. Too perfectly, repeating themselves until even the least discerning of fans were asking, "What else is on?". But, all of that said, the original Gamera series films are all *unquestionably* Gamera movies. And that means they are Noriaki Yuasa movies.

Chapter 38: *Godzilla vs Hedorah*

This chapter is a little different than the others in this book. The episode of *Record All Monsters* this essay featured in was recorded live and featured clips from the film. Since I was unsure of how familiar the audience was with the show, the history of Giant Monster Movies, and so on, I had to catch them up on almost 20 years of cultural history. Consider this essay a brief refresher.

First of all, how many of you are familiar with Record All Monsters, raise your hands

I hope you have a good time and enjoy our presentation tonight. You can take a look at the show on apple podcasts, spotify, and most other podcasting platforms.

The film we are talking about today, *Godzilla vs Hedorah*, or *Godzilla vs The Smog Monster*, as it was initially released here in the United States, is the 11th film in the Godzilla franchise, which began in 1954 and is still releasing films to this day, with a total of 36 theatrically released films over 68 years, and it's important to understand this movie to have an idea about what was happening not just in the Godzilla series, but in the Japanese Monster Movie industry, and yes, it was its own industry inside the film industry.

The polish (left) and American (right) posters for Godzilla vs Hedorah

When the Original *Godzilla* was released on November 3rd, 1954, it was a science fiction horror film, a disturbing meditation on the Post-War experience of the only nation to suffer a nuclear strike. It was closely modeled on the celebrated stop motion dinosaur movie from the previous year, *The Beast From 20,000 Fathoms*, and heavily inspired by 1933's *King Kong,* which is generally regarded as the foundational text of the Giant monster movie genre.

A sequel followed the next year, but wasn't quite as successful, and so parent studio Toho Productions shelved Godzilla for the next 7 years. During that time, they introduced the new monsters Rodan, Varan, the alien space robot Mogera, the giant walrus monster Maguma, and of course, Mothra. Over this period of time, the movies had grown more vibrant and upbeat, so when Toho obtained the rights to make a movie featuring King Kong in combat with their own King of the Monsters, some retooling was necessary.

1962's *King Kong vs Godzilla* changed everything for this type of movie. Once again, it's an allegory, but this time for how we interact with television and advertising. I seriously urge you to seek this one out, it can be found for relatively cheap on blu-ray, dvd, and streaming services fairly easily. This film was an out and out comedy, which made 1964's *Mothra vs Godzilla*'s somber tone feel… strange. For some, it was a breath of fresh air, but for others, a dull and uninteresting step backwards for Godzilla. Late that same year saw the release of *Ghidorah, the Three Headed Monster*, a sprawling monster brawl in which Godzilla, Mothra, and Rodan join forces to fight the golden space dragon King Ghidorah and prevent him destroying the earth. So in just ten years, we have seen Godzilla transform from the sacred beast of the Apocalypse and into a grumpy but likable hero and defender of the earth.

Around this time, we get the first Godzilla imitator from a competing studio. Daiei studio's *Gamera* released in 1965 and started its own series, which spawned 7 sequels between 1966 and 1980. The Gamera series very quickly made up for lost time by targeting an audience of children instead of families or young adults as the recent Godzilla films had done. 1967 saw 8 Giant Monster Movies released, they are:
Gamera vs Gyaos, The X From Outer Space, Gappa, The Triphibian Monster, King Kong Escapes, Space Monster Wangmagwi, Yongary, and *Son of Godzilla.*

While all of these movies took different approaches, most of them included an exploitable kid friendly element. *Gamera vs Gyaos, Gappa,* and *Yongary* all had child protagonists. *King Kong Escapes* was based in large part on the Rankin Bass produced Saturday morning cartoon, *The King Kong Show.* And both *Gappa* and *Son of Godzilla* featured baby monsters. This was clearly the direction that the Giant Monster Movie Genre was headed, and Toho, despite having innovated this type of movie, had to follow the lead of the Gamera series in order to keep their Godzilla and other sci-fi flicks profitable. They announced the end of the Godzilla series, which was to take place in a no holds barred monster bash called *Destroy All Monsters*, which brought back original Godzilla director Ishiro Honda, who had not directed a Godzilla film for 3 years at this point.

The send off film was successful enough that Toho decided to keep the Godzilla franchise going, and Honda put together the next film largely out of stock footage and a very heartfelt script by longtime series writer Shinichi Sekizawa. While this movie, *Godzilla's Revenge,* is widely disliked, I myself love it dearly and a previous episode of this show dedicated an unprecedented 90 minutes to its defense.

Box office returns were not as good for *Revenge*, and so the bosses at Toho determined that it was time to once again find fresh blood to direct their flagship monster series. Back in 1966, Honda had passed the baton to action director Jun Fukuda, who directed that year's *Godzilla vs the Sea Monster* and 1967's *Son of Godzilla*. But it was now the 70s, and the studio looked to even fresher, newer talent.

Yoshimitsu Banno had been an assistant director to Akira Kurosawa on four movies, *Throne of Blood, The Lower Depths, The Hidden Fortress,* and *The Bad Sleep Well,* and helmed his first feature as director in 1970, a special effects tour de force called *The Birth of the Japanese Islands*, which was designed as an attraction for The World's Fair Expo in Osaka in that year.
I couldn't find any promo materials directly related to *The Birth of the Japanese Islands,* but there was a Godzilla vs Gamera stage show at the expo. Think *Disney on Ice* with Giant Monsters.

Banno was brought in to reinvigorate and modernize the Godzilla movies. Around this same time, the main executive producer of the Godzilla series, Tomoyuki Tanaka, was hospitalized during production,and unable to supervise the shoot. He asked Ishiro Honda to watch a rough cut in his stead. Honda, being a very gentle natured man, had a difficult time giving Banno any criticism.

The resulting film, *Godzilla vs Hedorah* is without a doubt the strangest of the Showa era Godzilla movies. We're now going to go through some clips, and watch a somewhat abridged version of the film.

Yoshimitsu Banno

Chapter 39: *Godzilla vs Gigan*

The fallout from *Godzilla vs Hedorah* was… there. Depending on who you ask, Tomoyuki Tanaka either hated it, or thought it was fine and hated its low box office attendance numbers. In special effects director Teruyoshi Nakano's telling of events, Tanaka was so upset he fired Yoshimitsu Banno, that film's director, on the spot, shouting "You've ruined Godzilla!" and telling him he'd never work at Toho again[239]. None of that happened according to Banno, and since he continued to work at Toho as a writer[240], I think his story holds a little more weight. Either way, Banno was out as the new hope of the Godzilla series. Tanaka, in noticing *Godzilla vs Hedorah*'s low attendance at the Summer Champion Festival in 1971, noticed that reissues of *Invasion of Astro-Monster* and *Ghidorah the Three Headed Monster* at the spring and winter festivals did extremely well, bringing in more than twice *vs Hedorah*'s attendance each.

Tanaka, ever the visionary, noticed the common denominator was Godzilla's most popular foe, King Ghidorah, last seen being curb stomped by ten other kaiju in 1968's *Destroy All Monsters*, which had taken place in the impossibly far off year of 1999.

While King Ghidorah was meant to be the big draw, Gigan proved popular in his own right

So, he decided to have his two favorite screenwriters for the series each pitch a return for the Golden Terror from Outer Space[241]. We know a little bit about Shinichi Sekizawa, whose script entitled *The Return of King Ghidorah*, won out, with some changes to the monster cast, so let's look at Tanaka's other writer, who I personally like to call his Left Hand, Takeshi Kimura.

If Sekizawa was a dog, bright, playful, and full of optimism, Kimura, born Kaoru Mabuchi, was a cat; secretive, cynical, and brilliant. His credits as writer or co-writer in our little world of Gods and Monsters include *Rodan, The Mysterians, The H-Man, The Human Vapor, Gorath, Matango, Frankenstein Conquers the World, War of the Gargantuas, King Kong Escapes, Destroy All Monsters,* and the previous Godzilla movie. These include some of the best and bleakest kaiju movies that ever were, and you can see his more contemplative streak compared to Sekizawa's more exuberant approach. Sekizawa wrote *Mothra*. Kimura wrote *Matango*. That should tell you everything.

---

[239] *A Critical History*, pg 122
[240] *A Critical History*, pg 124
[241] *A Critical History*, pg 124

Tanaka also sought proven talent for the director's chair, turning to Jun Fukuda to helm the next picture since Ishiro Honda had retired[242]. The score would be made up of recycled Akira Ifukube cues from the Toho Library in order to save money, with the only original music in the film being *The Godzilla March*, or *Ganbare! Bokura no Gojira!* Which is a real banger, as the kids say. Do the kids still say that?

This film was meant to be a return to the mid-60s glory days of Toho's science fiction films, much like *Space Amoeba,* but budget concerns kept scaling things back[243]. Three villainous monsters became two, four heroic monsters became two, and, most stingily of all, roughly seven minutes of the film's runtime, all of them effects shots, were stock footage from previous Toho sci fi epics. With the belt tightened to its very last notch, effects director Teruyoshi Nakano was understandably upset. He said of the use of stock footage, "...it hurt me when I had to re-use those scenes, but there was no other way - we did not have the time or the money to film new scenes."[244] Two notable displays of the budget constraints include material visibly falling off the Godzilla suit during fight sequences, and King Ghidorah's strange immobility while in flight. It took twenty-four wires to operate the suit, and the effects department did not have the manpower to work him at full capacity. All the cost cutting paid off, though. *Godzilla vs Gigan* but more than double the butts in seats that *Godzilla vs Hedorah* or *Godzilla's Revenge* had[245].

Before we move on to the next segment, we really should stop and appreciate Haruo Nakajima, who makes his 12th and final appearance as Godzilla in this film. He had first portrayed the character in 1954, at just 25 years of age. 18 years later, the 43 year old stunt man hung up his rubber monster suit, and moseyed off into the sunset. As he said in an interview from 2008 with August Ragone and Brett Homenick: "It was my last movie, but I did about [2]8 kaiju movies [in total], and I made 10 *Ultra*[-series] episodes. It was my best career. Completing the last movie, I felt I had done what I wanted to do, so I have no regrets."[246] Nakajima passed away in 2017, leaving behind a legacy no one can compete with, having played both Godzilla and King Kong, the two most iconic monsters of all time, as well as helping to invent a new acting style and genre of science fiction. His work is monumental, and the closing theme from this song says it best: Ganbare! Bokura no Gojira!

Haruo Nakajima

---

[242] *A Critical History,* pg 124
[243] *A Critical History,* pg 124
[244] *Monsters Are Attacking Tokyo!,* pg. 112
[245] *A Critical History,* pg 127
[246] Homenick, Brett. "MR. GODZILLA SPEAKS! Suit Actor Haruo Nakajima on Playing the King of the Monsters!" *Vantage Point Interviews*, 18 May 2017, https://vantagepointinterviews.com/2017/05/18/mr-godzilla-speaks-suit-actor-haruo-nakajima-on-playing-the-king-of-the-monsters/.

Chapter 40: *Godzilla vs Megalon*

The story of *Godzilla vs Megalon* is, at its heart, really a story of contrasts. The contrasts between TV and movies, the contrasts between Japan and the US, the contrasts between Ishiro Honda, Jun Fukuda, and Yoshimitsu Banno. The contrasts between Masaru Sato, Akira Ifukube, and Riichiro Manabe. And, ultimately, the contrast of a good movie against a bad one, and where that line is drawn.

Godzilla vs Gigan had been pretty successful in Japan. Not only had the presence of King Ghidorah helped to put butts in seats, but the new monster Gigan had proven pretty popular in his own right[247]. Since that film had been made on a shoe-string budget, therefore increasing the profit margin, Tomoyuki Tanaka decided that if they made the next one even cheaper, the profit margin would be even bigger. What's cheaper than a shoestring budget? A cooking twine budget? Let's see… shoestrings are… about 9.3 inches for a dollar and cooking twine is… oh, wow, 83 feet for a dollar. Yeah we'll go with cooking twine budget.

The villainous monster of the title was initially conceived of as an opponent for Minya in *Godzilla's Revenge.* Instead of a beetle-like monster, the original concept for Megalon was a giant mole cricket named Gebara, who was replaced by the similarly named Gabara[248]. Megalon was once again considered during the planning stages of *Godzilla vs Gigan*, but was cut out due to budgeting issues. The monster cast of this film has another misfit, whose origin is a little better known, if only in an inaccurate version. I won't give anymore lip service to the rumor. According to the 2012 book *Toho Special Effects Movie Complete Works*, Seiyu, a grocery and department store chain, held a monster design contest for kids co-sponsored by Toho and Tsuburaya Productions. The contest, called the "Children Monster University", ran from late 1971 until January of 1972. A kid named Masaaki Sano was among a number of Japanese children who had submitted monster designs and were invited onto *Katsura Kokinji's Afternoon Show,* where it was announced that the winner's creature would be featured in the next Godzilla movie. You would think little Mr. Sano would have been excited to see that his Monster design, Red Alone, had been chosen as the winner. You would be wrong. Sano had intentionally left his monster all white, and the suit designers had given him a red, yellow, blue, and silver color scheme[249].

Red Alone (left) and Jet Jaguar (right)

When the time came for the next movie to begin production, Red Alone was changed into a robot by Shinichi Sekizawa[250], who wrote the story for this film. Director Jun Fukuda would finish the script to save time on the production[251].

---

[247] *A Critical History,* pg 132
[248] *Showa Completion,* pg 204
[249] *GODZILLA VS. MEGALON (1973) Audio Commentary by Steve Ryfle & Stuart Galbraith IV. www.youtube.com,* https://www.youtube.com/watch?v=Bo18EoH0T2s. Accessed 12 Sept. 2023.
[250] *GODZILLA VS. MEGALON (1973) Audio Commentary*
[251] *GODZILLA VS. MEGALON (1973) Audio Commentary*

Red Alone's design was also changed to match with his new designation as a robot[252]. Special effects director Teruyoshi Nakano supervised the redesign, begrudgingly at first. According to the audio commentary produced by Tokyo Shock for *Godzilla vs Megalon,* Nakano bristled at the suggestion to take the character in a more Ultraman-esque direction. He found the motivation, however, when he decided it would be kind of funny if the newly re-christened Jet Jaguar was ugly and a little off-putting[253]. And brother, he was right.

The film was shot in just 3 weeks, with the production taking about 6 months total. Then it was time to see if Tanaka's big gamble would pay off. It didn't. Though released as the main feature in 1973's Champion Festival, it was the first Godzilla movie to sell fewer than one million tickets[254]. The next Godzilla film would not be given a cooking twine budget, that strategy had failed. The next film was also slated for release in 1974, 20 years since the original film was released, so a shoestring budget would just seem downright disrespectful. Let's see… uhhhhhh.. It would need a Twisted Manila Three Strand Natural Fiber Rope budget. That stuff runs at about two dollars and fifty cents a foot. That's a lot of money for rope.

I'd said at the beginning that *Godzilla vs Megalon* was a study in contrasts, and the contrast I want to focus most on is the film's dismal reception in Japan, versus its enthusiastic welcome to the American movie house. Most of my sourcing for this section will come from the previously mentioned Tokyo Shock DVD commentary.

In the US, *Godzilla vs Megalon* was distributed by Cinema Shares, a now defunct distribution company. The movie was a big success for them, in part because of a major 2 prong advertising campaign focusing on major events coming up later in the year. First, there was the US presidential election[255]. Cinema Shares crashed the Democratic Party's National Convention, announcing Godzilla himself as a candidate and giving away free buttons and posters. I have one of these buttons, it's yellow with GODZILLA VS MEGALON in big bold letters around the outside. There were four, one for each monster[256]. Mine is the Godzilla one. The second prong focused on the upcoming Dino DeLaurentis produced *King Kong* remake, set to release in December of that year. The advertising blitz for that movie had started, very early for a December release, with a poster featuring King Kong straddling the top of the Twin Towers of the World Trade Center, screaming blonde in hand. Cinema Shares, in their poster for *Godzilla vs Megalon,* the two title monsters facing off on the top of the towers, one on each.[257] It proved hugely popular for them, even with three minutes of cuts to receive a G rating from the MPAA.

Cinema Shares' poster for Godzilla vs Megalon *(right) and its "inspiration" (left)*

---

[252] *GODZILLA VS. MEGALON (1973) Audio Commentary*
[253] *GODZILLA VS. MEGALON (1973) Audio Commentary*
[254] *A Critical History,* pg 136
[255] *Showa Completion,* pg 204
[256] *GODZILLA VS. MEGALON (1973) Audio Commentary*
[257] *Showa Completion,* pg 204

The film would be further cut for its primetime network television debut in March of 1977, initially to 67 minutes, and then to 48, so it could fit in a 1 hour time slot[258]. Both "hour long" versions fell into the public domain in the United States after the 1986 dissolution of Cinema Shares, which resulted in a wealth of cheap public domain VHS releases, often of the US theatrical version, still owned by Toho. The TV premier was hosted by John Belushi in a Godzilla suit, but these wrap-around segments are lost to time. The suit would be used later that week on Saturday Night Live, and that footage still exists. Stills of that sketch are sometimes passed off as being from the lost wrap-arounds[259].

The legacy of this movie is a complicated one. It's one of the many candidates among people who hate joy and happiness as the worst Godzilla film, but many others, myself included, find much to love in its unbridled lunacy. You've heard of so bad it's good? This is so bad it's *great*. It's almost like you're doing so poorly at a video game that the score counter goes backwards from zero and maxes out. It's like a pizza from Little Caesar's or a taco from Jack in the Box: you know it's junk, but it's there for you at your lowest lows and helps you find your feet to begin digging back up. And the series would do the same in the next film.

---

[258] *A Critical History,* pg 135
[259] *GODZILLA VS. MEGALON (1973) Audio Commentary*

Chapter 41: *Godzilla vs Mechagodzilla*

It has been said, by who? It depends on who you ask. But it has been said that there are only two stories: a man goes on a journey, and a stranger comes to town. This really could be boiled down to one story, as the stranger in town is a man on a journey, but I digress; I would like to add a third story: Godzilla vs Mechagodzilla. You think I'm joking, but I'm not. You see, I've had a very long time to think about this movie. Longer than I've ever had to think about anything, maybe. If you're a longtime listener, you know that I first saw this movie when I was but a lad of three years. I've told the story on guest appearances on other podcasts, in essays for friends publications, and once even as a stand up comedy bit that went over surprisingly well. I'll recount it here, briefly.

Me, at around 4 years old

When I was 3 years old, after being picked up from preschool, my mom took my 3 sisters and I grocery shopping. This was part of our usual Friday afternoon routine, getting groceries for the week and weekend. After the store, we would go to the Hollywood Video across the street and have around 15 minutes to pick out a movie. Like all three year olds since the mid 19th century, I was obsessed with dinosaurs and would usually rent something dinosaur related. As I walked down the aisle labeled "sci-fi", I saw one of the most beautiful things I had encountered up to that point- a tape. THE tape. I couldn't read super well, but I could recognize the word GOD, like a good Catholic boy, and the Z-I-L-L-A. Godzilla? Godzilla. It was a dinosaur fighting HOLY CRAP A ROBOT DINOSAUR?

Again, I've told this story many times, maybe more times than I've watched the movie, which is a lot. This is a movie that I can breathe in and out instead of air. I can drink it like water, eat it like food, watch it 4 times instead of sleeping. I've had this movie's babies. Record All Monsters is one of them. I've known it my whole life. It's a key part of my childhood, my young adult life, and now in my professional life. It introduced me to Godzilla, who has, no joke, been one of my best and most faithful friends since I was three years old. It is a part of my identity as a human being. And I think that carries no small amount of irony, since identity is one of the key themes of this movie.

The tape that started it all

I believe that this is a particularly good introductory film for new Godzilla fans. It's upfront and casual about its exposition, and whether or not you think it's lazy, you can't deny that it is brutally effective at moving the story along. That means that you can keep up with what's happening not just in the film, but in the Godzilla movies up to this point. He's a hero, but also a giant monster. Sometimes things get destroyed when he's around. And having Mechagodzilla act the way Godzilla did when he first arrived on the scene twenty years ago draws attention to this fact. While the story for this film was penned by our good friend

146

Shinichi Sekizawa[260], the actual screenplay was written by director Jun Fukuda[261], back at the helm for the third time in a row. I think much of the storytelling efficiency comes from his lack of patience working on the Godzilla movies, but his style is just too much fun, and he's too good of a director, for his lack of care to tank the movie. At least to me.

As much nostalgia as I have for this movie, I think it holds up remarkably well. There's a definite feeling of triumph at the series being around for 20 years, as well as a generally more adult tone. With Masaru Sato returning to do the score, it fits right in with Fukuda's earlier work from the franchise in the 60s. It's also just one of my favorite film scores in general. The bright, bold horns and the driving percussion make it unforgettable. Sato also makes several subtle callbacks to some of Akira Ifukube's themes, while keeping true to his own sensibilities as a composer.

This was the 20th anniversary film for the character of Godzilla, and he had progressed over that time from a destructive manifestation of humanity's sin to a friend, ally, and protector. I can't emphasize this point enough. Godzilla, as a character, was a villain, and now, is a superhero. And the same reasons he had been a villain were the very reasons he could be the hero he became. These facts are highlighted in *Godzilla vs Hedorah*, where our child protagonist tells his uncle that Godzilla and Superman are his favorite heroes. This characterization holds true over the next two movies as well. In *Godzilla vs Gigan,* he is a vigilant guardian, sending Anguirus to investigate strange noises coming from Japan, and then making a plan of action. In *Godzilla vs Megalon*, he is summoned by Jet Jaguar and his creators to help fight the invading monsters. So when we first see Godzilla in this movie and he's destroying things, and fighting his now established good buddy Anguirus, the movie tells us something is wrong. "Godzilla shouldn't be fighting his friend Anguirus!"

As a three year old, I remember feeling very comfortable being dropped into this world. The movie begins, after a wonderfully scored and atmospheric pre-credits scene, with the Princess of the Royal Azumi Family of Okinawa dancing for tourists. She is interrupted by a vision of a monster destroying the world, which conforms to an old Okinawan prophecy. Godzilla appears shortly after and begins destroying things. Is he the monster the princess foretold? He can't be, though. Godzilla is our friend. Right? The characters very casually and helpfully let you know, this is not how this normally works. He's acting suspiciously. We need to get to the bottom of this.

When the real Godzilla appears and beats the false skin off of Mechagodzilla, everything is made clear. In the past, I have referred to "mercenary screenwriting", meaning a no frills way of approaching scripts, and this film is a good example. All of what I described above happens in the first 30 minutes. The next 30 minutes set up the rest of our story, a race against time and some ape-faced spacemen for possession of the idol representing the protector god of the Royal Azumi Family of Okinawa, a big fluffy lion-dog named King Caesar. When the aliens fail to capture the idol, they unleash Mechagodzilla. Our human heroes summon King Caesar, but humanity seems to be doomed until Godzilla returns. The remaining half hour is the three monsters brawling with the fate of the world in the balance.

---

[260] *A Critical History,* pg 136
[261] *A Critical History,* pg 136

It's beautiful, and, if you're a three year old kid, life changing. I say that with no exaggeration. *Godzilla vs Mechagodzilla* changed my life.

The theme of identity runs throughout the film. The interpersonal relationships between our rather large cast of characters are strangely detailed, but also surprisingly simple. Spelunker Masahiko's brother Keisuke works with an archaeologist named Saeko who was a student of their uncle Professor Miyajima, whose daughter Ikuko assists him periodically. This complex web of familial/professional/academic relationships can be seen as a parallel to the complicated relationships between the four monsters in the film, though that may be a stretch. Less stretchy is the false identity of the sinister reporter who seems to be stalking our heroes, but turns out to be an INTERPOL agent named Namura making sure they return the statue of King Caesar to Okinawan Royal Family as a reflection of both Mechagodzilla's false identity as the real Godzilla, and the Ape-Faced Black Hole Aliens disguised as human men. The villains deceive to get close enough to attack, Namura deceives in order to be close enough to protect.

Godzilla (right) meets Mechagodzilla (left)

The Black Hole Aliens are, apparently, superior to humans in every way, but when Godzilla damages Mechagodzilla in their initial skirmish, they must rely on Professor Miyajima to do the actual repairs, and so they kidnap him and his daughter. In the same way, Mechagodzilla is apparently superior to the original in every way, but he is a robot and must function solely as instructed. Godzilla, however, as a flesh and blood animal can learn and adjust, and in the ballsiest, stupidest, most amazing deus ex machina ever put to film, is able to turn himself into a magnetic pole with little to no explanation (there's a possible explanation that made perfect sense when I was three), pulling a fleeing Mechagodzilla close enough to rip off his frickin' head.

The good guys blow up the alien base, King Caesar returns to his home in the mountains, and Godzilla returns to the sea. Our real finale, however, is a mirror of the film's first scene after the opening credits, the princess of the royal Azumi family running cheerfully towards her grandfather as our main characters look on. These two scenes act as bookends, continuing the theme of duality that runs through the film. The pride of the Azumis is restored. Their *identity* is restored.

It comes back to that little joke I made at the start of the episode about there only being 3 stories. "A man goes on a journey" can cover many classic monster and horror movies. *Frankenstein* comes to mind, as the titular doctor and his creation go on journeys of humility and self discovery, respectively. "A stranger comes to town" fits nicely over both *Dracula* and *The Wolf Man,* even the original *Godzilla* from 1954. Jokingly, I added "Godzilla vs Mechagodzilla", but in truth, it fits as an archetypal story about identity and duality within an individual, writ large in an actual opponent, the kind of bad guy who tells the hero, "we're not so different, you and I."

The story of John Henry is an obvious example. John Henry must assert his humanity over the cold, soulless efficiency of the steam drill. *The Dark Knight* is actually a good illustration of this as well, since the Joker is a reflection of Batman, bucking the system to meet his goals, taking the same measures to the extreme, and removing the humanity and compassion (what little there is) from what Batman does. The twin hero and villain are a very old trope, and are even found in the man going on a journey and the stranger coming to town. I find reducing this idea to "Godzilla vs Mechagodzilla" is actually extremely helpful; Godzilla is what is good, thinking, feeling, and even redeemed within us. He was the villain once, and now he's the hero. Mechagodzilla is an empty shell, driven by malevolent intent, a deadly saw blade meant to needlessly cut down the unruly tree, beautiful but mildly inconvenient, because they can't control how it grows.

My original idea for Record All Monsters was born the night I saw *Godzilla, King of the Monsters* in 2019. It was Legendary's sequel to their 2014 Godzilla reboot, and I was extremely excited. My youngest sister, who is older than me by about 18 months, took me to see it as a surprise when I got off work on its opening night. As I walked into the theater, I looked at the crowd already seated. It was mostly men in their late twenties and early thirties, around my age. Almost all of us were either black or Hispanic, like me. They were also visibly excited, wearing t-shirts with the various monsters we knew were going to be in the film. I was too. I'm not sure if I've ever felt as instantly welcome in a room in a public place in my life. It was like being in church, almost.

I thought a lot about the movie when it was over, but I also thought a lot about the audience I had been a part of, both physically and demographically. And I wondered, what had drawn us, all of us to Godzilla? I mean obviously, there was a boom of Godzilla merchandise and public awareness with the 1998 movie, which had come out when we were all relatively young, but what made it resonate with us more than twenty years later? What made us return? And as I thought about this, I thought about my family down in the Rio Grande Valley in South Texas. They almost all loved monsters. I thought about the few friends I'd made in my life who liked Godzilla or King Kong, and I noticed that so many of them, of us, were Hispanic or Black. This thought evolved into the question: Why are so many people like me drawn to these monsters and their stories. I think the answer can be found in my other great storytelling love: The Fairy Tale.

At the beginning of *Coraline,* which is probably Neil Gaiman's best book, he misquotes one of my favorite writers, GK Chesterton. Gaiman gives the quote as, "Fairy tales are more than true – not because they tell us dragons exist, but because they tell us dragons can be beaten.[262]" The correct version of the quote, from Chesterton's *Tremendous Trifles*, is, "Fairy tales do not give the child his first idea of bogey. What fairy tales give the child is his first clear idea of the possible defeat of bogey. The baby has known the dragon intimately ever since he had an imagination. What the fairy tale provides for him is a St. George to kill the dragon.[263]" He expands much on this idea in his later work *Orthodoxy*, which was just as influential on me as *Godzilla vs Mechagodzilla.* I myself would like to extend the logic here.

---

[262]Gaiman, Neil, *Coraline,* 2002
[263] *Tremendous Trifles by Gilbert Keith Chesterton: The Red Angel.* http://www.online-literature.com/chesterton/tremendous-trifles/17/. Accessed 12 Sept. 2023.

Showing us that the dragon can be defeated shows us its vulnerability. The dragon is persecuted for its monstrousness, which makes it a threat to society. And once we realize that not only *can* monsters be slain, but that many feel that they must be slain, it becomes easy to see them as victims of their own size, strength, and a society that rejects them. As Ishiro Honda said, "Monsters are tragic beings. They are born too tall, too strong, too heavy. They are not evil by choice. That is their tragedy."[264]

I live in a small town in Central Texas. Or, it was a small town. Over the nearly 30 years my family and I have lived here, it has grown and grown. Historically, blacks and Hispanics have been treated very poorly here. One of our major parks was built by enslaved people. Hispanics weren't allowed in that park until the late 1970s, when they were finally legally able to buy property outside of the city's impoverished West Side. This prejudice can still be found very easily. In 1996, just a little less than a year before my family moved here, a Klu Klux Klan rally was held in our town square. Louis Ray Beam Jr, former head of the KKK in Texas, lives here in quiet anonymity[265].

Now, I'm not saying that my formative years were spent fighting off Neo-Nazis and hooded Klansmen with pointy sticks, but when you're three years old, you don't understand why so and so invited everyone except for you and a few other dark skinned kids to his pool party. You don't understand why a parent in the park might tell her daughter not to talk to you on the playground. You don't understand why the daycare teacher called everyone in for cake except for you and the same handful of kids who didn't get to go to that pool party. But all of it hurts. You're aware of racial prejudice even if you don't have a name for it or know exactly why it is happening.

And then you watch movies and TV shows. You see Frankenstein's Monster trapped in a burning windmill while the townspeople cheer. You see Lawrence Talbot punished with an ancient curse for trying to help someone, and then hunted down like a dog by the same people who knew him as a child. The monsters are destroyed, everyone goes home and sleeps well, knowing their way of life is safe until the sequel. You run *away* from the monster, unless you are going to kill it.

And then, you see Godzilla. Monstrous by nature, outcast, cresting the hill, coming to destroy the very thing created to destroy him. And he proves superior to it, by the same unruly, monstrous virtues that made him an obstacle to his opponents. You see this, and you feel, through the language of cinema, *this* is the hero. His victory is what we have been hoping for all along. This is Cinderella, triumphing by turning her faults into virtues. This is Tom Thumb, using his size to his advantage. This is St. George, killing the dragon because he was born with that intimate knowledge of it. Because he has the potential to be the dragon. Godzilla has *been* the dragon. But even in his very first appearance, we see that Godzilla is truly a monster in accident only, as much our victim as we are his. This makes his heroic work resonate even more.

---

[264] Tucker, Guy Mariner. *Age of the Gods: A History of the Japanese Fantasy Film*. Daikaiju Publishing, 1996.
[265] "Louis Beam." *Southern Poverty Law Center*, https://www.splcenter.org/fighting-hate/extremist-files/individual/louis-beam. Accessed 12 Sept. 2023.

The first time I realized I had been racially profiled, I was 14 years old. I had a part time job working for my dad by assembling ductwork for his mechanical contracting business. I made good money for a 14 year old kid. My mom and sisters and I were downtown shopping and I decided to check out a store that looked like it might have some cool vintage stuff in it. I was about six foot two at the time, broad shouldered, and bronze from my manual labor in the sun most days of the week and outdoor basketball games on days off. As I walked up to the door, I saw a middle aged white woman rush to the door from inside. She locked the door. I could hear it. Then she went away. I had assumed she was unlocking the door, but when I put my hand on the handle, it would not open.

Godzilla, the dragon-slaying dragon

The temptation to be the monster people see you as is strong. Especially in the moment in which you realize that what has just happened to you has been happening your whole life. And every time it happens again, you see the white kids eating cake inside. You feel the door knob resist your gentle touch. You see the police lights when you tried to turn around in that culdesac because someone gave you bad directions. You see the man on the street in the Make America Great Again hat pointing his finger at you like a gun as you drive home from work. You hear the bride at the wedding you attended single you out to stay behind and pick up garbage. And in that moment you have a choice. A choice that isn't fair to you, but it's yours nonetheless. Do you become that monster? Or do you embrace your true, wild, unpredictable self, and walk away? Do you embrace Mechagodzilla and lash out? Or do you embrace Godzilla and be the better version, the real version? No matter what you do, they'll see you as a monster, so do you live with it and move on? Or let it eat you alive?

The truth is, once we know dragons can be beaten, we know that they are fragile and we can relate to them. Especially when we have been beaten throughout our lives. Once we can realize that you must take each dragon on a dragon by dragon basis, we can know which dragons will help us and which dragons will hurt us. Eventually, we know which dragon we are.

I didn't have any of these thoughts as I watched this movie for the first time as a three year old boy, sitting too close to the television with my feet turned inward under my butt, setting the stage for many knee and ankle problems in the future. All I could see was that Godzilla was a hero. Godzilla was a monster. Godzilla was a hero *because* he was a monster, and maybe someday, if I couldn't be a giant alien fighting hero, I could at least be comfortable being my monstrous self.

Chapter 42: *Terror of Mechagodzilla*

This is a victory lap. Record All Monsters has been a passion project, and always will be. But with the previous episode on 1974's *Godzilla vs Mechagodzilla*, I was able to say the thing that got stuck in my craw deep enough to get the ball finally rolling. I'm approaching this episode as not just a victory lap, though, but also as a chance to renew and reinvigorate myself as I look forward to what is coming on the horizon for myself and this show.

In many ways, *Terror of Mechagodzilla* is the perfect movie to reflect on both of these attitudes. The Godzilla series had reached its absolute peak of silliness with 1973's *Godzilla vs Megalon*, so it may seem like the next year's film, *Godzilla vs Mechagodzilla* couldn't help but be a little more serious and a little more thoughtful. But if you look at the trends of the Japanese box office in the mid-seventies, that seriousness may have been another deliberate effort to follow the trends of the day.

Toho was starting to make some blockbusters again. In the US, disaster movies like *Airport 1970, The Andromeda Strain, The Poseidon Adventure,* and *Earthquake* were making big bucks, and so it only made sense for Japanese filmmakers to try out the same thing. The dam broke, so to speak, with 1973's *The Submersion of Japan*, which wound up being the most successful domestic film of the decade in that country[266]. The next year, they had another hit with *The Prophecies of Nostradamus,* which got so dark as to depict cannibals and mutants roaming the earth in humanity's final days and a post-apocalyptic nuclear wasteland. Once again, it topped the box office[267], followed by another adult focused film, Jun Fukuda's heavily violent supernatural spy thriller, *ESPY*.

So the winds were blowing cold, and Tomoyuki Tanaka followed with the next entry in the Godzilla series. Initially he turned to none other than the screenwriter for *Prophecies of Nostradamus,* Yoshimitsu Banno, director of *Godzilla vs Hedorah,* who planned to use the chance to make the sequel that had been hinted at in that film's closing frames. But other Toho brass had different ideas, and since dark and documentary-like realism was in, they plucked Ishiro Honda out of retirement and told him to make another Godzilla movie. Partly at the request of the upcoming film's screenwriter.[268]

Yukiko Takayama, a recent graduate of a non-Toho affiliated writing academy, won a company wide contest to develop the next Godzilla film, with her treatment, *Godzilla vs the Titans.* They had her expand it into a screenplay, which was reworked by Honda to match his ideas of what Godzilla ought to be. Additionally, the studio mandated that the movie *must* feature Mechagodzilla, and be a sequel to that creature's debut[269].

The resulting film is probably the thing most people think of when they think of a Godzilla movie. Unlike the Gamera franchise, the Godzilla movies never quite developed a formula to guide the direction of sequels, and the sequels are almost all wildly different from each other. *Godzilla Raids Again* is moody and unfocused. *King Kong vs Godzilla* is tongue in cheek and spectacle driven. *Mothra vs Godzilla* takes the tongue out of its cheek and adds a dose of

---

[266] *A Critical History,* pg 141
[267] *A Critical History,* pg 141
[268] *A Life in Film* p. 266
[269] *A Life in Film* p. 266

dark fantasy. Finally, with *Ghidorah the Three-Headed Monster* and *Invasion of Astro-Monster,* we start to get something like tonal and thematic consistency before it gets thrown out the window as Jun Fukuda tries to balance his action oriented approach with the demands of the youth market in *Ebirah* and *Son of Godzilla*. *Destroy All Monsters* feels a lot like *Ghidorah* and *Astro-Monster,* but this time Honda himself tosses out the tone and makes a completely new kind of monster movie with *Godzilla's Revenge.* Yoshimitsu Banno reinvents the wheel again in *Hedorah,* and Fukuda's next three entries are so different in terms of tone that I didn't believe it when I first learned that he'd directed all 3.

With Honda at the helm of *Terror of Mechagodzilla,* it feels a bit like he really did put all of the best qualities of the previous films in the series into a blender and hit "puree". Even children figure into this film, as Godzilla intervenes when Titanosaurus is about to stomp on a pair of boys as the final battle begins. (Though it must be said that the film never shows the boys reaching safety.)

L-R: Godzilla, Mechagodzilla, Titanosaurus

Speaking of Titanosaurus, he is a somewhat divisive monster. Introduced in this film, he is a red and orange aquatic dinosaur with fins running from his head down his back, with another on the end of his tail that can be collapsed or fanned out. It seems like most folks think his design is pretty cool, but his roar seems to be what many dislike about him. Titanosaurus' roar is a gargling, warbling screech that sounds a little bit like revving up an elephant. I love him, warts and warbles and all. I don't know if I'm in the minority or the majority, but I do know that the other side of this debate is very passionate.

Mechagodzilla returns, and so does Akira Ifukube. While this is generally good news, and it is great to hear the classic Godzilla theme in full bloom, I miss the funky jazz score of Masaru Sato. *Terror of Mechagodzilla* is a very good film, so far as the late 70s Godzilla outings go, but it didn't put too many butts in seats, and while it was never officially declared a retirement of the character, the low box office ensured that Godzilla would be absent from movie screens for the next nine years.

At least, in Japan. 1976 saw the start of a mini-boom for Godzilla in the US. We talked a little bit about Cinema Share's two pronged ad campaign beginning at the Democratic Party's National Convention for *Godzilla vs Megalon*, and they rode the success and notoriety of that film by releasing it again on a double feature with *Godzilla vs Mechagodzilla,* which they released in early 1977 as *Godzilla vs the Cosmic Monster*, and as a triple feature with *Godzilla vs Mechagodzilla* and *Godzilla vs Gigan,* now rechristened as *Godzilla on Monster Island.*

This movie came out in 1978 in the US under two different titles, *Terror of Godzilla* went to theaters courtesy of Bob Conn Enterprises, who edited it down for a G rating, and *Terror of Mechagodzilla* was released to TV by our old friend Henry G Saperstein, who left the film mostly uncut, and even edited in a 10 minute prologue to catch the audience up on not just the previous movies, but the entire Godzilla franchise!

I feel this is the most appropriate place to end this essay, with a recap of Godzilla's journey from villain to hero, scourge to savior, enemy to friend. As we draw the curtain shut on this troubled season of Record All Monsters, we're saying goodbye to Godzilla for a long time. However, his influence will still be felt as we examine the genre in his wake. Sayōnara kyūyū.

The US theatrical release poster for Terror of Mechagodzilla

PART II: THE RECORD ALL MONSTERS GAME SHOW QUESTIONS AND ANSWERS

APING THE APES: Game for *King Kong*

King Kong is one of the most influential movies of all time, which of course means it has had its fair share of knock-offs produced over the years. Not only that, but apes and gorillas in particular have always been popular movie monsters, due to their uncanny resemblance to men in costumes. So today, I'm going to read to you the descriptions of some lesser known ape movies, and your job will be to guess if I'm describing actual films, or am I making them up. Aping the films about apes, if you will. There are no prizes.

Q: A mother gorilla adopts a baby doll after losing her own infant, and becomes violently protective when zoo managers try to take it away from her. Bill Paxton features in an early role as a zoo employee.
Is it real? Or am I Aping the Apes?
A: Aping the Apes

Q: *Batman Forever*'s Michael Gough plays a mad scientist who is using mad science to make plants grow to extreme sizes. When his wife finds out he's having an affair, she feeds the serum to his pet chimp, who turns into a giant gorilla and rampages through London.
Is it real? Or am I Aping the Apes?
A: It's real. *Konga* is a 1961 british monster movie

Q: A petty crook, a woman under intense pressure to get married, a suicidal farmer, and a recently fired family man team up with a chimpanzee to rob a bank.
Is it real? Or am I Aping the Apes? It's real.
A: *Gorilla* is a 2019 Tamil language Indian comedy

Q: A bonobo steals a valuable diamond from a mob boss, and a team of other marginalized great apes come together to keep her out of the mob's hands despite their own differences and separate motivations.
Is it real? Or am I aping the Apes?
A: Trick question, that's a simplified version of 2020's *Birds of Prey* but with monkeys.

Q: Bela Lugosi is a mad scientist whose experiments with animal DNA are slowly turning him into an ape man, and he needs human spinal fluid to delay the change. When his partner won't help him any longer, he seeks aid from an actual ape, who kills him.
Is it Real? Or Am I aping the Apes?
A: It's real! *The Ape Man* is a 1943 horror film that ends with the film's writer telling the hero it was a "screwy" movie before driving off in a stolen car.

FAMOUS RAY'S ORIGINAL QUOTES: Game for *The Beast from 20,000 Fathoms*

Ray Harryhausen and Ray Bradbury who were involved with the making of today's film, are two very famous Rays, and Ray appears to be a fairly good choice of name if you want your baby to be famous. I have gathered some quotes from various famous Rays, and I'll ask you to choose between two Rays as the quotes originator. There will be no prizes or penalties. It's FAMOUS RAY'S ORIGINAL QUOTES!

Q: Who said, "I'm very happy that so many young fans have told me that my films have changed their lives. That's a great compliment. It means I did more than just make entertaining films. I actually touched people's lives--and, I hope, changed them for the better." Was it special effects whiz Ray Harryhausen or noted actor Raymond Burr?
A: Harryhausen

Q: Who said, "A lot of it starts with playing instruments and working with other people. Some of the new generation is doing it on computers and they don't have a clue as to how to play anything. That's probably one of the problems. They don't know how to make the melody, go through the chord changes. They're not starting from that same school of thought." Was it legendary soul singer Ray Charles, or legendary Ghostbusters theme singer Ray Parker Jr.?
A: Ray Parker Jr

Q: Who said, "My theory has always been that everyone in show business is there because they were deprived of some attention as a child." Was it Kink's frontman and songwriter Ray Davies, or Comedian and Actor Ray Romano?
A: Romano

Q: Who said, "Since I've retired, I eat less, weigh less, train less and care less." Was it boxer and Warren Zevon song subject Ray "Boom Boom" Mancini, or convicted domestic abuser and former Baltimore Ravens running back Ray Rice?
A: Mancini

Q: Who said, "The moment a man begins to talk about technique, that's proof that he is fresh out of ideas." Was it deceased mystery writer and alcoholic Raymond Chandler or deceased science fiction writer and father of four Ray Bradbury?
A: Chandler

THE GEOGRAPHY THAT I STANDS TO YOU SUPERIOR:
Game for *Godzilla* vs *Godzilla, King of the Monsters*

Bringing a hit film from another country that largely speaks a different language can present a unique challenge, especially since idioms and turns of phrase don't always translate exactly. But sometimes there is no excuse, and strange ways of saying simple things crop up in the translation process. So in our game tonight, THE GEOGRAPHY THAT I STANDS TO YOU SUPERIOR, I'll read you a questionable translation, and you need to tell me if it's a real line from an official dub of a Godzilla movie, or if I'm pulling on your legs, as Google Translate says the phrase is from Japanese. There will be no prizes, penalties, or points awarded.

Q: Is "Space titanium, you mean it's from outer space" a real line from a dub? Or am I pulling on your legs?
A: It's real

Q: Is "His head looks like Jack Nicholson. Don't smile like that. It'll stay that way." a real line from an official dub? Or am I pulling on your legs?
A: False. It's from the MST3k version of the Jet Jaguar theme song from Godzilla vs Megalon

Q: is "Godzilla and Biollante aren't monsters. It's the unscrupulous scientists who create them that are monsters." a real line from an official dub?
A: real

Q: Is "Oh, Godzilla, what terrible language!" a real line from an official dub?
A: Real

Q: "I guarantee you it will go through Godzilla like CRAP through a goose"
A: Real

WHAT'S IN A NAME: ANGUIRUS EDITION: Game from *Godzilla Raids Again*

Like we discussed in last week's game, translation is not an exact science, especially when it comes to idioms, expressions and turns of phrase, but it's also true for names. Doubly so for made up names like Anguirus. It has been translated a number of different ways before Toho settled on the official version around 2006. In today's Anguirus edition of our game, What's in a Name, I'll ask you if these translations of Anguirus were ever used in reference to the monster in English language media. If you win, you get to marry me, if you lose, you have to stay married to me. There are no other prizes or penalties.

Q: Angweenis
A: Real, from *Godzilla Final Wars*

Q: Boryu
A: Real, his official nickname, meaning Fierce Dragon

Q: Angila
A: Real, from *Godzilla vs Gigan*

Q: Anzilla
A: Real, from various books in the 1970s, including the Crestwood House Monster Book Godzilla by Ian Thorne

Q: Angoorus
A: Fake

TYRANNOSAURUS-SEX: Game for *Rodan*

Today's movie dealt with two monsters in love with each other, kind of. There was also a human love story. But what happens when prehistoric monsters and humans share love together? I'm not here to kink shame anybody, so I'll leave that question open ended. Seriously, you do you, as long as you both consent. Anyways, today's game is called TYRANNOSAURUS SEX, and this is how it works. I'll read you the title of a book from the Amazon Kindle Series *Dinosaur Erotica*, and you tell me if it's actually real or if it's one I made up. There will be no prizes, or penalties, though you may feel like I'm punishing you as you reckon with the reality of some of these titles. I was going to read the descriptions, but, uh… no.

Q: *Dinosaur Lover*
A: Fake

Q: *Taken By the T-Rex*
A: Real

Q: *Fifty Shades of Feathers and Scales*
A: Fake

Q: *Taken at the Dinosaur Museum*
A: Real

Q: *In the Velociraptor's Nest*
A: Real

Q: *Ravished by the Triceratops*
A: Real

Q: *Taken by the Pterodactyl*
A: Real

EL SANTO CONTRA EL CACA DEL TORO: Game for *The Giant Claw*

Today's movie featured a marionette as our monster that was made in Mexico City for $50. Mexico has its own proud tradition of monsters and horror movies, some of which are just as outlandish to American audiences as some of the Japanese ones we'll discuss later. So in our game today, El Santo contra el Caca del Toro, I'll read you a brief synopsis of a Mexican monster movie, and you'll tell me if it's real or not. There will be no prizes or penalties. I considered offering $50, like the cost of the puppet, but I wanted to keep them for myself.

Q: A scientist cures his son's leukemia by replacing his heart with a gorilla's, but it turns him into a murdering were-ape, who is brought to justice by a lady luchador. Is it real or el Caca del toro?
A: Real. Released in the US in 1972 as *Night of the Bloody Apes*, in Mexico in 1969 as *The Horrible Man-Beast*, and in Europe as *Horror y Sexo*

Q: A teenage orphan finds an alien dying of a gunshot wound in the street the night he is told that he's too old to live at the orphanage. It gives him an alien ray-gun in its dying moments, which he uses to get revenge on those who have wronged him.. Is it real, or el caca del toro?
A: Fake, but inspired by *Laserblast* an early Charles Band movie that was featured on MST3K

Q: Two Alien Women gather male aliens to reproduce with from around the galaxy before landing on earth and falling in love with and fighting over a singing vaquero, who tames the one he loves. Is it real or el caca del toro?
A: Real. *Ship of Monsters* is a 1960 Mexican horror/sci-fi/comedy, and stars Ms. Mexico 1953 and 1960

Q: A serial killer uses his helicopter to stalk and seduce women who he takes to his castle and feeds to his cats. One woman escapes and makes a hole in the fence which allows the cats to escape and they turn on their master. Is it real? Or el Caca del toro?
A: Real. *Night of 1,000 Cats* is a 1972 Mexican horror film, released two years later in the US as *Blood Feast*, a different movie from the 1963 Herschell Gordon Lewis movie, *Blood Feast*.

Q: A handsome bandito helps a woman trapped by a witch escape from her prison, only for both of their pasts to separate them just as they begin to fall in love. The witch kills him as they declare their feelings for one another. Is it real or el cac del toro?
A: Fake, but it was inspired by the 2009 animated Disney musical *Tangled*, which is much better than *Frozen*.

VARAN THE UNAVAILABLE: Game for *Varan the Unbelievable*

Varan is a cool looking monster and I'm not the only person who thinks so. Despite only officially appearing in 3 movies, he was considered for numerous projects in the Godzilla franchise. So many, in fact, that I have a hard time keeping them straight. In our game today, I'll read the synopsis of a movie from the Godzilla franchise, some of which never made it past the conceptual stage. Your job is to tell me if Varan was ever considered to appear in that movie. There will be no prizes, and there will be no penalties.

Q: The monsters Gigan, Megalon, and King Ghidorah under the control of the Alien Miko, WHO IS A LIVING BRAIN, invade earth. Everyone is very concerned about airplanes. Scientists build a Godzilla shaped tower in a place called "SCIENCE LAND". Godzilla and a monster buddy fight and win! Was Varan the Unbelievable considered for this film?
A: Nope! This concept, Godzilla vs. the Space Monsters: Earth Defense Directive, would go on to be reworked into 1972's *Godzilla vs Gigan*, which featured Godzilla and Anguirus fighting Gigan and King Ghidorah.

Q: Godzilla and his offspring fight the monster of the end times in 1999! Little Godzilla learns how to use their atomic breath in the fight! The movie ends with a countdown to the year 2000! Was Varan the Unbelievable considered for this film?
A: Yes! He was! Godzilla vs Giant Monster Varan was one of several concepts for the seventh and final Godzilla movie of the Heisei series. It was abandoned in favor of *Godzilla vs Destoroyah*.

Q: The listeners will probably know this one. Three guardian monsters rise up to protect Japan from Godzilla, who hasn't been seen in 50 years. The Gotengo from Atragon is an 11th hour, deus ex machina which kills Godzilla after he murders the guardian monsters. Was Varan the Unbelievable considered for this film?
A: He was! The Guardian Monsters were to be Varan, Anguirus, and Baragon. Baragon was the only one to make it to the screen for *Godzilla, Mothra, King Ghidorah: Giant Monsters All-Out Attack* from 2001. Varan and Anguirus were replaced by Mothra and King Ghidorah.

WHAT'S IN A NAME: DINOSAUR EDITION: Game for *The Giant Behemoth*

Today's monster was a radioactive dinosaur that hews a little closer to known paleontology than most of the ones we've seen on this show, but the paleosaurus has a really boring name. There are real dinosaurs with much funnier and more interesting names, some so strange that you'd swear I was making them up. And so I made some up. Your job is to tell me which names I invented and which ones were made up by real paleontologists. There will be no paleo-prizes or paleo-penalties.

Q: Gasosaurus. Is that a real dinosaur name? Or one I made up?
A: Real! Gasosaurus Constructus was a carnivorous Chinese theropod from the mid Jurassic whose only fossil evidence was discovered on the construction site of a gas facility in 1985.

Q: Citipati. Is that a real dinosaur name? Or one I made up?
A: It's real! Citipati Osmolskae was a late cretaceous oviraptor discovered in the Gobi desert and scientifically described in 2001.

Q: Otterdon. Is that a real dinosaur name? Or one I made up?
A: Fake! But if it were real, it would have been a semiaquatic, quadrupedal herbivore from the Hell Creek Formation described in 1977.

Q: Animantarx. Is that a real dinosaur name? Or one I made up?
A: Real! Animantarx Ramaljonesi is a nodosaurid ankylosaur whose name means "living fortress" in Latin who was discover in 1999

Q: Caprasaurus. Is that a real dinosaur name? Or one I made up?
A: It's phony. If it had really existed, Jimmy Stewart would have discovered it accidentally while visiting an archeologist friend's excavation site. He was too humble to name it after himself, so he named it after his friend, Frank Capra.

Q: Servoceratops. Is that a real dinosaur name? Or one I made up?
A: Somebody is LYING to you. It's me. I am lying to you. Servocertops Tomsoni, if it were real, would have been discovered by some nerds in 1996.

Q: Kosmoceratops. Is that a real dinosaur name? Or one I made up?
A: Somebody is telling you the TRUTH! Kosmoceratops Richardsoni was discovered and described in 2010. Its name means "ornate horned face".

BATMAN OR NOT, MAN?: Game for *Konga*

Today's movie stars British genre film icon Michael Gough, who appeared in several Hammer Horror movies, episodes of The Avengers and Doctor Who, BBC Shakespeare productions, and numerous hard working starring and character roles in nearly 200 productions over 65 years. But you probably know him best as Alfred Pennyworth from the Tim Burton and Joel Schumacher movies of the 90s. That tenuous connection was just enough for me to justify making this episode's game all about Batman, who in his 80 year career has had some flat out stupid adventures. So stupid in fact, you'd swear I was making them up. So I did. I made up some of them. The rest are real Batman stories from across his many media appearances. There will be no bat-prizes or bat-penalties.

Q: Batman is abducted by an alien to help stop another alien race from invading his home planet. The alien abductor wants to be his planet's Batman and dresses in a multicolored bat suit. Answer Batman for a real Batman story, and Not, man, if you think I'm making it up.
A: Batman! It's a real Batman story from 1958 called "Batman- The Superman of Planet X!" written by France Herron, who was not a bird, and drawn by Dick Sprang, whose name I will not make fun of.

Q: The Joker steals a gem from the Gotham Museum that turns out to be a mystical link to either an alternate reality or past life where he and Batman are warring medieval chieftains. Is it Batman or Not, man?
A: Not, Man! I made it up. If it had been real, it would have been an unusually light story for the mid 70s when it was published.

Q: Batman subs in for a kidnapped quarterback while Robin looks for the missing athlete. There's a bunch of stuff about crooked football coaches betting on the game too. Robin saves the quarterback and Batman scores a touchdown. Batman, or Not, man?
A: Batman! This story was in Batman #4 and was called "Touchdown for Justice"

Q: Bruce Wayne is shanghaied by a brutal sailor he hired to hunt down a white whale that has been sinking merchant ships he owns a stake in. It turns out to be an insurance fraud scam by one of his business partners. Batman or not, man?
A: Batman! This was the second story in Batman #9, cover dated March 1942. The fourth story in that issue was about Santa Claus.

Q: Alice in Wonderland, but with Batman instead of Alice. Like, an actual one for one where Catwoman is the Cheshire Cat and the Joker is the White Rabbit and the Riddler is the March Hare. Batman or not, man?
A: Not, man! At least I couldn't find one, but I wouldn't be surprised if it happened. Honestly, I was gonna give you a point for this one no matter what.

YOU CAN'T DO THAT IN A MONSTER MOVIE: Game for *Reptilicus*

Today's movie, *Reptilicus*, featured a ridiculous monster that was also called Reptilicus. Now, being a giant snake with vestigial legs isn't what makes Reptilicus a ridiculous monster, but the fact that it can fly and spit acid goo does. Lots of monsters in lots of movies have loopy powers, though. Some are so bizarre that you'd swear I was making them up. So, of course, I made some up. In today's game, You Can't Do That in a Monster Movie, I'll ask you about some dumb monster abilities, and you'll answer true or false if that monster has been depicted with that ability. There will be no prizes or penalties because we don't really have the budget for either.

Q: King Kong can shoot electricity from his fingertips. True or false?
A: True! He develops the ability to combat Godzilla in 1962's *King Kong vs Godzilla*

Q: Dracula can climb walls like a spider. True or False?
A: True! In Bram Stoker's original novel, he is described as doing so on several occasions

Q: Dr. Jekyll's alter-ego Mr. Hyde has the strength of ten men in the original novella. True or False?
A: False! Mr. Hyde in the story and in pretty much all adaptations until *League of Extraordinary Gentlemen*, is just a younger, angrier, less socially conscious and inhibited version of Dr. Jekyll

Q: Godzilla can fly. True or False?
A: True! In 1971's *Godzilla vs Hedorah*, AKA *Godzilla vs The Smog Monster*, he tucks his tail between his legs, bends his neck forward, and uses his atomic breath to launch himself into the air and after his opponent.

Q: Brundlefly from David Cronenberg's 1986 remake of *The Fly*, can only be killed by someone who loves him. True or False?
A: False! Anybody could have blown that thing's head to bits, Geena Davis just happened to be the one to do it.

Q: The Japanese mythological creatures known as kappa can speak and use tools, including weapons. True or False?
A: False! Kappa are not real. Probably.

Q: Frankenstein has the ability to regenerate from any part of his body. True or false?
A: False! While his creation is depicted as having this ability in Frankenstein Conquers the World, Frankenstein is the name of the doctor who created him, and not the name of the monster himself. But when you think about it, isn't Frankenstein the ACTUAL monster?

FATHER OF THE BRIDE OF FRANKENSTEIN: Game for *Gorgo*

Today's movie featured an adolescent monster who was rescued by their mother. This got me thinking, what other monsters have children? How many do they have? Are they sons, or daughters, or non-binary or what? What's the deal with these monster babies? So, in today's game, Father of the Bride of Frankenstein, I'll be giving you the name of the monster, and your job is to tell me if that monster is a parent. And, if you want some bonus points, what the kid's deal is. The bonus points do nothing, as there are no prizes. But, lucky you, there's also no penalties.

Q: Is Dracula a parent?
A: He is! At least according to 1936's *Dracula's Daughter* and 1943's *Son of Dracula*. Also, he attended the Monster Mash with his son.

Q: Is King Kong a parent?
A: He is! In 1933, we got a quickie sequel called *Son of Kong* starring an albino giant gorilla named Koko who also fought some dinosaurs. Additionally, in 1986's *King Kong Lives* we see a baby Kong frolicking with his mother after Kong himself gets her pregnant.

Q: Is the Wolf Man a parent?
A: He is not. But in the 2010 remake starring Anthony Hopkins and Benicio Del Toro, his father is also a wolf man. So make of that what you will.

Q: Is Godzilla a parent?
A: He is! His son Minilla, better known as Minya, debuted in 1967's *Son of Godzilla*, and then *Destroy All Monsters* and *All Monsters Attack* the following years. In 1993's *Godzilla vs Mechagodzilla 2*, he had another child, called Baby, then in the following films, *Godzilla vs Spacegodzilla* and *Godzilla vs Destoroyah* called Little and Junior, respectively.

Q: Is Gamera a parent?
A: Maybe! In *Gamera the Brave* from 2006, we see Gamera die at the start of the movie, and then a little boy finds and raises a baby Gamera named Toto. So, the answer, once again, is maybe!

Q: Is Frankenstein's Monster a parent?
A: He isn't! But Doctor Frankenstein had 2 sons, at least according to the Universal Horror Cycle of the 1940s. One was played by Basil Rathbone in *Son of Frankenstein* and the other was played by Lionel Atwill in *Ghost of Frankenstein*. Basil Rathbone's son from *Son of Frankenstein* would grow up to be played by Gene Wilder in *Young Frankenstein*.

Q: Is The Blob a parent?
A: Yes, it is! 1972's *Beware! The Blob!* was also called *Son of the Blob,* which was justification enough for me to include it in this game.

FAIRY TALE OR FAKE-Y TALE: Game for *Mothra*

Today's movie featured some fairies, and an overall fairy tale tone. Well, the way we think of fairy tales now. Initially, fairy tales were pretty terrifying and featured far fewer singing princesses and a lot more fart jokes and weird sex. Like an R-rated Shrek 2. One of the best and earliest examples of this is Giambattiste Basile's Pentamerone, or Tale of Tales, in which the cursed Princess Zoza who can't laugh until she witnesses an old lady get mad that someone broke her jug of oil. The old lady turns out to be a witch who curses her to only marry a prince who's asleep forever and will only wake up when she fills a jar with 3 days worth of tears. She falls asleep before crying the last few drops, when another woman cries the last couple of tears and steals the prince away. She infiltrates their house disguised as one of ten female storytellers to entertain the now pregnant new queen. These stories are absolutely cuckoo bananas. So cuckoo bananas that you'd swear I was making them up. So I made some up. In today's game, Fairy-tale or Fake-y Tale, I'll read you the summary of a fairy tale, your job is to tell me if it's actually a part of the Pentamerone, or if I'm pulling your legs. If you lose, your hands will be cut off and fed to donkeys. Just kidding, there are no prizes or penalties.

Q: A guy, who is dumb, and who everyone hates because he is dumb, including his own mother, and also, he is ugly, does a favor for some fairies while he is out gathering wood. They give him a magic charm so that all of his wishes come true. He wishes for the wood he was carrying to carry him, and a sad princess laughs at him riding the wood like a horse. They get married against her father's wishes, so he drowns them in a barrel. The ugly man uses his charm to turn the barrel into a boat and they escape and live happily ever after. Is this a real fairy tale from the Tale of Tales? Or a fake-y tale?
A: Peruonto is a real story in the Pentamerone! It is the third story told on the first day.

Q: After astrologers prophecy danger in the form of a flax splinter for a king's newborn daughter, he bans all flax from his house. As a young woman, she still gets some flax under her fingernail, and dies, maybe. Years later, a king finds her body and takes advantage of her. Nine months after that, she has two babies, who suck the flax from her finger and wake her up. When the king returns, he sees her and her kids and brings him to his castle to live. His wife gets jealous for what are extremely valid reasons and tries to have the girl and her kids cooked, but the chef saves them. The king then has his wife killed and maries the girl he raped in the woods. Is this a real fairy tale from the Tale of Tales? Or a fake-y tale?
A: Sun, Moon, and Talia is a real story from the Pentamerone and is the fifth story of the fifth day. It's also the earliest known version of Sleeping Beauty.

KING KONG VS GODZILLA: Game for *King Kong vs Godzilla*

King Kong and Godzilla are two of the most famous monsters of all time, and pretty much everyone knows the basics about them. King Kong is a big monkey that climbed the Empire State Building and got shot by airplanes, Godzilla is a spiky dinosaur who breathes fire and smashes Tokyo, specifically. They're so famous, and their names so well known, that they are often used for shorthand to mean someone or something that's really big, cool, and tough. So here's how this game works. I'll mention either an exploit or mention of King Kong or Godzilla, and I need you to tell me which one is being referenced. There will be no prizes if you get them right, and no penalties if you get it wrong, so it is ultimately meaningless.

Q: In 1973, this monster was voted as the Most Popular of All Time in The Monster Times Magazine.
A: Godzilla! King Kong came in 3rd place, after Dracula. The Wolf Man and The Mummy rounded out the Top Five.

Q: This monster was the star of a Rankin-Bass Cartoon that ran for three seasons and was an American-Japanese co-production.
A: King Kong was the star of *The King Kong Show*, which ran 26 episodes from 1966 to 1969.

Q: This monster was referenced in *The Rocky Horror Picture Show* song "Science Fiction/double Feature"
A: King Kong strikes again! The lyrics read: "Then something went wrong for Fay Ray and King Kong"

Q: This monster was briefly played by Bobcat Goldthwait in the 1986 comedy *One Crazy Summer*
A: Godzilla, is the correct answer. Whether or not you refer to this as God-cat Zillathwait or Bobgod Zillathwait is entirely up to interpretation.

Q: In a remake 4 decades after the original, this monster had a now difficult to watch effects scene featuring the World Trade Center.
A: The answer is King Kong… AND Godzilla! Dino De Laurentiis' 1976 *King Kong* remake, 43 years after the original, moved the climax to the twin towers. And in Dean Devlin and Roland Emmerich's 1998 *Godzilla* remake, 44 years after the original, the towers are used as a landmark when fighter jets attack Godzilla.

WHAT'S IN A NAME: CELEBRITY EDITION: Game for *Mothra vs Godzilla*

Today's movie is originally called *Mothra vs Godzilla*, but when it was brought over to the United States and other English speaking territories, it was called *Godzilla vs The Thing* and no actual explanation has ever been given. Mothra is far from the first or last celebrity to change their name in hopes of reaching a greater audience, so in today's game, What's in a Name? Celebrity Edition, I'll tell you a celebrity's real name and the name they go by now. Your Job is to tell me if they actually changed their name or if I, like a celebrity using a fake name, am lying to you. There will be no prizes or penalties. There never are. Stop asking.

Q: Is Whoopi Goldberg's real name Caryn Elain Johnson?
A: It is! I have no further trivia about her.

Q: Is Richard Gere's real name Reeshard Geeray?
A: Not unless you're French! Which he is not. Both of his parents are Mayflower descendants, which makes him instantly insufferable.

Q: Is depressed pop icon Lorde's real name Ella Maria Lani Yelich-O'Connor?
A: It most certainly is. I don't know anything about her.

Q: Is Human Tuba Tom Jones' real name Thomas Woodward?
A: It absolutely is. Jones is his middle name, so I'm not sure how big a lie you would consider this one.

Q: Is Vin Diesel's real name Vincent Peters?
A: No it is not! His real name isn't Vin Diesel or anything that even sounds remotely like that. His name is Mark Sinclair. He has a twin brother named Paul.

Q: We all know Charlie Sheen's real name is Carlos Esteves, but is his middle name actually Irwin?
A: Yes, it is. Charlie Sheen's real name is Carlos Irwin Esteves.

Q: Is Kat Dennings real name Katherine Litwack?
A: Sadly, it is. As Joe E. Brown said in Some Like it Hot, well, nobody's perfect.

WHEN WORLDS COLLIDE: Game for *Ghidorah the Three-Headed Monster*

Today's film brought three of one studio's most famous characters together and introduced a new one. This happens basically every day in major studio movies now, but for the longest time, these sorts of meetings between intellectual properties took place only in our imaginations and in pop cultural peripheries, like tie-in comic books and Saturday morning cartoons. This has led to some strange team ups and cross overs over the years, some so strange, you'd swear I'm making them up. So I did. In today's game, WHEN WORLDS COLLIDE, I'll propose a ridiculous crossover, and you'll tell me if you think it has really happened in some official form or not. If you're right, hey good for you. If you're wrong, well that's too bad. Lucky for you, there are no penalties, though. Conversely, there are also no prizes.

Q: Have Spider-Man and Cap'n Crunch ever crossed over?
A: Yes! In 1985, Quaker Oats, the owners of Cap'n Crunch ran an ad campaign in Marvel comic books where kids would use clues from the back of cereal boxes to help Spider-Man find the missing naval officer.

Q: There have been a bunch of weird Batman crossovers, but was one of them with Godzilla?
A: No! Though it came close to happening twice, once in 1965, and again in 1966. Neither project ever made it past the writing phase.

Q: Has Ash from the *Evil Dead* series ever clashed with Freddy Krueger and Jason Vorhees?
A: No, but once again, it came close to happening in a sequel to 2003's *Freddy vs Jason* set in 2008. They never did make it.

Q: Has Batman ever met Hellboy?
A: He has indeed, in a comic where the two team up to locate Starman, who has been kidnapped by Neo-Nazis.

Q: Have Ray Barone from *Everybody Loves Raymond* and Fran Fine from *The Nanny* ever met?
A: They have! In a 1998 episode of *The Nanny* she runs into him at their high school reunion. Interestingly, the actors Ray Romano and Fran Drescher were actual highschool classmates, both graduating from Hillcrest High School in Jamaica, New York in 1975.

FRANKENSTEIN OR FRAUDENSTEIN: Game for *Frankenstein Conquers the World*

The real star of today's movie is Frankenstein, who is in the Public Domain, which means nobody owns him as an intellectual property. He's free, baby. Free like the wind. Now that also means anyone can use the character in whatever they want. This has resulted in some strange Frankenstein movies. You know the drill. Some were so strange I made some up, blah blah blah. Here are the synapses of some weird Frankenstein movies. Your job is to tell me which ones are real and which ones I invented specifically to fool you. There are no prizes if you win, which is bad. But there are no penalties if you lose, which is good. Let's play FRANKENSTEIN OR FRAUDENSTEIN

Q: Dr. Frankenstein's Monster isn't horny enough, so he cuts off the head of a man leaving a brothel who turns out to be a prospective monk who was only there because his friend insisted that he stay out of the monastery, so the monster remains chaste. Is this a real Frankenstein movie? Or is it a Fraudenstein?
A: Frankenstein! 1973's *Flesh for Frankenstein* was released as *Andy Warhol's Frankenstein* in America, despite the artist's merely financial involvement.

Q: A Mexican Dr. Frankenstein enters his creation in a lucha libre tournament, but has to repair him between fights. Can he keep the secret of El Muerte's identity from being revealed? Is this a real Frankenstein movie? Or is it a Fraudenstein?
A: Fraudenstein! I made this one up! But if it were real, it would have been from 1961 and featured a young Mil Mascaras as one of the monster's opponents.

Q: After seeing 1931's Frankenstein in Franco's Spain, a little girl thinks a wounded republican soldier hiding in an abandoned sheep pen is the monster, and she makes friends with him. He is killed by El Guarda, and she becomes isolated and weird. Is this a real Frankenstein movie? Or a Fraudenstein?
A: Frankenstein! *Spirit of the Beehive* is a 1973 Spanish movie that was a major influence on Guillermo del Toro.

Q: After villagers lynch a caveman, Dr. Frankenstein and his cronies bring him back to life and of course he escapes and rampages. Is this a real Frankenstein movie? Or a Fraudenstein?
A: Frankenstein! *Frankenstein's Castle of Freaks* is from 1974 and was featured on *Elvira's Movie Macabre*.

Q: The Frankenstein Monster, Dracula, and the Wolf-Man help a bullied preteen find the courage to stand up to the teenagers who make his life a living hell by putting together a haunted house that literally scares them to death. Is this a real Frankenstein movie? Or a Fraudenstein?
A: Fraudenstein! But it's an idea I've had kicking around in my itty-bitty brain for a while now.

YOU KNOW, FOR KIDS!: Game for *Gamera*

Gamera is a movie that suffers a little bit from tonal whiplash, a grim Godzilla imitator in some scenes, and a family friendly, child focussed adventure film in others, like if *ET* was a gigantic turtle who killed people. This got me thinking about things that are for kids, but maybe shouldn't be. Or maybe work better when oriented toward children. So, in today's game, "You Know, for KIDS!" I'll ask you whether or not you believe that a particular R-rated or otherwise adult-oriented franchise has an iteration made explicitly for children. There are no prizes, which sucks, I'm sorry, but there's also no penalties, so I feel like it kind of evens out.

Q: Is there a version of *The Rocky Horror Picture Show* for kids?
A: No, there isn't. Although there was a Glee episode that spotlighted songs from *Rocky Horror*, I don't think it was very good. From what I've heard.

Q: Has the *Rambo* franchise ever had a kid friendly iteration?
A: Yes! In 1986, there was an animated series called *Rambo: The Force of Freedom*, which ran 65 episodes and spawned a line of toys.

Q: Was there ever media in the *Alien* franchise intended for children?
A: Yes! In 1992, Fox began production of an animated series called *Operation: ALIEN*, which would have followed as a direct sequel to James Cameron's 1986 film. But *ALIEN³* bombed, and Fox put all of their eggs in the *X-Men* and *Batman* animated series baskets. The *Operation: ALIENS* pilot never aired, but Kenner released a tie-in toy line anyway.

Q: Did Danny Trejo's character from the *Machete* movies ever appear in children's media?
A: Yes! Machete actually first appeared in 2001's *Spy Kids* and it's sequels

Q: Was Freddy Krueger ever the star of a children's series?
A: No! But there was a TV spinoff of *Nightmare on Elm Street* called *Freddy's Nightmares* that aired 2 seasons in syndication between 1988 and 1990

WHAT'S IN A NAME: ALIEN EDITION: Game for *Invasion of Astro-Monster*

Today's movie introduced intelligent, humanoid aliens to the Godzilla franchise, through a race from Planet X called Xillians. This is an objectively silly and wonderful name for a race of aliens and it got me thinking about other movie aliens with weird and funny names, so I decided to make some up and try to make you guess which ones are real and which ones I invented for the specific purpose of making you look foolish on my podcast. You must do so under the penalty of death. Just kidding, there are no prizes or penalties. I may have used that one already.

Q: Are Luphomoids a real pop culture alien race?
A: They are! The Luphomoids are an alien race from Marvel comics, one notable member of which is Nebula from the Guardians of the Galaxy films.

Q: Are Margs a real pop culture alien race?
A: No, but they are what some obnoxious people call margaritas, a delicious Mexican cocktail with origins that are foggy at best.

Q: Are Quarrens a real pop culture Alien race?
A: Yes indeedy. From the *Star Wars* franchise! The Quarrens are a race of squid headed aliens from the planet Mon Calamari, and share it with the better known race Mon Calamari, who are also squid headed aliens. They appear in *The Clone Wars* animated shorts, as well as comics and other *Star Wars* ephemera.

Q: Are the Zetoxians a real pop culture alien Race?
A: Yes! The Zetoxians are the progenitors of the Great Gazoo from the Flintstones cartoons.

Q: Are Alphabetamen a real pop culture alien race?
A: They are not! I made them up. If they were real, they would be a race subservient to Doomsday from Jack Kirby's *New Gods* comics, and be shaped like letters of the alphabet. They would also feature in Zack Snyder's recut of *The Justice League* so you have to take them seriously, *TRIXIE!*

ANIMANIA!: Game for *The Magic Serpent*

Today's film was based on a traditional Japanese fairy tale, *The Tale of Gallant Jiraiya,* which was also one of the earliest novels in the Japanese language. The novel also served as the inspiration for the manga and anime *Naruto*, which I have never read or seen and have no desire to read or see. That little factoid did, however, get me thinking about how many unusual anime adaptations of the canon of Western Literary classics there are, something I used to find endlessly amusing. And still kind of do. Anyway, In our game today, which I'm calling Animania, I'll ask you if a given piece of respected classical lit has an anime adaptation. You must tell me whether or not it does by answering "animyay" for yes, and "animnay" for no. There are no prizes or penalties, but I will try to make you feel ashamed whether you win or lose.

Q: Is there an anime adaptation of GK Chesterton's Fr. Brown Mysteries?
A: No, there is not.

Q: Is there an anime adaptation of *The Diary of Anne Frank?*
A: There is. Produced in 1995, *Anne no Nikki* was made by Madhouse Inc., which also produced *Chobits, Beyblade,* and the first season of *One Punch Man*. The less said about it the better.

Q: Is there an anime adaptation of Laura Ingalls Wilder's *Little House on the Prairie?*
A: There is indeed! *Sougen no Shoujo Laura* or, *Prairie Girl Laura,* ran from 1975 to 1976 for 26 episodes and was produced by Nippon Animation for the Tokyo Broadcasting System, the same network that originally ran *Ultraman*.

Q: Is there an anime adaptation of Michael Bond's *Paddington* series?
A: No! There isn't, but there was a 1989 American and British animated series from *Flintstones* creators Hanna-Barbera

Q: Is there an anime adaptation of Louisa May Alcott's *Little Men,* AKA *Jo's Boys?*
A: There sure is, Mathilda. In 1989, Fuji TV aired Nippon Animation's *Tales of Little Women,* which they followed up in 1993 with *Little Women 2: Jo's Boys* which ran from January to December and ran for 40 episodes.

BACK IN THE HABIT, CRUISE CONTROL, ELECTRIC BOOGALOO: THE GAME: THE SEQUEL: Game for *Gamera vs Barugon*

Today's movie is the first sequel to the movie *Gamera the Giant Monster*. Despite this, the film is quite different tonally from the original, and this angle was abandoned with the third film, *Gamera vs Gyaos*. So for today's game, we'll be talking about movie sequels that weren't quite what audiences were expecting. You have to tell me what movie the plot I summarize is a sequel to. So let's play "Back in the Habit, Cruise Control, Electric Boogaloo: the Game: The Sequel!" No prizes will be awarded and no penalties will be taken.

Q: In what movie's sequel does Dolph Lundgren go undercover as a substitute kindergarten teacher to catch a Russian crime lord who has stolen a USB drive with sensitive information on it?
A: That is the sequel to *Kindergarten Cop*. Creatively titled *Kindergarten Cop 2,* it was released in 2016, 26 years after the original and with no returning cast, creatives or characters.

Q: In what movie's sequel does a Chicago Fire Department arson investigator track down a weapons dealer who may be using the fires as cover?
A: That's the sequel to 1991's *Backdraft*. Kurt Russel does not return, but Donald Sutherland and a Baldwin do!

Q: In what film's sequel does Jessica Harper of *Phantom of the Paradise* and *Suspiria* leave her husband to be a TV star at a studio where people are forced to play inane game shows around the clock? Also there's some mad science.
A: That would be *The Rocky Horror Picture Show*'s sequel, *Shock Treatment!* Which I personally think is the better film, though I don't think either is particularly good. Sue me.

Q: What movie's third installment kills Jim Carrey offscreen before following his son as he tries to prove his mother's innocence in the case of a kidnapped panda?
A: That is the third movie in the *Ace Ventura* series, *Ace Ventura Jr.: Pet Detective*. That's all anyone knows about it because no one has actually seen it.

Q: What movie's sequel recasts Daryl Hannah with Maid Marian from *Robin Hood: Men in Tights*, and basically ignores everything that happened in the original so that some guy who used to be Tom Hanks can save his failing business in New York City and she can steal a dolphin?
A: That's the sequel to *Splash, Splash, Too.* I'm sorry about this game, much like Daryl Hannah in the first movie, the idea didn't really have legs.

O! BROTHER, WHERE ART THOU?: Game for *War of the Gargantuas*

Today's film is one of high drama, a Shakespearian tragedy between giant, hairy Frankenstein brothers. I don't have any brothers, at least not brothers of flesh and blood but do you know who does? Famous people! That's right, many, if not all famous people, have brothers, it's practically a requirement. So in today's game, O! Brother Where Art Thou?, I'll tell you about a celebrity's brother, and your job is to tell me if this mysterious brother is real or if I made them up, as is my way. There will be no prizes or penalties, for you or any brothers you may have.

Q: Does one-time heart throb and current inhuman monster Mel Gibson have a brother named Donal who looks like somebody hit Mel Gibson in the face with a barstool?
A: He does! Donal Gibson has 19 credits on IMDB, 2 of which are him standing in for his brother's voiceover roles in sequels.

Q: Is there a fourth Hemsworth brother named Kyle?
A: There is not! However, if there was, he would be the tallest and handsomest Hemsworth that there ever was.

Q: Does soft rocker John Mayer have an older brother named Carl?
A: He does! Apparently he also has a younger brother named Ben, but this question wasn't about him, so don't change the subject.

Q: Does That Bastard Oscar Isaac have a younger brother named Mike?
A: He does! His younger brother, Mike Hernandez, is a journalist with the Miami Times News.

Q: Do Zooey and Emily Deschanel have a younger brother named Christopher?
A: They do not, but if they did, his middle name would be Clovis and he would play banjo in some hipster band. Probably that one band where their album cover has a lady with a coconut head.

Q: Did Fred Rogers, of *Mr. Rogers' Neighborhood,* have a brother named Nathan?
A: He did not! He did, however, have a sister named Nancy Elaine, who was adopted by his family when he was 11. He named the frightening puppet, Lady Elaine Fairchilde, after her.

Q: True or False, Zach Braff of *Scrubs* fame has a brother named Adam, who looks like a leather muppet.
A: True! They co wrote a movie about being a struggling actor in LA that looks painfully hipstery.

CHANGING OF THE GUARDIANS OF THE GALAXY: Game for *Ebirah, Horror of the Deep*

Behind the scenes of today's movie, the main creative forces of the Godzilla franchise were shifted, a changing of the guard if you will. However, some of the team stayed the same, with Tomoyuki Tanaka as producer, Haruo Nakajima as Godzilla, and Shinichi Sekizawa as screenwriter carrying over from the previous set of films.

Long running teams like this frequently change out members, both in real life and in fiction. So in today's game, Changing of the Guardians of the Galaxy we'll be looking at team line-ups of Marvel Comics' roving gang of space weirdos. Here's how it works. I'll give you the name of a character from Marvel Comics, and ask if they have ever been a member of the Guardians of the Galaxy in the comics. There will be no prizes if you win, there will be no penalties if you lose. The Stakes have never been lower! Do you understand? Are you ready? Let's do it!

Q: Has Kitty Pride ever been a member of the Guardians of the Galaxy?
A: Yes! As a matter of fact, she was their leader for 19 issues, all the way through the crossover event Civil War II!

Q: Has Moon Knight ever been a member of the Guardians of the Galaxy?
A: No! Not at the time of this writing anyway. With his newfound popularity, who knows what the future may bring?

Q: Has Tony Stark, the Iron Man, ever been a member of the Guardians of the Galaxy?
A: Yes! After determining that he needed to better understand threats in outer space, Tony Stark was joined up with Star Lord and the Guardians by writer Brian Michael Bendis in 2013!

Q: Has any version of Ghost Rider ever been a member of the Guardians of the Galaxy?
A: Yes indeedy! Specifically, Cosmic Ghost Rider, who is Frank Castle from Earth TRN 666! Writer Donny Cates brought him over from his own series when he took over the Guardians title in 2019!

Q: Has Johnny Storm, AKA, The Human Torch ever been a member of the Guardians of the Galaxy?
A: No, he hasn't, but fellow Fantastic Four member Ben Grimm, AKA The Thing was a member of the team until the end of Civil War II, when they were stranded on earth and he joined up with SHIELD.

MONSTER BLOOD: Game for *Gamera vs Gyaos*

This Gamera film, like most, features copious amounts of pink and green, Eastmancolor monster blood, which happens to be the title of a Goosebumps book. Those things were very weird, and eternally present through my childhood. This tenuous connection was enough for me to decide that today's game should be called Monster Blood and about Goosebumps books. What's gonna happen here is I'll read you the name and a brief summary of a classic Goosebumps book, and you have to tell me if it is real or if I made it up to trick you. As always both prizes and penalties are prohibited by state and federal law.

Q: Is *I Was a Fourth Grade Frankenstein*, where a kid is experimented on by his estranged grandpa over spring break, a real Goosebumps book?
A: No it is not! There's no such thing. If it were real, though, it would have been published in 1995 and been the 24th book in the series

Q: Is *Ghost Camp*, where two brothers attend a summer camp for the living dead, a real Goosebumps book?
A: Yes! Published in 1996, *Ghost Camp* is the 45th book in the original series.

Q: Is *Let's Get Invisible*, where a kid finds a magic mirror in his attic that turns him invisible, a real Goosebumps book?
A: It is indeedy. It was the 6th book in the series and originally going to be the final one when published in 1993.

Q: Is *The Barking Ghost,* where the scaredy cat new kid in town and his only friend swap bodies with some ghost dogs, a real Goosebumps book?
A: It is. Published in 1995, it is the thirty second book in the series.

Q: Is *The Haunted Department Store,* where a kid stocking shelves as a summer job discovers a coven of witches selling cursed clothes and toys owns the store, a real Goosebumps book?
A: No it is not! Though I think it would be a good one.

Q: Is *The Blob that Ate Everyone*, where an aspiring horror writer accidentally brings his stories to life with a magic typewriter, a real Goosebumps book?
A: I didn't need a magic typewriter for this one to be true! Published in 1997, it's the 55th book in the series.

Q: Is *Monster Blood VI*, where the kid from the other Monster Blood books discovers that his school cafeteria now serves a fruit juice that contains Monster Blood as an ingredient, a real Goosebumps book?
A: Nope. But it would have been the 73rd and last book in the series if it were real.

X MARKS THE SPOT: Game for *The X from Outer Space*

The Letter X has been used from olden times to denote different things. In today's game, X Marks the Spot, I will ask you trivia questions about various famous people named "Mark". As usual, prizes and penalties are BOTH forbidden by state and federal law.

Q: Is it true that Mark Whalberg is a fan of all but one of the Boston Area sports teams? If true, which team is he NOT a fan of?
A: It is false. Insert the Marky MArk and the Funky Bunch joke of your choice here.

Q: True or False, Mark Strong was almost cast as Anton Chigur in The Coen Brothers' film *No Country for Old Men?*
A: True! He was, of course, beaten out by Javier Bardem, who is not named Mark, and so will not be featured further in this game.

Q: True or False, Mark Duplass is the third name to come up when you enter the name "Mark" in the IMDB search bar.
A: True! At least it was for me. This may have changed, but I don't know who Mark Duplass is outside of this context.

Q: Does Mark Ruffalo share a birthday with scream queen and John Carpenter muse Adrienne Barbeau?
A: No! He does, however, share a birthday with scream queen and John Carpenter muse Jamie Lee Curtis!

Q: Did Mark Hamill go to High School in Hokkaido, Japan?
A: No, but he DID go to high school on a military base in Yokohama, Japan, The Nile C. Kinnick High School, which was locally referred to as "Yo-Hi"

REMAKE OR RE-FAKE: Game for *Gappa the Triphibian Monster*

In his book *Japanese Science Fiction, Fantasy, and Horror Films*, Stuart Galbraith erroneously calls *Gappa the Triphibian Monster* as a remake of 1961's British monster movie *Gorgo*. While the stories are similar in that they revolve around parent monsters coming to a major city to save their children, the writers of *Gappa* had never seen *Gorgo*, and as such could not have been intentionally remaking it. However, more movies are remade for an international market than you might think, so I decided to round up a few and make up a few and make you guess which is which. If you think the movie I'm describing is an actual remake, say "remake"! If you think I'm full of bull, say "re-fake!" There will be no prizes or penalties, because this episode has already gone waaay over budget.

Q: Is 1974's *Willy Wonka and the Chocolate Factory* a remake?
A: Refake! While it is based on the children's novel *Charlie and the Chocolate Factory* by Roald Dahl and was remade under that name in 2005, *Willy Wonka and the Chocolate Factory* is not a remake of a previous feature film

Q: Is 1983's *Scarface* a remake?
A: Remake! Oliver Stone and Brian dePalma's iconic work is based on a 1932 gangster movie loosely based on the life of real life mobster Al Capone, and was directed by Howard Hawks, who produced alongside Howard Hughs, which is convenient because I always mix those guys up anyway.

Q: Is Wes Craven's 1972 exploitation hallmark *The Last House on the Left* a remake?
A: Remake! Ingmar Bergman's controversial 1960 drama *The Virgin Spring* won the Academy Award for best Foreign Film, and was a nominee for the Palme d'or at the Cannes film festival.

Q: Is the 1966 Spaghetti Western masterpiece *The Good, the Bad, and the Ugly* a remake?
A: Refake! While the finale of Sergio Leone's *Dollars* or *Man with No Name* trilogy is not a remake of a previous feature film, the first film in the trilogy, *A Fistful of Dollars* is, legally speaking, an unofficial and unauthorized remake of Akira Kurasawa's *Yojimbo*. While Leone disputed this, citing Dashiel Hammet's 1929 novel *Red Harvest* and the 1746 Italian play *The Servant of Two Masters*, which share similar stories, he did eventually settle out of court with Kurasawa, who received royalties from the later film.

Q: Is the 2000 Ben Stiller comedy *Meet the Parents* a remake?
A: Remake! 1992's original *Meet the Parents* was produced by Emo Phillips, written, directed by, and starring Greg Glienna, who also wrote the remake 8 years later.

DR. *WHO?*: Game for *King Kong Escapes*

Dr. Who, played by Hideo Yamamoto in today's movie, *King Kong Escapes,* is not the same Dr. Who from the long running British science fiction drama. But he's not the only character in the film canon with a more famous name-fellow, as our game today, Dr. *Who?* explores. The way this works is this way: I will ask you if a given character, like the British Dr. Who, shares a name with a less mainstream character, like Yamamoto's Dr. Who. We've been forbidden by recent court cases on a local level from offering prizes or penalties on this podcast, so I'm sorry that we can't offer you any at this time. Thank you for your understanding.

Q: We know King Kong as the Giant Primate Star of today's film, but is there a Hungarian wrestler from the 1960s of the same name?
A: There is! Born Emile Czaja in 1909, he frequently starred as the malevolent yang to Indian actor Darah Singh's heroic yin in both wrestling matches and feature films.

Q: There is a very famous series of children's and young adult novels starring a boy wizard named Harry Potter. Was there also a low budget family film starring *Lost in Space* actress June Lockhart as a witch who shares an apartment building with someone else named Harry Potter and his son, Harry Potter Jr?
A: There is! *Troll* was released in 1986, and was successful enough that the unrelated Claudio Fragasso film *Goblins* had its title changed to *Troll 2* before being distributed on home video.

Q: Does the towheaded American newspaper icon Dennis the Menace have a counterpart of the same name from across the pond?
A: He does indeed! The British comic strip *Dennis the Menace and Gnasher* focused on a dark haired 10 year old in a red and black striped sweater causing actual mayhem and mischief, like, as in petty crimes, on the streets of the fictional Beanotown.

Q: Does *Space Jam* star and one time professional athlete Michael Jordan share his name with a character played by Gene Wilder?
A: He does! Gene Wilder plays Michael Jordan in 1982's *Hanky Panky,* the movie where he met Gilda Radner. The movie was also directed by Sidney Portier.

Q: Does Jay Sherman of the 1990s animated TV show *The Critic* share his name with a guitarist who has collaborated with indie darling rock band They Might Be Giants?
A: Yes! He does! And no, he doesn't. The real person in question, Jay Sherman-Godfrey, hyphenates his sherman with a godfrey, which the cartoon character does not do. I was gonna give you this one either way.

WHAT'S IN A NAME: INTERNATIONAL TITLE EDITION:
Game for *Yongary, Monster from the Deep*

One of my favorite bits of Giant Monster Movie trivia is that, when released in Germany, this movie was called *Godzilla's Death Paw,* or *Godzilla's Paw of Death*. So, in today's game, What's in a Name, International Title Edition, I'll ask you if certain movies we've already talked about on the show were released under certain, stupid sounding titles in Germany. There are no prizes if you win, because I'll make sure you don't win, but there's also no penalties if you lose, because I will make sure you don't lose. Does that make sense? No neither do these titles. Let's get going!

Q: Was 1965's *Invasion of Astro Monster* released in Germany under the title *Command from the Dark*?
A: It was indeed! It sounds cool when translated into English, but in German it's called *Befehl aus dem Dunkel,* which is just silly.

Q: Was *Gorgo* released in Germany as *The Dinosaur Takes Revenge*?
A: No! That was not even a title used for *Gorgo* that I could find! That was one of the Greek titles for *Reptilicus,* its other Greek title, used when it was released on home video, was, *Threat to the City*.

Q: When it was released to German TV, was *King Kong vs Godzilla* called *Godzilla - Slaughter Festival of the Giants*?
A: It was! Once again, the actual German sounds less cool: *Godzilla - Schlachtfest der Giganten*

Q: Was the German release of *Mothra vs Godzilla* called *Godzilla and the Primeval Caterpillars*?
A: Yeah it was! And this one actually sounds ok in German too: Godzilla und die Urweltraupen

Q: Was the original *Rodan* from 1956 called *Rodan: The Bird of Death* when released to German TV?
A: No, it was not! That is actually the Polish title of the film, and I'm not even gonna try to pronounce that.

SON OF GODS: Game for *Son of Godzilla*

Ok, so while I was doing research on this episode's movie, whenever I went online, they always asked if I meant *Son of God*, a 2014 drama about the life of Christ that was edited down from a miniseries about the Bible on the History Channel. While I did eventually train my search engine to fill in that extra "z-i-l-l-a", this got me thinking about the game for the episode, and how many other religions have gods who had more than one begotten son, born of the Father before all ages, God from God, light from light, true God from true God, begotten not made, consubstantial with the Father-

Excuse me, my Catholicism is showing. Anyway, answer true or false if this Greek demi-god or hero is the child of the Greek god or goddess I ask you. We wanted to sacrifice some goats and have a feast if you won, but we couldn't get the permits, so there will be no prizes or penalties.

Q: Was Dionysus, God of Wine and Revelry, the son of Zeus and the mortal woman Semele?
A: Yes! And no. while Zeus is pretty uniformly considered Dionysus' daddy, his maternal heritage changes from story to story. In several tellings, yes, Semele is his mother. I'll give this point to you anyway.

Q: Was Thesus, who slew the Minotaur and solved the Labyrinth of King Minos of Crete, the son of Zeus?
A: No! He was the son of Poseiden! The paternity lawsuits for those two guys must have cost the Olympians a fortune

Q: Was Tantalus, from whose name we get our word tantalize, a son of Zeus?
A: Yes! And his mother was a nymph named Pluto, whose father may have been Cronus the titan, which would make her Zeus's half-sister, which is very, very icky.

Q: Was Pelias, King of Iolcos and enemy of Jason, the son of Poseidon?
A: Yes! I won't get into the story because it is icky, but both he and his twin brother Neleus are the sons of Poseidon and the mortal woman Tyro, who seems to have had a thing for water deities.

Q: Was Hercules the son of Zeus?
A: No! I know what you're thinking, "uh, I saw the Disney movie", but guess what? Disney LIED to you. Hercules was the son of Jupiter, the chief god of the Roman pantheon, whereas Zeus was the chief of the Greek pantheon. He did have a son who would be considered the equivalent to the Roman Hercules named Heracles.

FORMULA FRENZY: Game for *Gamera vs Viras*

We focussed on how formulaic the Gamera series has become by this point in our essay segment of the show, and also how child-centric it had become. For today's game, Formula Frenzy, I have combined these two lines of thought. I will read to you the name of a brand of baby formula, and it's your job to tell me if it's a real brand, or one I made up. If you win, we will give your baby back to you. If you lose, we'll give the child to the strange little man who helped us spin straw into gold so that we could marry the king. Just kidding, there are no prizes or penalties.

Q: Is Baby's Only Gentle Dairy Toddler Formula a real brand of baby formula?
A: It is! Despite being called Baby's Only, this is, in fact, made by Nature's One with the intention of feeding toddlers, who are not babies, but toddlers.

Q: Is Enfamil Aluminum Free Extra Protein Formula a real brand of baby formula?
A: It is NOT! You'd think that you wouldn't have to advertise baby formula as aluminum free, but there's a lot of aluminum in a lot of formulas and I don't know why. Maybe a real journalist should look into that.

Q: Is "Hello Baby! Dairy Based Powdered Baby Formula" a real brand of baby formula?
A: It is. NOT! I made it up using words, which can be used for good or evil.

Q: Is Jarrow Formula Baby's Big Support a real brand of baby formula?
A: Yes, it is! Big, by the way, is an acronym in this case, standing for Brain, Immune, and Gut.

Q: Is Bobbie Organic Infant Formula Milk Based Powder with Iron a real Brand of baby formula?
A: It is! Its website advertises it as being Inspired by European Formulas, Our Babies, Real Life, Modern Parenting, and Breast Milk.

DESTROY ALL BAND NAMES: Game for *Destroy All Monsters*

In 1973, a Detroit Michigan based band named Destroy All Monsters began to be a band. I want you to know that that sentence was poorly written as an attempt at comedy and I do know how to actually do a good writing from time to time. Anyway, *Destroy All Monsters* is also the name of the movie we talked about today. This made me wonder about other bands named after movies, monster and horror movies specifically. Now, you must pay for my curiosity, as I ask you five questions, each one kind of the same. I'll say the name of a movie, and you have to tell me yes or no, is there a band named after this film. If you win, you will have the pride of knowing that you won the derivative game show segment of a z-grade podcast. If you lose, you will have the shame of knowing that you lost the derivative game show segment of a z-grade podcast. Other than that, there are no prizes or penalties. Are you ready? It doesn't matter, here we go.

Q: *Witchfinder General* is a 1968 Vincent Price witch-hunting movie, and it featured, by his own accounting, one of his finest performances. There was also a song of the same name by Carl Douglas of "Kung Fu Fighting" fame. But was there a band called "Witchfinder General"?
A: Yes, there was! I have never listened to them, but apparently, they were an English heavy metal band that formed in 1979 and broke up 5 years later.

Q: *Adam and Eve vs The Cannibals* is a 1983 Erotic Biblical Cannibal Drama where-in Adam and Eve get cast out of the Garden of Eden and fight dinosaurs and cannibals. It stars cult film celebrity Mark Gregory who has not been heard from since 1989's *Afghanistan- The Last War Bus* where he played a character named Johnny Hondo. But was there a band of the same name?
A: No! While the movie *is* real, the band is not. If they had been real, though, their reputation would have made them seem much more hardcore than they actually were.

Q: *Suspiria* is considered one of the all-time great Italian horror films and one of my personal favorites. It focuses on an American ballet student at a German dance school in the late 70s who discovers it is secretly run by a coven of witches. It was remade in 2018, and I sometimes like to sing the title to the tune of the Activia jingle. "Suspiria!" But was there ever a band named after it?
A: There was! The two man British goth band had formed in 1993 and lasted for five years. According to Wikipedia, they combined the older synth based goth music with the then current guitar based sound of the goth scene. Their MySpace page is still active.

Q: The 1965 American International Pictures produced film *Die Monster Die* is loosely based on the HP Lovecraft story "The Colour Out of Space". It stars Nick Adams, a famous TV actor who was also featured in two of our previous films, and Boris Karloff, who most famously narrated Dr. Seuss's How The Grinch Stole Christmas animated special and also played Frankenstein's Monster. But, was there ever a band called Die Monster Die?
A: There is! They're still active, and have been since 1995! That's all I know about them.

Q: Have I run out of room on my question sheet?
A: Yes! I have!

WHAT'S IN A NAME: GAMERA MONSTER EDITION: Game for *Gamera vs Guiron*

The Gamera monsters have very interesting names, and even more interesting origins to those names. I've explored them before, but how much attention were you paying? I suspect not enough. To test this suspicion, I will tell you the name of a Gamera monster and propose an origin for it. Your job is to tell me if that is the real origin of that particular monster's name. If you succeed, you will be my best friend for 15 seconds, starting immediately. If you fail, my friendship will be lost to you for 5 seconds, and a colder five seconds you will never know.

Q: Is Viras's name a play on the Japanese word for squid?
A: No! It was not! Though Daiei studios advertised the monster as having been named by the winners of a contest, Viras's name was in fact a play on the word "bai" which means to fold. His name was initially going to be Gesso, the Japanese word for squid legs.

Q: Was Gyaos's name a portmanteau of the Japanese words for Vampire and Bird?
A: No! Gyaos's name is an onomatopoeia that the child protagonist of *Gamera vs Gyaos* used to describe the monster's roar and named him after.

Q: Is Barugon's name a combination of an Australian Aboriginal word for crocodile, and the end of the word dragon?
A: It is!

Q: Is today's monster's name a combination of the words Guillotine and Dragon?
A: Yes, it is!

Q: Is Gamera's name a combination of the Japanese word for Turtle and the suffix "la".
A: It is! You should have known that

MIGHTY MIX UP: Game for *The Mighty Gorga*

Mighty, as in, the Mighty Gorga, is a great descriptor. It conveys a kind of rugged and casual strength. It's one of my favorite adjectives. So in today's Game Mighty Mix Up, I will ask you if the word "Mighty" is describing a person, place, or thing. So, as a burner question and example, if I say "The Mighty Quinn", you would say, "Thing" as the correct answer, since it is the name of a song. And yes, the song is about a person, but we don't know anything about him except that pigeon's think he's cool and that he makes people sleepy. There are no prizes or penalties, mighty or otherwise.

Q: Freak the Mighty. Person, place, or thing?
A: Thing. A novel to be precise. A 1993 young adult novel by Rodman Philbrick about a large mentally disabled boy and a brilliant but small physically disabled boy who team up to have very sad adventures and one of them dies. To be even preciser.

Q: Mighty Mule: Person, Place, or thing?
A: Thing. Mighty Mule is a company that sells automatic gate openers and other gate opening accessories.

Q: The Mighty Howlin' Wolf. Person, place, or thing?
A: Person. Born Chester Arthur Burnett in White Plains, Mississippi, Howlin' Wolf was one of the most loved and skilled performers of blues music in both West Memphis, Arkansas and Chicago, Illinois.

Q: The Mighty Five. Person, place, or thing?
A: Place. Or should I say places? The Mighty Five refers to any of the five state parks in the state of Utah.

Q: The Mighty Cone. Person, place, or thing?
A: Place. The Mighty Cone is a restaurant in Austin, Texas, that specializes in fried, hand held foods, served in a paper cone. Ideal for festivals like Austin City Limits Music Festival, though they're open all year, I think. I've never been there.

WE HATES IT!... OR DO WE?: Game for *Godzilla's Revenge*

For a long time, the realm of film criticism seemed to be populated solely by people who hated movies. Kings among them were Harry and Michael Medved, who have published several books about what movies they think are the worst since 1978's *The Fifty Worst Films of All Time*. Like many such lists, they mostly focus on low hanging fruit like *Robot Monster* and *Santa Claus Conquers the Martians*, neither of which deserve to be on that list. I try to focus on the positive here, so in that spirit, for today's game show, I have gathered five movies from their various "Worst Movies" lists. Your job is to tell me if I secretly love these accepted bad movies or not. If you think I love a movie, answer "You LOVES it!" if you think I hate it, say, "You HATES it!" There will be no prizes or penalties because there never are.

Q: *Alakzam the Great*- A 1960 anime musical in which a very smart monkey who is studying to be a magician overestimates himself and comes to learn humility. Do we loves it? Or do we hates it?
A: We LOVES IT! I first saw this movie on Comet TV about 7 years ago and have been looking for a dvd or blu-ray of it ever since. I will even undertake my own Journey to the West to obtain a copy.

Q: *The Bible: In the Beginning*- A 1966 American-Italian religious epic film produced by Dino De Laurentiis and directed by John Huston which covers the first 22 chapters of Genesis. Do we loves it? Or do we HATES it?
A: We Loves it! Huston makes some very interesting and theologically informed artistic choices.

Q: *The Brain that Wouldn't Die*- a 1962 American science fiction horror film directed by Joseph Green and written by Green and Rex Carlton, a doctor and his fiancée, are driving to his lab when they get into a horrible car accident. She is decapitated, but he is not fazed by this seemingly insurmountable hurdle. Do we LOVEs it? Or do we HATES it?
A: We LOVES IT! One of half a dozen or so *Eyes Without A Face* knockoffs from the early 60s, it's dumb and sleazy and has a surprise monster attack near the end!

Q: *The Car*- a 1977 American horror film directed by Elliot Silverstein and written by Michael Butler, Dennis Shryack and Lane Slate,

WHAT'S IN A NAME: SURGERY EDITION: Game for *Gamera vs Jiger*

During *Gamera vs Jiger*, Gamera is infected with a parasite by his opponent. This is illustrated for the audience through stock footage of an elephant having thousands of works removed from its nose in a grizzly surgical operation. That got me curious. What is the name of that operation? Well, it seems like it's just called surgical parasite removal. That's no fun. So, I went and looked up the names of some actual unusual and uncommon surgeries. Your job will be to tell me if the name of the surgery I give you is the same as the correct moniker for the procedure I describe, or if it has a different official name. If you win, you will not have to undergo any unnecessary surgery today, if you lose, well, I can't make any promises.

Q: Is an osteotomy the resetting or modifying of bones?
A: It is!

Q: Is a frenotomy, or a frenulotomy a procedure to heal diseases of the ear?
A: It is not! It is, however, a procedure to allow the tongue greater movement by removing the little fold underneath, which is called the frenulum.

Q: Is blepharoplasty the technical name for lip modification surgery?
A: It is not! Blepharoplasty is the surgery to repair droopy eyelids.

Q: Is metatarsal surgery the repair of knees?
A: It is not! It is the surgery to repair deformities of the foot.

Q: Is a cholecystectomy a surgery for removal of the gallbladder?
A: It is!

YOG OR NOG?: Game for *Space Amoeba*

Today's movie's official English language title is *Space Amoeba,* but when originally released to theaters by AIP in 1971, they called it *Yog, Monster from Space.* At no point does any character say the name Yog, but if you try it yourself, you'll see that it is very fun to say. Yog. Yog. Yog. Yog yog yog yog yog. Any, most words that end with -og are fun to say. So we're gonna see if these -og things are real or not. If you think it's real, say "Yog". Otherwise, answer "Nog".

Q: Is King Zog a character in a show?
A: Yog! King Zog is a character in the excellent Netflix Matt Groening series *Disenchantment* and is voiced by Jon Dimaggio. If you like D&D and Abbi Jacobson, watch it!

Q: Was there a television show from the 1990s called *Mike, Lu & Og*
A: Yog! This odd animated series with a catchy theme song ran for 2 seasons on Nickelodeon from 1999-2001 and was about a foreign exchange student who applies to be on a remote island partially populated by shipwreck survivors.

Q: We all know about The Mighty Throg, a frog version of Marvel's Thor, who I hope gets his own MCU movie someday. But is there a place that shares the name with him?
A: Yog! Throg's Neck is a neighborhood in Brooklyn, New York, across the East River from Long Island Sound.

Q: First century Jewish historian Josephus was quite concerned with Gog and Magog, two nations of people or possibly one person named Gog from a place called Magog, foretold in the book of Ezekiel, destroying the second Temple in Jerusalem. Did Josephus believe these invaders to be the Parthian Empire from modern day Iran?
A: Nog! While Josephus was concerned about Gog and Magog, he ascribed their characteristics to the Scythian people of southern Siberia.

Q: The National Dog Groomers Association of America, or NDGAA is a society for professional dog groomers that requires both registration and training in order to gain membership. Do they also have an organization for amateur dog groomers called Amateur North American League of Groomers, or ANALOG, that only requires registration and code compliance?
A: Nog! I made it up purely for the fun of there being an organization called ANALOG. Buy physical media when you can, kids.

GAME SHOW: MOVIE: THE SERIES: THE GAME: Game for *Voyage into Space*

Voyage into Space is an example of a movie based on, or really compiled from, a television show. This used to be much more common, but the most recent examples that come to mind are *The Bob's Burgers Movie*, and *El Camino*, the *Breaking Bad* movie, which I have not seen and will not see because I haven't watched the show. You might say that I never broke a single bad.

But sometimes, it works the opposite way, and a successful movie spawns a TV show. In today's game, *Movie: The Series: The Game* your job will be to identify which of these is real and which of these is phony. If you win, a detailed HBO mini-series on your life will be made. If you lose, Bret Ratner will make a paint by numbers biopic of your life with a score by John Debney, and not a good one, like his score for *Elf*. A bad one. Like his score for *Daddy Day Care,* an otherwise delightful film. Just kidding, as usual, prizes and penalties are forbidden by a recent federal court ruling. Thanks, Obama.

Q: *Planet of the Apes* was a 1968 film starring Charlton Heston and based on the 1963 novel *Monkey Planet* by French author Pierre Boulle. It spawned 4 sequels, a remake in 2001, and a series of prequels running from 2011 to 2017. But did it also spawn a television series?
A: It did! 2 actually. A 14 episode live action series simply titled *Planet of the Apes* ran from September to December in 1974 and was a loose remake of the original film that expanded into an *Incredible Hulk* style adventure travelog through the titular ape world. The animated series *Return to the Planet of the Apes* followed in 1975, and incorporated elements from the book, film series, and live action TV show.

Q: *Aliens* was a popular sequel to the equally popular science fiction horror film *Alien*, and they've also had a few sequels. But was there an animated TV Spin off?
A: No! There wasn't! Though one was attempted to be produced when toy manufacturer Kenner was promoting their line of children's action figures under the title, *Operation: Aliens*, and even went so far as to produce 3 commercials animated in the style of the proposed show to sell the idea to FOX Kids in 1992. Nothing came of it.

Q: Walt Disney Studios was nominated for a Best Picture Oscar with their 1991 hit *Beauty and the Beast,* but did their critical success lead to an animated series?
A: No it didn't! Though Disney did make a habit of adapting other renaissance era films into TV shows, including *The Little Mermaid, Aladdin,* and *The Lion King*.

Q: *An American Tail* was one of my favorite films as a kid, and I liked its sequel *Fievel Goes West* pretty good too, but was there also an animated series based on the beloved little Jewish immigrant mouse in search of the American dream?
A: There was! *Fievel's American Tails* is set after the second film and follows Fievel and his family through adventures in the old west. It aired 13 episodes in 1992 and is currently available to stream on peacock, if you're one of the 7 people who have it.

Q: The 2011 film *Limitless* stars Bradley Cooper as a man who takes a pill so he can have, like, double brains, and gets really good at business and fights Robert DeNiro. It's based on the book *The Dark Fields* by Alan Glynn. But was a television show in turn based on the movie?

A: Yes, one was. *Limitless* served as a sequel to the film of the same name and followed the adventures of somebody who was not Bradley Cooper taking the double brain pills and using the resulting double brains to help the FBI solve crimes. I believe Bradley Cooper was there sometimes, but I, much like the rest of the United States, never watched the show, so I'm not sure.

SHARK JUMPING: Game for *Gamera vs Zigra*

To Jump the Shark is an expression that usually means a long running series has reached the point where it is so ridiculous it has lost its audience and popularity. The phrase originates with the 70s sitcom *Happy Days*. In the show's 5th season, popular character Arthur "Fonzie" Fonzarelli wore his leather jacket to the beach and jumped over a shark on water skis. Despite the fact that the show was still incredibly popular in the aftermath, most people look back on this moment as the beginning of the end for the series, which would run for 6 more seasons. Today's film is a definite moment of shark jumping for the Gamera franchise.

Long ago, in the days of old, pop-culture on the internet was discussed not in the current forms of video essays and podcasts, but in the now dated video review. While not dissimilar to the modern video essay, the online video review was usually focussed on a particular movie or tv show with an eye towards comedy instead of actual textual analysis. One of the online video review series that began this shift toward the proper video essay was written and performed by Beth Elderkin, former editor at I09, Gizmodo, and others, along with her husband Tim, *Shark Jumping*, which looked at popular TV shows to determine when, if ever, they jumped the shark, and if it conformed to the conventional wisdom. In today's game, I will mention a TV show and your job will be to tell me if it was ever featured on the no longer extent video series. If you win, you will get to be the star of their own popular network sitcom. If you lose, you'll be forced to enter an already popular sitcom in decline as a gimmicky character. Just kidding, no prizes or penalties blah blah blah.

Q: Was *How I Met Your Mother* covered on *Shark Jumping*?
A: Yes! Though I don't remember what *Shark Jumping* determined to be the definitive moment, most contemporary sources say it was season 5's finale, with even positive reviews noting it wasn't particularly funny.

Q: Was *Laverne & Shirley* covered on *Shark Jumping*?
A: No, it wasn't and *Laverne & Shirley* was a perfect show against which I will hear no slander!

Q: Was *Community* covered on *Shark Jumping*?
A: No! Although the conventional wisdom says that Season 4, or "The Gas Leak Year" was a blow the show never recovered from, to my memory, the quality was consistent throughout all six seasons and hopefully a movie?

Q: Was *Glee* covered on *Shark Jumping*?
A: Yes! Though Shark Jumping's catalog has been wiped from the internet and I therefore can't see what they said, however, looking at a combination of Nielsen Ratings and contemporary critical reception, the show took a hard nosedive after the second season.

Q: Was *Boy Meets World* covered on *Shark Jumping*?
A: No! But kind of! They did an episode on ABC's long running teen focused programming block, TGIF, which featured a brief look at *Boy Meets World* within the larger context of TGIF, but they never dedicated an episode to the series. I'll give you a point anyway.

NEW HOTNESS OR OLD AND BUSTED: Game for *Godzilla vs Hedorah*

The movie we discussed today took some big swings in an attempt to update the Godzilla series for the 70s. I wasn't around then, but I was around during the 90s, when many older intellectual properties were updated in anticipation of the coming millennium. However, there were also a number of iconic 90s franchises and characters native to the decade. This balance between nostalgia and the current day is very well represented in the 1997 summer blockbuster, *Men in Black*, where Will Smith is recruited by Tommy Lee Jones into a secret organization founded in the 1950s to deal with the increased presence of extraterrestrial aliens by making sure their intentions on earth are peaceful. Once he is on the job, Will Smith refers to himself as "The New Hotness", and Tommy Lee Jones as "Old and Busted". OR something like that. Maybe it was in *Men in Black II*. Whatever.

In today's game, "New Hotness or Old and Busted", I will present a beloved nineties film, and your job is to determine if it is 1990s New Hotness, or a remake of something Old and Busted. If you think the movie being discussed is original to the 90s, say, "New Hotness". If not, say, "Old and Busted. Ordinarily, due to a federal court order, we are not permitted to award prizes or inflict penalties, but seeing as this is a live performance, we'll say that that ruling doesn't apply to the present situation, and the winner will be awarded this certificate entitling them to the love and respect of their peers until the end of the universe in perpetuity.

Are you ready? It doesn't matter, here we go.

Q: 1999's *The Mummy* was a big hit. But was it also 1990s new hotness? Or based on something old and busted?
A: Old and busted! Inspired by the 1932 Karl Freund directed Universal Horror film *The Mummy*. It starred Boris Karloff. And I'll put a disclaimer here to let you know, just because I'm calling something "old and busted" doesn't mean I don't like it. I love this movie, but I needed a conceit for the game show.

Q: Is 1997's *Flubber* starring Robin Williams 1990s new hotness? Or based on something old and busted?
A: Old and busted! It's a remake of the 1961 Disney film starring Fred McMurry, *The Absent Minded Professor*, who did not have a weird robot that fell in love with him.

Q: Is the 1990 film *Edward Scissorhands* 1990s new hotness? Or is it based on something old and busted?
A: It is 1990s new hotness! Tim Burton created the character from sketches in his high school notebooks.

Q: Is 1991's *Cape Fear*, starring Nick Nolte and Robert De Niro 1990s new hotness? Or based on something old and busted?
A: Old and busted! It is a remake of 1962's *Cape Fear*, starring Gregory Peck and Robert Mitchum.

Q: Is 1993's *The Sandlot* an example of 1990s new hotness? Or is it based on something old and busted?
A: New hotness! It was inspired by writer-director David Mickey Evans memories growing up as a nerd who liked baseball in the 1960s.

TUMMY TROUBLE: Game for *Godzilla vs Gigan*

Today's film features Gigan as the main antagonist monster, some sort of cyborg with hook hands and a buzzsaw-tummy. Gigan isn't the only character in fiction with something special about their belly. In today's game, Tummy Trouble, I will bring up another character with some kind of gut gimmick, and ask you a more or less unrelated, yes or no, true or false-type trivia question.

If you win, we'll give you a gut worm to help you digest things that would ordinarily make your stomach hurt pain free. His name is Walter. If you lose, we'll give you a different gut worm who looks at the things that make your tummy hurt and laughs at your pain. You can't hear him, but you know he's there, and that makes it worse, somehow. His name is also Walter, but he spells it weird, with an "h" after the "t": WALTHER. Absolute madman.

Anyway, while Walter and Walther are both very real, we can offer no prizes or penalties until such time as the Texas Supreme Court overturns the decision in *State of Texas v Kelly and Noble Walrus Media*, so I wouldn't hold your breath.

Q: Bender, the cigar smoking, beer swilling robot from Matt Groening's *Futurama* has a compartment in his stomach where he can keep pretty much anything, and does. The question I pose to you is: Is the corn plant a type of grass?
A: Yes! I will not elaborate further.

Q: Tinky Winky was one of the four main characters in the unusual and slightly disturbing British children's TV show *Teletubbies*. There was some controversy in the late 90s regarding the Tinks, as I call him, due to his being characterized as male while carrying what looks like a purse, being purple, and having an antenna shaped like a triangle. Jerry Falwell, a normal person, identified him as the pop cultural gay role model for kids. My question to you is: Are Grizzly Bears still extant in California?
A: No! Grizzlies were driven from and killed off in the golden state over a hundred years ago. Black bears, also native to the state, have adapted to fill their niche.

Q: The Care Bears began as toys made by a greeting card company before spinning off into a tv show. Wikipedia describes their trademark "Care Bear Stare", where multiple care bears project beams from their tummy symbols at the same time to form a light wave of happiness as their "ultimate weapon". My question to you is: Is the vegetable corn a type of grass?
A: No! It is a grain. I will not elaborate further.

Q: Charlie Brown, from the popular *Peanuts* newspaper comic strip, which ran from 1950 to 2000, has a zigzag stripe across his shirt, running over his stomach. Was former Mexican president Antonio Lopez de Santa Anna born on Christmas Day?
A: No! He was born on February 21, 1794.

Q: Before it was known that Bill Cosby was a terrible person, it was suspected that he was a terrible person. During that time of being a suspected terrible person, he starred in and produced a cartoon series called *The Adventures of Fat Albert and the Cosby Kids*. The title character of the series, Fat Albert was fat. Why are the corn plant and the corn vegetable not both either a grass or a grain?

A: Grains, while considered separate things in terms of food, are in fact the seeds of various types of grasses. Rice, corn, wheat, and quinoa are all grass seeds, and therefore, grains.

CALLOUSED THUMBS UP OR DOWN?: Game for *Godzilla vs Megalon*

Stephen. You host the video game podcast Super Mega Crash Bros. Turbo. This is an indisputable fact. Another indisputable fact is that there are a bunch of Godzilla video games. Not all of them are good. But there have basically been Godzilla video games as long as there have been video games, so of course there is what could be generously described as a wide variety of quality when it comes to them.

In today's game, Calloused Thumbs Up or Down, I will briefly describe a console released Godzilla game, including release year, console and a short gameplay overview. Your job is to tell me if it received a thumbs up, meaning 5 stars or more in my research of various game review sites, or a thumbs down, meaning fewer than 5 stars. If you think IT was well received, say thumbs up. If not, say thumbs down.

If you win, you will get to play any Godzilla game you wish. If you lose, you will be forced to play the Godzilla mobile game *Run Godzilla* from 2021. Just kidding. We can not award either prizes or penalties due to the Texas Supreme Court Ruling in *State of Texas vs Kelly and Noble Walrus Media*. Don't worry, our legal team is appealing.

Q: *Godzilla: Monster of Monsters* was made for the Nintendo Entertainment System and released in the US in 1988. You play as both Godzilla and Mothra, moving through various levels across a virtual game board before facing a boss monster. Does this game have a general thumbs up or down?
A: Thumbs up! Barely! Across HonestGamers.com and GameFAQ.gamespot.com, the game is rated 5/10.

Q: *Godzilla Generations* was one of four launch titles for the Sega Dreamcast, and was released exclusively in Japan. It is a 3D open world city destruction game where you can unlock variations of Godzilla, as well as his son Minya and a giant Dr. Serizawa carrying the Oxygen Destroyer. But is it a thumbs up or down?
A: Thumbs down! Across the same websites, the game averages 3.2/10

Q: *Godzilla: Save the Earth* was the middle game in a trilogy of Godzilla games from Pipeworks and Atari. It was released for XBox and PlayStation 2 in 2004. The game is a multi-level 3D fighting game. Thumbs up or down?
A: Up! Across the same sites and Metacritic, *Save the Earth* has a 6/10.

Q: *Godzilla 2: War of the Monsters* was the 1992 sequel to *Godzilla: Monster of Monsters*, and was also released on the NES. You play as the military, setting up various outposts to hold off invading monsters and aliens. Thumbs up or down?
A: Thumbs down! It got an aggregated score of 2/10 between all previously mentioned sites.

Q: *Godzilla* was released for Game Boy in 1990. You play as a tiny little Godzilla climbing through various puzzles and punching enemies in the face with a giant boxing glove. Thumbs up or down?
A: Thumbs up! Thumbs waaaaaaaaaay up! It has an average score of 9/10, and yes, it is surprisingly fun.

WHAT'S IN A NAME- ROBOT EDITION: Game for *Godzilla vs Mechagodzilla*

Mechagodzilla is not the only evil robot doppelganger, as a matter of fact, there are so many that I decided that's what this episode's game show should be about. If you win, I will make a good robot clone for you to perform your more unpleasant jobs. If you lose I will create an evil robot version of you to go around town and make it look like you are doing crimes. Just kidding, I'm not allowed to do any of that. There are no prizes or penalties.

Q: Alvin and the Chipmunks are a popular cartoon singing group. In the 2015 iteration of the franchise, evil record executives make a robot version of the band to eat up their market share. Was the name of this imposter band Calvin and the Hipmunks?
A: True!

Q: King Kong is a big monkey. There have been many giant monkeys, but King Kong was first. Was his robot doppelganger named MechaKong?
A: False! MechaniKong

Q: Popular 1980s cartoon *He-Man and the Masters of the Universe* was about a space-barbarian who fought a skeleton. Was He-Man's robot doppelganger named Faker?
A: True!

Q: Your son-in-law, who is my brother-in-law, is a big fan of *The Transformers*. The good guys in *The Transformers* were called the Autobots, and their leader was Optimus Prime. When Megatron, leader of the evil Decepticons, made a fake Optimus Prime to infiltrate the Autobots, was the fake Optimus named Scourge?
A: Yes! He was.

Q: The Kelly family loves Christmas and Christmas movies. Almost uncritically. Among those we love uncritically are *The Santa Clause* franchise starring Tim Allen. In *The Santa Clause 2*, when he has to find a wife before Christmas and leave the North Pole, he creates a robot Santa to run things while he is gone. Was this fake Santa named S.A.N.2.?
A: No! He was simply called Toy Santa.

MY CANADIAN-ROBOT GIRLFRIEND GOES TO A DIFFERENT SCHOOL: Game for *Terror of Mechagodzilla*

There's some confusion about who Katsura is for a little while in today's film, especially regarding her relationship with Ichinose. I get big "I have a girlfriend but she goes to another school/lives in Canada" vibes off of the whole thing. So, that got me thinking about our game show segment. Look at it. In all of its majesty. This game is called "My Canadian Robot Girlfriend Goes to a Different School", and your job, dear friend, is to answer in the affirmative or the negative when I ask you if a particular fictional character had an invented or robotic significant other or not. If you win, you will be issued a standard robot of your preferred gender to do with as you see fit. If you lose, you will be modified into a standard robot to be used as seen fit by someone for whom you are the preferred gender. You signed the contract, you already agreed to this, so don't complain to me.

Q: Did Bart Simpson's fourth grade teacher Edna Krabapple ever have a fake boyfriend?
A: She did! Though she didn't invent him herself, Mrs. Krabapple had a whirlwind romance with Woody Wilson, who, by some coincidence, looked just like Hockey Legend Gordy Howe.

Q: Did Fox Mulder, absolute madman and FBI special agent from the TV show *The X-Files* fall in love with a realistic Robot Woman named Diana 2 who said she had corroborating evidence of his wider investigation into the international conspiracy known as The Syndicate?
A: No, he didn't, but I feel like this was a missed opportunity.

Q: In weird fiction pioneer ETA Hoffman's 1816 short story *The Sandman,* main character Nathanael falls in love with two women, Olimpia and Clara, both of whom try to dissuade him of the belief that the Sandman, in the form of the scientist Coppelius, murdered his father. Were either of these women robots?
A: Yes, Olimpia was, in fact, a robot made by another scientist and Coppelius. I may have spoiled the big twist in a 203 year old sci-fi story, but it is still worth reading.

Q: Sometime in the late 12th Century, a volume of twelve romantic poems was published. It survives to this day and is known under the title *The Lais of Marie de France*. It contains an Arthurian tale titled *Lanval*. When Queen Guinivere seduces the titular knight, he rejects her by saying he is currently bound to a fairy woman who is extremely jealous. Is he telling the truth?
A: He is! The unnamed fay is real, but their relationship is contingent upon his keeping it a secret. When he tells Guinivere, he breaks their agreement, and the queen accuses him of seducing her! Will the fay woman come and testify to King Arthur and save her errant lover's life? Find out when you read *Lanval!* Only in the *Lais of Marie de France*, available in a shady PDF download near you, TODAY!

Q: The Middle Grade graphic novel *Ghosts* by Raina Telgemeier is about Catrina and her family moving to southern California where she meets a boy who helps her deal with her little sister's terminal illness. Was this boy one of the ghosts of the title?

A: No, he's just a kid, no older than my son. That was a reference to the end of the famous train sequence in *Spider-Man 2*. I must say, that man's son probably had a son of his own, might have been divorced, had a mortgage, and was thinking about buying a convertible.

PART III: SUNDRY THINGS

SPECIAL EDITION GAME SHOW FOR 1ST MONSTER KID RADIO APPEARANCE

Between the release of my first and second episodes of *Record All Monsters*, I made a guest appearance on *Monster Kid Radio* to swap favorite Non-Godzilla and Non-Gamera Kaiju movies with *MKR* host Derek M. Koch. In the intervening years, Derek and I have become terrific long distance friends and appear on each other's shows regularly.

What follows is a little promotional version of the *Record All Monsters* Game Show that I whipped up for that first guest spot. I can't recall, but I think Derek went 1-2 on this. He got a better handle on the Game Show after a few appearances on *RAM*, but I was worried I was annoying him the first few times he played. Maybe I was, but he played anyway and somehow we became pretty good friends. Thanks for having me on, Derek, and thanks for giving my fledgling little show a little bit of a platform to jump from to learn to fly.

Godzilla and Gamera are the poster boys for Daikaiju Eiga, or Giant Monster Movies, however, today, we discussed Giant Monster Movies in which they do NOT appear. These movies are popular all around the world, and, until recently, their local distributors could call them whatever they wanted to sell more tickets in their home countries. So in this Special Monster Kid Radio edition of our recurring game "What's in a Name?" I'll give you the title of a Giant Monster Movie in a foreign country, and your job is to let me know if that movie really was billed as that name in that country. There will be no prizes or penalties, since this is your show and I have no authority here.

Q: Was *Frankenstein Conquers the World* titled *The Terror with an Ape Face* in Germany?
A: It was! It was originally called *Frankenstein vs the Subterranean Monster Baragon* when released in Japan

Q: The banned film produced by Thai super producer and alleged forger of documents Sompote Sands *6 Ultra Brothers vs the Monster Army* released in the US as *Space Warriors 2000*?
A: It was! The film stars Sands' own superhero creation Hanuman, based on the Hindu and Buddhist deity of the same name, and is extremely violent.

Q: Was 1967's *Yonggary, Monster from the Deep* released in Italy as *Gamera's Death Paw*?
A: It was not! However, its German title was *Godzilla's Death Paw*.

WRITTEN ESSAYS FOR *PODCASTERS ASSEMBLE*

Around the time I started *Record All Monsters*, I was invited by some internet friends to participate in a roundtable show called *Podcasters Assemble*, where podcasters from a variety of different shows send in recordings of themselves talking about movies in long running franchises, usually with a new installment being released soon.

Podcasters Assemble, or PODASS, as I took to calling it in my own notes, was beginning its 4th season, called KONG-ZILLA-THON, and wanted opinions on the original *King Kong* and *Godzilla,* as well as their most recent remakes and Monsterverse incarnations. I jumped at the chance to get *Record All Monsters* into more ear-holes, but also to look at movies that I would not get to examine through the lens of my show until its possible 5th season. Presented here, without much if any reformatting, are my entries as written for *Podcasters Assemble*'s fourth season. You'll notice that there is no entry for Episode 9, which was on 2021's *Godzilla vs Kong*, as my contribution to that episode was done off the dome the night I first saw that movie on release. Enjoy.

PODCASTERS ASSEMBLE SEASON 4 EPISODE 1: KING KONG (1933)

Hello, I'm Robert Kelly, host and writer of Record All Monsters.

Let's talk about 1933's KING KONG.

The first time I saw that particular film, it was the summer before I started 4th grade, and we were visiting my recently divorced uncle. His apartment was very beige, and the only TV was in his bedroom. He let me and my older sisters watch TV there, while he and my parents caught up in the living room.

As we were flipping through the channels in his enormous satellite TV program, we shot past a movie I knew on sight was KING KONG, despite never having seen it before. I begged my sisters to stop and watch it. It seemed to surprise them that I hadn't seen it yet; I'd been a fan of Monster Movies since I was 3 years old, and Godzilla was particularly dear to my heart. So how had I not seen the original King Kong? I'd even seen the Dino DeLaurentis version from the 70s! Recognizing the importance of this movie to me, my sisters, by a vote of 2 to 1, agreed that we would watch KING KONG. And it was wonderful. So far as immersive movie experiences go, only *The Wizard of Oz* had ever engulfed me so completely before.

Of course, Kong is the star of the show, even if Robert Armstrong, Bruce Cabot, and Fay Wray are all billed above him, and the monstrous menagerie of dinosaurs and other prehistoric reptiles he faces off against during our time on Skull Island dazzle almost as much. But there's something like a humanity in Kong, and we see it from the first image of his grim, grinning visage leering over the treeline at Ann Darrow, to the last, pleading, soulful glance he has of her as he loses his grip on the world's tallest building.

We can't ignore the above mentioned human characters, and the one most deserving of praise is Robert Armstrong's Carl Denham. He has, in my opinion, the best line in the film : "I'm goin out to make the greatest picture in the world!" and captures a sense of awe and wonder in his performance, making it hard for us to realize that he really is the antagonist by the time he declares kong to be the 8th wonder of the world, and that the film's perspective has, intentionally or not, shifted to the King of Skull Island over the course of the film.

As I researched this film for my own show, I came across a behind the scenes fact that brought a tear of joy to my face; while Kong was animated by the renowned Willis O'Brien, he was built and sculpted by Marcel Delgado, a Mexican-American man, like myself, who had been hired by O'Brien for his keen and artistic eye. Here at the beginning of my research into the beginning of my favorite film genre was a man who looked like me, who shared my heritage, and who was key in bringing it to life.

For my full thoughts on KING KONG, check out Record All Monsters, where we look at the history of Giant Monster Movies as a narrative story, starting with this very film. It's a great way to beef up on your Kaiju Knowledge before Godzilla vs Kong arrives in theaters and on HBO MAX on March 31st, that way YOU can be the obnoxious nerd who knows too much about the films references and deep cuts who all your friends ask to explain when the movie is over.

PODCASTERS ASSEMBLE SEASON 4 EPISODE 2: GODZILLA (1954)

Hello, I'm Robert Kelly, host and writer of Record All Monsters.

Let's talk about 1954's GODZILLA, and 1956's GODZILLA, KING OF THE MONSTERS.

First of all, I'm fairly certain most of this episode's contributors will extol the virtues of Ishiro Honda's 1954 masterwork, and that is right and just. But, sometimes, when it comes to Terry Morse and Joseph E Levine's 1956 US import version, I find myself in the role of John the Baptist, the lone voice, crying out in the desert "ACTUALLY, THIS MOVIE IS PRETTY GOOD! AND ALSO, WAS COMPLETELY NECESSARY AT THE TIME!"

Looking at the foreign film landscape in America today, you might be tempted to think that it was sometime around the birth of the Criterion Collection that it occurred to western distributors to simply subtitle movies not made in English when releasing them in English speaking markets. This is not the case. No, as a matter of fact, this was incredibly common. I go into the reasons in more depth in the third full episode of Record all monsters, but it was also detrimental to the film's box office potential. So when Joseph Levine saw Godzilla, and decided to distribute it in the US, he knew changes to this uniquely Japanese film would be necessary to make it work for an American audience in the mid 1950s.

Raymond Burr brings a believable gravitas to his role as international reporter Steve Martin, and while his integration into the story isn't always seamless, it's definitely well and artfully done. Though some scenes are cut or shortened, this does frequently improve the film's pacing, I'll leave it up to you if that's worth losing almost 20 minutes of footage though.

What is NOT cut, for the most part, are the real reasons that people are still watching these movies today, the scenes featuring our monSTAR, if you'll forgive a very bad and overused pun. Even in this Americanized version of the film, the power, terror, and poignancy of Godzilla's appearances is intact. The visual effects, masterminded by Eiji Tsuburaya, a personal hero of mine, give us a number of iconic and meaning-laden images. Two that always resonate with me are Godzilla, framed through a window behind a bird cage, as if he is also imprisoned within it, and Godzilla again, moments before his death, simply walking peacefully along the seafloor in Tokyo Bay. These images emphasize an uncomfortable truth: Godzilla is our victim as much as we are his.

For my full thoughts on Godzilla and its imported US version, check out episode 3 of RECORD ALL MONSTERS. We talk more about everything discussed above, and also go over our Godzilla fan bona fides. We tell a few stories about growing up as Godzilla fans which will make for great conversation fodder you can claim as your own life experience while you drive with friends to see Godzilla vs Kong on March 31st, if you live in a place where theaters have safely opened. That way everyone will know you're not some kind of FAKE NERD like that guy, *Timmy.* And I know we all feel the same way about him.

PODCASTERS ASSEMBLE SEASON 4 EPISODE 3: GODZILLA (1998)

Hello, I'm Robert Kelly, host and writer of Record All Monsters.

Come with me (doo doo doo doo dodo) and let's talk about 1998's *Godzilla*

Think back to the summer of 1997. You're gonna turn 5 in a few months. It's Fourth of July Weekend, and you're going to the movies with your family. The Will Smith classic *Men In Black* has just been released and you couldn't be more excited. You love the *Fresh Prince of Bel-Air*, which you watch in syndication after school at your grandma's house, and this summer movie season has already been packed with treats for you specifically. Back in May, T*he Lost World: Jurassic Park* was a fun but pretty scary experience. *Batman and Robin* was a little more your speed, and Disney's *Hercules* was everything you had hoped for, even if you were already enough of a dork to notice the inconsistencies with the few Greek myths you know about, who cares, the Danny DeVito goat-man was hilarious!

So you're sitting down, fighting with your sister over who gets to sit between Mom and Dad in case things get scary, and the credits start rolling. A bunch of kids are in a museum, and there's a slow build to reveal the skeleton of a Tyrannosaurus Rex. Cool! T-Rex! Yih! And as the museum guy drones on, the earth starts to shake, the security guard looks nervous and then- CRASH! STOMP! CRUNCH! A great big monster foot smashes through the roof! It's the same size as the absolutely decimated T-Rex bones! It lifts away and you see a huge, lizard-like tail swish through the museum's brand new sun roof. Green text on the now black screen says: Guess who's coming to town? Slowly the word GODZILLA appears in slick looking black text, outlined by a dangerous looking, lime green aura. A familiar Skreeonk is heard and the screen flashes MEMORIAL DAY, 1998.

You're shaking, folks. Hell, I'm shaking, even remembering the excitement. When 1998 rolled around, all of a sudden, I wasn't so lonely. Let me explain: When I was 3 years old, my mom took me and my sisters to Hollywood Video, and as I walked down the aisles, looking for something to satisfy my dinosaur obsessed child brain, I saw one of the most beautiful things I had encountered up to that point- a tape. THE tape. I couldn't read super well, but I could recognize the word GOD, like a good Catholic boy, and the Z-I-L-L-A. Godzilla? Godzilla. It was a dinosaur fighting HOLY CRAP A ROBOT DINOSAUR? For close to 2 years I tried to share my discovery with my friends, who reacted with the full range of emotions, from indifference, all the way to not caring. Finally, the marketing blitz began, and Godzilla was EVERYWHERE! I was thrilled, and I wasn't alone, not only were my friends into Godzilla now too, but there were suddenly toys, books, and tapes of the movies that you could buy and keep!

The whole thing culminated for me the day the movie came out. It was Wednesday, May 20th, 1998. My dad picked me up from school early, with the local paper open on his truck's passenger seat, an article detailing the then 40 plus years of the Godzilla Franchise faced me. I couldn't read well enough to get all of it, but I knew where we were going. My dad says I wasn't that thrilled with the movie, though I don't really remember it that way. I remember waiting for Godzilla to fight something, and I do remember not liking that Godzilla died, but I was optimistic that the promised sequel would get it right.

There was no sequel. There was a cartoon, I guess, and that was pretty good. I went through the whole hate thing for this movie when I was a teenager, but now when I think of this entry in the series, I don't think of the many things I don't like about it, I think of the year leading up to its release, and the community and camaraderie that grew up around me, and how for a few months in the late nineties, everyone was a Godzilla fan.

For my thoughts on movies in the Early Godzilla franchise, Check out my show RECORD ALL MONSTERS, where we look at the entire history of Giant Monster Movies from King Kong to the Present day! We're just now starting to touch on the films of the sixties, so if you want to be the guy with all the knowledge about Monster Movies in your friend group as you gear up to see Godzilla vs Kong on HBO Max on March 31st, it's a good cliffs notes version of watching the 88 years of legacy these two icons carry with them, without having to watch 88 years of movies.

PODCASTERS ASSEMBLE SEASON 4 EPISODE 4: KING KONG (2005)

Hello, I'm Robert Kelly, Host and writer of Record all Monsters, and today, I'm gonna talk to you about Peter Jackson's 2005 remake of *King Kong*

I have good memories of this movie. I hadn't seen it all the way through since I saw it in theaters, instead opting to jump around to my favorite parts. But I rewatched the whole thing recently, and woof. Insert that meme of naked Spongebob leaning against a wall with one hand and breathing hard.

I like to start with the positives, and there's actually a lot of them, but everything is so intertwined, it's hard to discuss the good and the bad separately. So now, we find ourselves engaging in the time honored tradition of the PROS and CONS list. (to that's what makes the world go round): For ev'ry Con there is a pro, each thing that rocks has one that blows and that's what makes this a mixed bag!

Pro: Our main characters are more fleshed out! This version of Jack, played by Adrien Brody is actually a character and not a cardboard cut out who occasionally kisses someone. Naomi Watts Ann Darrow has a background in vaudeville, which makes Denham's appeals to her slightly less predatory, but still super creepy. And of course, our perfect boy, sleazy director Carl Denham, is played as a self deluded con-man who's bought his own lies by Jack Black in a delightful and unjustly maligned performance. He's honestly the only actor who seems to understand what kind of movie this ought to be.

Con: Pretty much every other returning human character is done dirty. Englehorn goes from the voice of reason to a trigger happy German WWI vet? And the new characters are terrible. Especially Jimmy. There's a special place in Hell for Jimmy. Kyle Chandler is pretty funny.

Pro: Kong looks good! And Andy Serkis does a good job in his motion capture performance.

Con: Making Kong just a very big gorilla makes him a little less Kong to me, somehow. He's not a monster, he's just an animal. Trying to make a story like this more realistic undercuts some of its wonder, and I think this was a big misstep. It turns it into a boy and his dog movie, where the boy is a vaudeville actress and his dog is a 25 foot tall gorilla.

Pro: Skull Island and its residents look photo realistic!

Con: Until they're placed next to something that is actually real. Then something just doesn't sit right. Peter Jackson has this very documentary-like way of filming his actors, and it clashes with his much more dynamic way of filming action scenes, especially since the action scenes here are so CGI heavy. It creates a disconnect between the effects shots and the drama, and I never really could reconcile it.

Pro: The Skull Island natives aren't dressed like Screamin' Jay Hawkins!

Con: They're dressed like extras from *Cannibal Holocaust*. I understand that with Jackson's background as a horror director, that particular film has probably been in the back of his mind for some time, but, uh… yikes. Needless aggression and smashing heads with clubs, yeah this is even closer to the mischaracterizations of native peoples than the comparatively reasonable group the party encountered in the 1933 film.

I know I seem to have come down pretty hard on this one, but, c'mon, there's seventy two years and a bad 1970s remake between this movie and the original. Sure, they steered clear of Dino De Laurentiis' mistakes but they made a whole bunch of new ones. The truth of the matter is, this movie would have been a lot better if it had been an hour and forty minutes long. As it stands, the updated version of the T-rex fight is a perfect analogy for this movie as a whole: It's almost twice as long as the original, ends the exact same way, and you can't tell if you're actually feeling the intended emotions, or just too tired from everything you just saw to think clearly.

For my thoughts on other Big Monkey Movies, including the original (and still the best!) King Kong, check out Record all Monsters, new episodes every other Friday, and usually a special little something in between. Until next time, remember that Monsters are your Friends.

PODCASTERS ASSEMBLE SEASON 4 EPISODE 5: GODZILLA (2014)

Hello, I'm Robert Kelly, host and writer of Record All Monsters, and I'm here to talk to you about the 2014 American version of *Godzilla*

The first mistake people make with this movie is that they come to watch Bryan Cranston, as this came out the summer *Breaking Bad* ended. I always think of him as the dad from *Malcolm in the Middle* as I had never and still haven't ever broken a single bad. So before you watch it, drop that expectation from your mind.

Second mistake, this was a lot of people's first Godzilla movie, and Godzilla movies are largely defined in the popular imagination as 90 straight minutes of men in rubber suits smashing each other into cardboard buildings. This is not what Godzilla movies are, and even the silliest ones spend a lot of time establishing what the threat is and why Godzilla, who is an established character in most of these films, is needed to stop the monster. So drop that misconception from your mind as well.

Those are the mistakes most people who dislike this movie make. Not all, but most. The Marketing for this film also held up the false expectation that it was about Bryan Cranston trying to stop Godzilla, and not about Godzilla stopping an even worse threat. What we have here is essentially a late Showa era Godzilla movie, reimagined through a Spielbergian lense for a modern American audience. Once you're in the right headspace, this is a great Godzilla movie.

Part of getting into the right headspace is having the right background info, and understanding the kind of story being told, and outside of the late Showa era, are ancient stories of heroes and saints. Let me explain: Once upon a time, there was a butcher, and it was a time of famine. When he caught some kids stealing what little he had, he killed them. Horrified at what he'd done, he sealed them in a pickle barrel. Now, it just so happened that Nicholas of Myra was in town. He was a bishop and was told that some children were missing. After some quick detective work, he tracked them to the butcher's shop, and raised them alive and well from the pickle barrel. The End. Once upon a different time, a farmer's cart got its wheel caught in the road, and he was unable to move it. And then, Hercules showed up and pulled the cart free. The End again. This is that kind of story, except substitute Godzilla for Hercules or St. Nicholas. We're talking about how extraordinary figures influence the everyday people around them.

Now that we're all on the same page, I think this movie is fantastic. It feels like a Spielberg movie in all the best ways, and feels like a Godzilla movie in all the best ways. As someone who already loves Godzilla, and has their whole life, the way this movie builds tension, only to release it all like so much atomic breath down another monster's throat, is perfect. I cried in the theater as The Big G's tale plates illuminated the first time he blasted that deadly breath at one of the MUTOS, and cheered through the whole fight. This is the American Godzilla movie I wanted in 1998, and I'm so glad I finally got it.

To get a handle on why this movie fits so well alongside the established Godzilla mythos, check out my show, Record All Monsters!

PODCASTERS ASSEMBLE SEASON 4 EPISODE 6: KONG: SKULL ISLAND

Hello, I'm Robert Kelly, Host and Writer of Record All Monsters, And I'm gonna talk with y'all about 2017's *Kong Skull Island*.

I do not envy the makers of this movie. In a lot of ways, they had a much more difficult task than the team Legendary Pictures had working on 2014's *Godzilla*. There had really only been one kind of King Kong Movie up to this point. Sure there were a couple of outliers, like 1933's *Son of Kong*, and 1967's *King Kong Escapes*, but even those share some broad similarities. Add in the not so subtle goal of making this movie tie in to 2014's *Godzilla* and create a Monsterverse, and they had a tremendous challenge on their hands, I tell ya what.

With that in mind, they made all the right choices. Instead of focusing on the beauty and the beast angle, they focus on the Lost World style of storytelling. And instead of just dinosaurs, we get a whole array of wild-ass monsters! There's the big water-cow, the log-bug, the giant, fresh-water squid, the bamboo-leg-spider, the saw-nosed pterodactyls, the skullcrawlers, and of course, Kong himself. By the way, there's a *Cannibal Holocaust* reference in this Kong movie too, only it's not done at the expense of the native peoples, who are portrayed with great dignity and as an actual society. Take note, Peter Jackson.

Another thing Peter Jackson could take note of is how to impart the subtext of a film without hitting your audience over the head with it. Yeah, eventually Tom Hiddleston explicitly says something about how no one can really come home from war, which ties this film in nicely with the previous one thematically, but overall, the movie with a giant monkey ripping the organs out of a lizard's mouth has a much lighter touch when it comes to messaging.

Like with *Godzilla* three years earlier, the monster fights here are savage and brutal, like when real animals fight, and upon my rewatch today, I found myself cheering during the final confrontation once again.

For more on where Lost World Cinema comes from, check out episode 1.5 of Record All Monsters, where we take a Quick Look at 1925's *The Lost World*, based on Arthur Conan Doyle's novel of the same name that basically typified the genre. And check out all of our big monkey episodes, including our recent look at *Konga*, with the artist Nathanael Ross Smith, to understand why it's such a big deal that they finally told a new kind of big monkey story in this film.

PODCASTERS ASSEMBLE SEASON 4 EPISODE 7: GODZILLA: KING OF THE MONSTERS (2019)

Hello, I'm Robert Kelly, host and writer of Record All Monsters, and we're gonna talk about *Godzilla, King of the Monsters* from 2019

When this movie was announced, pretty much immediately after 2014's film came out, I was hyped. I had loved Legendary's first foray into Godzilla's world, and wanted to see more of what Gareth Edwards and Thomas Tull had in store for us. And then in 2016, Gareth Edwards stepped away from the project, and Thomas Tull sold Legendary Pictures to the Chinese media company WANDA. I was scared. How would this affect the upcoming sequel? *Kong: Skull Island* assuaged many of my fears, but surely most of it had been produced under the previous team? My fears were further assuaged when Michael Dougherty was announced to write and then later to direct.

Finally, the day came. I was planning on seeing it opening weekend, but my sister surprised me with opening night tickets. From here on out, I'm just gonna gush.

The movie works mostly as a big love letter to the classic Godzilla movies of the mid-60s, and I can understand why some people didn't like it, but c'mon, give me a break and stop taking yourself so seriously. This is a Godzilla movie, and sure, maybe it started out as a deadly serious meditation on a nation's trauma, but it evolved away from that a long time ago, and the spectacular monster fights and silly pseudoscience are as much a part of this franchise's history as the brooding masterpiece that got the ball rolling.

Ghidorah is extremely well realized, as are Mothra and Rodan, remodeled under the same ethos that had worked so well for Godzilla 5 years earlier. And as much as I liked the human characters in the previous film, I'm happy we got a new cast, with the only returning actors being Ken Watanabe and Sally Hawkins, with David Strathain making a cameo appearance. I really like that we see more about MONARCH and how they operate. Though the worst character comes with them, in the form of Bradley Whitford, who I generally like, but he wears a little thin over the course of the film.

This film also delves deeply into the many spiritual implications that the monsters carry, especially as written by original series writer Shinichi Sekizawa, who wrote, among other entries, *Mothra, King Kong vs Godzilla, Mothra vs Godzilla, Ghidorah, the Three-Headed Monster,* the pilot episode of *Ultraman,* and, just so much more. Sekizawa's debut as a writer for Giant Monster Movies was on 1958's *Varan,* where a giant monster is worshiped as a god by natives cut off from the rest of the world, so he was very much the force behind the deification within these films of the kaiju, and this movie updates those attitudes.

Everything about the original series that is paid subtle tribute to in the 2014 movie is paid loud, blatant, bull in a china shop tribute here and I love it.

PODCASTERS ASSEMBLE SEASON 4 EPISODE 8: KING KONG VS GODZILLA (1962)

Hello, I'm Robert Kelly, host and writer of Record All Monsters, and strap in boys and girls, we're talkin' about 1962's King Kong vs Godzilla

Let's get some context all up in here. Godzilla was last seen in the quickie sequel to his 1954 debut, 1955's *Godzilla Raids Again*, which is chiefly noteworthy because it introduced the monster vs monster concept into the franchise and as the story centerpiece in Giant Monster Movies in general. At the end of that movie, Godzilla was buried in ice by a daring team of bombers, and not heard from for 7 years. That film had left behind director Ishiro Honda and composer Akira Ifukube, swapping them out for Motoyoshi Oda and Masaru Sato respectively, while special effects wizard Eiji Tsuburaya and producer Tomoyuki Tanaka stayed on. In the seven years Godzilla was sleeping, though, the original team of Tanaka, Honda, Tsuburaya, and Ifukube made *Rodan, The Mysterians, Varan the Unbelievable* and *Battle in Outer Space.* Without Ifukube, they made *Half Human, The H-Man, The Human Vapor, Mothra,* and *Gorath.*

On the other side of the Pacific, *King Kong* effects titan Willis O'Brien had been having a really tough go of things. And I'll give a word of warning here, regarding self harm and violence toward children. The same year that *Kong* and *Son of Kong* were released, his ex-wife shot and killed their two sons, Willis Jr and William, shooting herself as well. She survived, and the bullet actually prolonged her life by a year, she had tuberculosis and it had drained her lung as it passed through.

His professional career was in a sorry state too, though things did begin to look up, culminating in an Oscar win for his work on 1949's *Mighty Joe Young*. Looking to get back on top, O'Brien teamed up with producer Irwin Allen to remake *The Lost World* in 1960. Allen's corner cutting eventually resulted in an inability for O'Brien to use stop motion animation, and he was instead forced to glue fins, horns, and other threatening appendages onto iguanas and baby alligators. If revisiting his first giant hit hadn't revitalized his career, maybe his second would. O'Brien began working out the idea for another King Kong sequel, *King Kong vs Frankenstein*, unsure of the copyright on the Frankenstein name, he later changed it to *King Kong vs Prometheus,* in which a descendant of Dr. Frankenstein puts together a patchwork beast from discarded animal parts called The Ginko. It all culminates in The Ginko and Kong fighting in San Francisco before tumbling off the Golden Gate Bridge.

O'Brien's treatment was picked up by producer John Beck, who more or less absconded with it to Japan, tricked Toho into paying RKO's $200,000 licensing fee to use Kong, and then worked out an exclusive distribution deal with Universal Pictures in the US and English speaking territories. O'Brien never saw a cent from it, and it remained the top grossing Godzilla movie until 1992, and still holds the record for most attended Godzilla movie in Japan to this day.

Now that all of that is out of the way, let's talk about the movie itself. There are two versions of this movie out there, and depending on which version you're watching, it's either pretty good or very good. Not that it's not without its problems, like the Japanese actors in black-face portraying the Faro Island natives, but it's a fun movie overall. This is the first time we're seeing both Kong and Godzilla in color, and also the beginning of the use of the "maybe this monster is less of a threat than that monster" style story that would come to dominate the Godzilla series in the future. Only Godzilla is explicitly the bad guy here, and would later be more regularly cast as the lesser of two evils.

We get lots of fun and goofy moments. The islanders get Kong drunk with berry juice! The Japanese Self Defense Force carries him around by tying him to balloons! Godzilla flaps his arms up and down! King Kong develops lighting powers!

It's important to look at this movie in the context of Japanese cinema at the time. One of the most popular genres was something called a salaryman comedy, where a Martin and Lewis style duo are forced into ever more ridiculous and dangerous assignments for an unreasonable over the top boss. In this case, the wonderfully played Mr. Tako sends two of his underlings to Faro Island, initially to bring back some of those berries, but then to bring back King Kong as a mascot to use in their TV commercials! Eventually, it all comes down to King Kong vs Godzilla on the slopes of Mt Fuji. This movie is deliberately silly, as it tries to comment on TV and capitalism coming together and putting everyone around them in danger, much like Godzilla and Kong themselves. Unleashed by arms races and corporate greed, Godzilla and Kong could have been stopped. It's a very silly way to make us look more deeply at our society and our roles within it.

For my full takes on the original King Kong and Godzilla, check out Record All Monsters, where I cover both movies quite in depth! And keep an eye out for our episode on this movie coming out soon! We'll have an all-star round table of new and returning guests.

PODCASTERS ASSEMBLE SEASON 4 EPISODE 10: BEST AND WORST OF GODZILLA AND KONG

Hello, I'm Robert Kelly, Host and writer of Record All Monsters, and we're gonna talk about the best and worst in both the Godzilla and King Kong franchises.

My favorite Godzilla movie is 1974's *Godzilla vs Mechagodzilla*. It has a terrific jazz score by Masaru Sato, and introduces my second favorite ever kaiju, Mechagodzilla, and features another favorite monster, Godzilla's friend Anguirus! There are ape-faced aliens, space-titanium (you mean it's from outer space?), ancient prophecies, Shisha dog guardian statues, a musical number, INTERPOL, and a boat. I highly recommend it.

Most people will probably decry either the 1998 movie, which we've already discussed, or Godzilla's Revenge from 1969. These people are wrong for a number of reasons. I feel the only way to discuss Godzilla's Revenge is using the structure of articles in Thomas Aquinas' *Summa Theologica.*

First, the Question: Is *Godzilla's Revenge* a good or bad movie? Now onto the Arguments or Objections, that is arguments against my position.

Objection 1: This movie is silly and too focused on children
Objection 2: This movie does not live up to the 1954 original

On the contrary, the focus on children is appropriate, and it is as clear an artistic vision as 1954's *Godzilla*

My answer: *Godzilla's Revenge* is a good movie.

My replies to the objections are as follow:

Objection 1: This movie is silly and too focused on children. That's because it is a movie for children. This movie came out in 1969, and by that time, the *Gamera* series had steered the entire genre squarely into the territory of children's films. When compared to the Gamera films of the previous years, *Godzilla's Revenge* is a well crafted if budget constrained Kaiju film for children. As a children's film, silliness is not only permissible, but welcome!

Objection 2: This movie does not live up to the 1954 original. To address this, let's look at the Godzilla sequels in comparison to the original, just at a glance, using IMDB's 10 star ratings: the original holds a rating of 7.6 stars out of 10. *Godzilla Raids Again* has 5.9. *King Kong vs Godzilla* has 5.9. *Mothra vs Godzilla* has 6.6. *Ghidorah the Three-Headed Monster* has 6.7. *Invasion of Astro-Monster* has 6.4. *Ebirah Horror of the Deep* has 5.5. *Son of Godzilla* has 5.3, and *Destroy All Monsters* has 6.9. *Godzilla's Revenge* has the lowest score, at 3.9, but none of the sequels come close to matching the reputation of the original, so this is not a valid grounds for criticism. And this movie isn't trying to do the same thing the original was. Additionally, this film shares a director with the original. Ishiro Honda was tired of making Monster Movies, and wanted to make a movie about people. But when he was told to make another Godzilla movie, built around stock footage ala the last few *Gamera* movies, he made a movie that deals with the corrupting influence of industrialisation on Japanese culture, and the people left behind by modernization, especially the children. I sincerely urge you to watch this movie with a childlike, open mind and heart.

Now for Kong, The best Kong movie is still the original. Check out the very first episode of Record All Monsters for my full reasoning. The worst is *probably* 1976's *King Kong*, which is just a not great remake, BUT it does feature a great gorilla suit by Rick Baker, the special effects makeup man behind *An American Werewolf in London, Men in Black, Harry and the Hendersons,* the original *Star Wars* trilogy, *Batman Forever, How the Grinch Stole Christmas,* and Ron Perlman's beast makeup front he 1990's TV show, *Beauty and the Beast.* But that movie is redeemed in my mind thanks to its absolutely bonkers sequel from ten years later, *King Kong Lives.*

In *King Kong Lives*, we open with the revelation that Kong didn't die when he fell in a bloody puddle from the top of the World Trade Center, and has been in a coma for ten years. Linda Hamilton is his doctor and she gives him a heart transplant with a giant artificial heart and they use a construction crane like a freakin' claw machine. He's losing blood, and a transfusion is necessary. The only problem is that no known living animal matches Kong's blood type, until they find Lady Kong in Borneo. That's right, they find a lady Kong and just straight up name her Lady Kong. They bring her back and do the transfusion, which succeeds. King Kong and Lady Kong escape, then get it on. This results in a pregnancy.

Samuel L. Jackson's Colonel Packard has a predecessor in John Ashton (not John Astin) playing Lt. Col. Archie Nevitt, who captures Lady Kong and seemingly kills King Kong. He survives however, and comes to liberate his lady love, and smashes Nevitt very much like Kong would Col Packard in *Skull Island* 30 years later. It makes, like, a bug squishing sound.

Honestly, there's a lot of stuff that's not very good in both franchises, but so much of that is dependent on your attitude going into it. I love these movies for the same reasons I love fairy tales, as Neil Gaiman paraphrased GK Chesterton, they don't tell us that dragons exist, but that they can be beaten, but ALSO because they take a deep look at that which is monstrous in each of us, and ask us if we think our worst attributes exclude us from being worthy of redemption, while answering a resounding no! Godzilla began as the incarnation of one of humanity's greatest sins, but over time, he became a superhero and savior. When the series was rebooted in the 80s and 90s, he again started out as a terror beast before turning into our only defense against a universe of worse monsters out to destroy us. It's been the same for Kong. In the 1933 sequel to the original, Koko, the son of Kong, is noble and heroic. Sure, we may all be monsters on some level, but King Kong and Godzilla teach us that, even as monsters, we're worthy of love, and better than we are often given credit for. So remember that Monsters are your friends.

Godzilla vs The World: The "Villains" of Destroy All Monsters

This is an article I wrote for *Kaiju Ramen* at the request of Travis Alexander, who is in charge of that wonderful site and magazine. I tried to take a different approach from my initial look at *Destroy All Monsters* featured earlier in this book. This was difficult for me, but ultimately, my idea was to separate it from the rest of my work and try to look at the film in isolation. *Record All Monsters* follows chronologically, so if you're listening in order, you know what came before, and even if you're not listening in order, I try to give a little bit of context to the time and place of the movie I'll be discussing. With a magazine article, you don't know how much information your reader may have, so you have to bring them up to speed quickly. I faced this same problem in preparing the two live shows we've done at the time of this writing.

Where do you begin when you talk about a movie like *Destroy All Monsters*? I'll tell you. You begin with the story. In these hallowed pages, I have waxed oh so very lyrical about many lofty ideas about stories and storytelling, and I've gone even further, verging on windbaggery, on my podcast, *Record All Monsters*, which, if you've never listened to, would you? Pretty please?

Now that that run-on sentence is out of the way, let's get back to the story of *Destroy All Monsters*. All of the world's monsters have been, uhhh, let's not say imprisoned. Let's say…. Let me check my thesaurus… Ah! Immured! All of the world's monsters have been *immured* on Ogasawara Island in a compound called Monster Land. They have free run of the island and its resources, with the only real restriction being that they can't leave. This is enforced through energy fields and unpleasant smelling gas.

Man has also set up a base on the moon. It's neat. Kenji Sahara is there. And so is Akira Kubo, and he has a spaceship, the *Moonlight SY-3*. When communication with Monster Land is mysteriously cut, Kubo takes his ship down to investigate. What he discovers is an abandoned laboratory, shrouded in mist. Eventually, the people he expected to meet do show up, but they are… different, somehow. Robotic. We soon see that this is because they are being controlled by a race of invading aliens called the Kilaaks, who are exercising the same mind control on the monsters themselves as they are on the Monster Land staff.

In the history of the Godzilla movies, the traditional narrative roles of "protagonist" and "antagonist" have been inexact and rather murky. In the 1954 original, Godzilla could be said to operate as our antagonist, but there are actually several stories being told in the film. In Dr. Yamane's story, fear and a societal lack of curiosity are the antagonists. In Emiko and Ogata's story, it's Serizawa, and in Serizawa's story, it's his own conscience and the broader scientific community. These threads do come together in Godzilla himself, but he is unaware of any of this going on. Narratively, to be an antagonist means to actively oppose the protagonist, which Godzilla is *not* doing. He's just existing. In fact, he's the one who is being opposed. *We* are his enemies in the original film.

In *Godzilla Raids Again*, we repeat ourselves in the role of antagonist to a mostly unaware Godzilla. We even chase him down as he is minding his own business. Why do we do this? Why do we oppose ourselves to giants? Well, we have to. I have spoken and written about the controversial poet and commentator GK Chesterton on Record All Monsters and in this revered publication. Well, hold on to your hats, folks, I'm back on my BS.

Chesterton wrote at length on the subject of giants in fairy tales, and how their purpose in those stories is to teach us to be humble. "Humility was largely meant as a restraint upon the arrogance and infinity of the appetite of man... Even the haughty visions, the tall cities, and the toppling pinnacles are the creations of humility. Giants that tread down forests like grass are the creations of humility. Towers that vanish upwards above the loneliest star are the creations of humility. For towers are not tall unless we look up at them; and giants are not giants unless they are larger than we. All this gigantesque imagination, which is, perhaps, the mightiest of the pleasures of man, is at bottom entirely humble. It is impossible without humility to enjoy anything— even pride."[270] This natural instinct toward humility can be perverted into hatred. Again, from Chesterton: "If you care to hear it I will tell you the real story of Jack the Giant-Killer. To begin with, the most awful thing which Jack first felt about the giant was that he was not a giant. He came striding across an interminable wooded plain, and against its remote horizon the giant was quite a small figure, like a figure in a picture--he seemed merely a man walking across the grass. Then Jack was shocked by remembering that the grass which the man was treading down was one of the tallest forests upon that plain. The man came nearer and nearer, growing bigger and bigger, and at the instant when he passed the possible stature of humanity Jack almost screamed. The rest was an intolerable apocalypse."[271]

In *King Kong vs Godzilla*, Godzilla faces another giant as his opponent, but we're still there, terrified by the Giant Monsters walking not only among us, but *above* us, over us, on top of us, and fighting them with everything we have. In *Mothra vs Godzilla*, we ally ourselves to another Giant Monster in hope of stopping him. At last, in *Ghidorah, the Three-Headed Monster*, we form an uneasy alliance with him, in the hope of stopping an even bigger threat than he has been. We see the planting of the seeds for *Destroy All Monsters* in *Invasion of Astro Monster*, as a race of invading aliens mind controls Godzilla to act as part of a colonizing force along with Rodan and King Ghidorah, until the mind control is broken and he once again fights by our side, but in his own interest. At this point, Godzilla and humanity have an uneasy peace between them: we'll try to leave you alone if you fight off invading alien monsters. We don't really hold up our end of the bargain, getting all up in his business in *Ebirah Horror of the Deep* and *Son of Godzilla*, but these minor infractions by individual humans seem to pass mostly unnoticed. We, however, are still frightened by his enormity, and mostly try to stay out of his way.

This brings us back to *Destroy All Monsters*, where we once again find ourselves in opposition to the King of the Monsters, working furiously around his feet to find a way to break the mind control of the Kilaak aliens. And Godzilla is supported not just by the Kilaaks, but by the other monsters, attacking around the world simultaneously, before they converge on Tokyo in one of the finest effects sequences in the entire Toho canon. Among the devastating aftermath, one thing has become painfully clear: humanity cannot defeat these monsters.

---

[270] Chesterton, G.K. *Orthodoxy*, Chapter 3, "The Suicide of Thought"
[271] Chesterton, *Tremendous Trifles,* "The Giant"

Colloquial wisdom dictates that if you can't beat 'em, it may be time to join 'em. There aren't a whole lot of options for the people of earth at this point, in terms of who to join. Sure, the Kilaaks are winning, but they're using the monsters to do so. So, what if the monsters were on our side? We know they can be controlled because the Kilaaks are already controlling them, but how? Probably in a similar way to how they are controlling the humans from Monster Land, with relatively small transmitters hidden on their persons. This knowledge helps them to find similar transmitters hidden in rocks and even in a coconut, which they destroy and reverse engineer. They even find where the signal is coming from; it turns out the Kilaaks also have a base on the moon, where they broadcast their orders to the earth monsters. A quick trip on the *SY-3 Moonlight* up there gets the power to the signal tower cut, and now we're in control of the monsters, ready to attack the Kilaaks at their base in Mt. Fuji.

What follows is the highlight of a movie in which almost every other effects scene would have been the highlight, where King Ghidorah takes on all 10 of the other monsters in the movie. Well, really, he takes on Godzilla, Minilla, Mothra, Rodan, Anguirus, Gorosaurus, and Kumonga. Varan, Baragon, and Manda just kind of hang out, which is what I would have done. "Godzilla and those other guys have got this. Do you think we're far enough away?" After Ghidorah is literally stomped into the ground, the aliens send out "The Fire Dragon", which they use to sever our control over the earth monsters. What happens next is very, very important as we look at the history of Godzilla's relationship with humans. He, along with the other monsters, continue to attack the Kilaak base. It's commented at this point that "the monsters know their enemies by instinct!" Godzilla is now firmly on our side. We are no longer his enemy.

Even though *Destroy All Monsters* takes place in the far flung future year of 1999 (199X in the original Japanese), how Godzilla interacts with humanity is greatly changed from here on out. In *All Monsters Attack* (can I just call it *Godzilla's Revenge*? It always has been and always will be *Godzilla's Revenge* in my heart.) Godzilla is curious about our small human hero, but it's his own fantasy, and I personally think that Ichiro has not seen *Destroy All Monsters* yet, so his understanding of Godzilla's character evolution is incomplete. However, if you move through the rest of the Showa era from here, Godzilla is unquestionably our staunch defender, our hero, fighting for humanity despite being a living embodiment of our sins against the earth and each other.

Nobody questions Godzilla's intentions for the entirety of the 1970s, even in *Godzilla vs Mechagodzilla,* the audience is supposed to realize that something is wrong when he begins attacking and destroying cities again. The Hanna-Barbera cartoon traded on this perception, and it carried through all the way to the late 90s, when the Dean Devlin and Roland Emmerich remake came under fire for numerous digressions from the public perception of what a Godzilla movie was supposed to be. One of the pillars that I distinctly remember of the arguments against the film was that Godzilla was *the bad guy*. What I observed was not people complaining that Godzilla is a dark representation of blah blah blah 1954 blah blah now I am become death blah blah atomic blah- no. It was "why isn't he punching a bad monster in the face?" That's because of Godzilla's perception as our hero against worse creatures from the dark reaches of space, or deep beneath the earth, or the prehistoric past was the overwhelming one, and that began in *Destroy All Monsters*.

I think the Kilaaks are in the running for Godzilla's most important enemy for this very reason. They completed what Ghidorah began, the Kylo Ren to his Darth Vader. And they got there by displacing us, by turning Godzilla and humanity into a united front against space men and monsters. I believe this is an inevitability in every incarnation of Godzilla, and the time in between his horrific introduction and his heroic assent grows shorter in each era. Godzilla became our hero, and he still is. And it's all because of those foxy devils in silver sequin jumpsuits and wimpled capes, the Kilaaks.

Selected Bibliography

- Galbraith, Stuart IV. *Monsters Are Attacking Tokyo! The Incredible World of Japanese Fantasy Films*. 1st ed, Feral House, 1998.

- LeMay, John. *The Big Book of Japanese Giant Monster Movies: Showa Completion (1954-1989)*. 3rd ed., 2020.

- Ryfle, Steve, and Ed Godziszewski. *Ishiro Honda: A Life in Film, from Godzilla to Kurosawa*. Wesleyan University Press, 2017.

- Wynorski, Jim, editor. *They Came from Outer Space: 12 Classic Science Fiction Tales That Became Major Motion Pictures*. Doubleday, 1980.

Printed in Great Britain
by Amazon